Organizing Modernity

New Weberian Perspectives on Work, Organization and Society

Edited by Larry J. Ray and Michael Reed

London and New York

First published 1994
by Routledge
11 New Fetter Lane, London EC4P 4EE

Simultaneously published in the USA and Canada
by Routledge
29 West 35th Street, New York, NY 10001

Typeset in Baskerville by LaserScript, Mitcham, Surrey
Printed and bound in Great Britain by
Mackays of Chatham PLC, Chatham, Kent

British Library Cataloguing in Publication Data
A catalogue record for this book is available from the British Library

Library of Congress Cataloging in Publication Data
Organizing modernity: new Weberian perspectives on work,
   organizations, and society/edited by Larry J. Ray and Michael Reed.
   p.   cm.
   Includes bibliographical references and index.
   ISBN 0–415–08916–6: $65.00. – ISBN 0–415–08917–4 (pbk): $17.95
   1. Organizational sociology. 2. Weber, Max, 1864–1920. I. Ray,
   Larry, J. II. Reed, M. I. (Michael I.)
HM131.075   1994
302.3′5 – dc20   94-7259
                                                                   CIP

ISBN 0–415–08916–6
ISBN 0–415–08917–4 (pbk)

Contents

List of figures   vi
List of contributors   vii

Weber, organizations and modernity: an introduction   1
Larry J. Ray and Michael Reed

1 **Bringing the text back in: on ways of reading the iron cage metaphor in the two editions of** *The Protestant Ethic*   16
David Chalcraft

2 **Max Weber and contemporary sociology of organizations**   46
Stewart R. Clegg

3 **Work and authority: some Weberian perspectives**   81
John Eldridge

4 **Accounting for organizational feeling**   98
Martin Albrow

5 **Max Weber on individualism, bureaucracy and despotism: political authoritarianism and contemporary politics**   122
Bryan S. Turner

6 **Commerce, science and the modern university**   141
Keith Tribe

7 **Max Weber and the dilemmas of modernity**   158
Larry J. Ray and Michael Reed

Conclusion: autonomy, pluralism and modernity   198
Larry J. Ray and Michael Reed

Index   205

List of figures

I.1   Nation state and globalization   7
7.1   Occidental rationalism   162
7.2   Typology of social action   164
7.3   Multi-dimensional Weberian control model   167

List of contributors

Martin Albrow is Research Professor in the Social Sciences, Roehampton Institute, London. He was founding editor of *International Sociology*, the journal of the International Sociological Association and is currently writing two books, *The Global Age* (Polity) and *Do Organizations Have Feelings?* (Routledge).

David Chalcraft is Lecturer in Sociology at Oxford Brookes University and the current field chair in the sociology unit. He is the founding member and current convenor of the BSA's Max Weber Studies Group. He is currently working on the problem of the two editions of *The Protestant Ethic and the Spirit of Capitalism*.

Stewart R. Clegg is the Foundation Professor in Management, University of Western Sydney Macarthur. He has just completed a research project on 'The Leadership and Management of Embryonic Industries' for the Australian Federal Government. He is currently developing this research and working on a number of book projects in management and organizations.

John Eldridge is Professor of Sociology at the University of Glasgow. He has published in the sociology of work and organizations, mass media and Max Weber. He is currently completing a book on Raymond Williams.

Larry J. Ray is Senior Lecturer in Sociology at Lancaster University. He has recently published *Rethinking Critical Theory* (Sage, 1993) and is currently working on a book for Edward Elgar on sociological theory and the transition in post-socialist societies.

Michael Reed is Professor in the Department of Behaviour in Organizations, Lancaster University and his recent publications include *The Sociology of Organizations* (Harvester, 1992). He is currently working on a book on new forms of work organization for Sage.

Keith Tribe is Senior Lecturer in Economics, Keele University. He has recently published *The Market for Political Economy* (ed. with Alon Kadish, 1993) and *Strategies of Economic Order* (1994) and is currently working on the development of economics in British universities 1870–1960.

Bryan S. Turner is Dean of the Arts Faculty and Professor of Sociology at Deakin University, Australia. He was previously Professor of Sociology at the University of Essex and Professor of General Social Science at the University of Utrecht. He has published a number of books on the work of Max Weber, including *Weber and Islam* (Routledge, 1974), *For Weber* (Routledge, 1981) and *Max Weber: From History to Modernity* (Routledge, 1992).

Weber, organizations and modernity: an introduction

Larry J. Ray and Michael Reed

The initial inspiration for this volume arose from a conference held at Lancaster University in April 1991, on Weber, Work, Organizations and Modernity, organized by the Weber Study Group of the British Sociological Association. However, the present collection is more than a publication of the conference proceedings. Martin Albrow's chapter ('Accounting for organizational feeling') has been written specifically for this volume, and represents a development of the themes addressed in his paper to the Study Group. The chapter by David Chalcraft ('Bringing the text back in') and that by the editors ('Max Weber and the dilemmas of modernity'), were also written especially for this volume. Each of the other chapters is based on a paper presented at Lancaster, but they appear here in significantly elaborated form. Even so, the intentions both of the conference and of this volume coincide in their attempt to assess Weberian sociology from the standpoint of contemporary social developments, and to re-examine Weber's work itself in the context of nearly a century of interpretation and critique. Each of the contributions in this volume provides detailed interpretations of the continued relevance of Weber's theoretical analysis and substantive work on modern organizations for understanding the trajectory of institutional change in both Western and Eastern Europe.

Such an evaluation is timely and perhaps overdue. As we approach the end of the century, and indeed of the millennium, it is probably inevitable that publications in the social sciences will indulge in a degree of retrospective and prospective speculation. Both of these attitudes might be appropriate to Weber's sociology, which was the product of a complex set of social and intellectual developments in the first two decades of this century, and yet now, at the *fin de siècle*, retains resonance with our concerns in ways which are explored in this book. The objective of assessing Weberian sociology from the standpoint of contemporary social developments raises questions about the validity of the Weberian model of bureaucratic organization and the trajectory of modernity, understood in terms of progressive rationalization and captured in Weber's epithet, 'the future belongs to bureaucratization' (1978, II:1401). Yet how does this expectation, and its implicit evolutionism, fare in the light of contemporary intellectual and social developments? Intellectual developments include the postmodernist rejection of progressive societal rationalization, and theories of cultural globalization that might leave Weber's focus on the national political and economic space rather anachronistic. Social developments include the emergence of more decentralized, flexible organizational forms (a process itself described as 'postmodernization' by Crook *et al.* 1992); the collapse of bureaucratic structures in the former communist countries, which for some signals a major breach in the bars of the iron cage; and the rise of ethnic nationalism and religious fundamentalism, which call into question the notion of a globally rationalized culture. Do these developments refute Weber's expectations about the expansion of secular, rational and formal modes of organization in society?

This question might be answered partly through the second objective here, a re-examination of Weber's work, which queries whether 'iron cage' pessimism actually exhausted his view of the trajectory of modernity. Perhaps there is another Weber, less prominent in organizational analysis, but more nuanced and open to alternative possibilities within the present. Indeed, a recurrent theme, addressed in different ways by the contributors to this volume, is the need to rectify the narrowness of interpretations of Weber's work that concentrate on his ideal-typical analysis of formal bureaucratic structures. The contributors here reflect more recent scholarship that has rediscovered deeper and more nuanced themes in Weber's work on organizations. Thus for Stewart Clegg, Weber's central contribution is as a cultural theorist; Bryan Turner argues that it is Weber's political sociology, rather than his theory of values, that remains his key contribution; whilst John Eldridge and Ray and Reed suggest that from beneath iron cage pessimism a more hopeful Weber might be recovered. Indeed Clegg, Albrow, Turner and (on the basis of close textual interpretation) Chalcraft, each offers grounds for rereading Weber as a critical analyst of (post)modernity.

These chapters can be located in relation to three different, but interrelated, ways of treating Weber. First, critiques of Weber, concerning his closed rather than open concept of organizational structure (Clegg; Ray and Reed); his lack of attention to affective dimensions of organizational behaviour (Albrow); his over-rigid distinction between 'traditional' and 'rational' behaviour (Eldridge). Secondly, as indicated already, there is a shift of emphasis as to what is most important about the Weberian legacy; and finally, a rediscovery of the 'other' Weber in contrast to Weber of the 'iron cage'. This Introduction will outline the integrating themes of the volume in terms of: (a) the 'iron cage' of bureaucratic rationalization; (b) forms of rationality and modalities of social action; (c) rationalization, globalization and modernity; (d) scholarship and politics; (e) the classical tradition and modern sociology; (f) the fate of modernity.

THE IRON CAGE OF BUREAUCRATIC RATIONALIZATION

The 'iron cage of bureaucratic rationalization' is often regarded as the central feature of modernity to which Weber's sociology is directed. Bureaucratic rationalization, its limitations, discontents and alternatives, is therefore a pivotal theme in this volume. For modernization theorists (e.g. Bell 1973; Kerr *et al*. 1960; Parsons 1966) complex organizations served as the institutional exemplar of modernity, in terms of their unrivalled technical precision, speed, rationality and control. Hence there arose a fateful convergence of 'organization' and 'modernity' in which bureaucracy was regarded as the unstoppable fate of our times, a phenomenon that Clegg in Chapter 2, characterizes as 'TINA' (There Is No Alternative). That is, 'The iron cage shuts, the lock bolts, the key turns. Some suggest that the lock is size and the key efficiency.' After the Aston studies (Pugh and Hickson 1976) the link between size, bureaucracy and efficiency became so closely associated, argues Clegg, that organizational theory forgot the broader cultural context and comparative concerns of Weber's analysis.

Thus Weber came to be interpreted as a theorist of bureaucratic rationalization, who predicted the convergence of different political and social systems, driven by an industrial and organizational logic. Theories of convergence that had been widely rejected during the past two decades have been given a new lease of life following the fall of communism, and the expectation that the whole of the industrialized world is following a single organizational trajectory after all. Francis Fukuyama's 'end of history' thesis is perhaps one of the most explicit statements of such a view, and his Nietzschean imagery of the 'last man' echoes a Weberian pessimism about impending dullness (Fukuyama 1992). However, the notion of a convergence of modernity and the organizational form of bureaucracy is increasingly being questioned both in theory and practice by fundamental structural and cultural transitions in capitalist and socialist societies. This critique has been prompted by a number of considerations.

First, there is a dark side of this vision of modernization which is not actually universalistic. Again, as Clegg points out, in reality it has excluded most women and colonial people from the white male community of moderns. Thus 'modernity' was Eurocentric and eliminated difference, and at its most extreme this could involve the genocide of 'non-European' peoples. This raises the theme of the violent tragedy of rationalization that was addressed in Adorno and Horkheimer (1973) and more recently in Bauman (1989, 1992) who describes modernity as 'a long march to the prison' (1992: xvii). This question is further addressed by Turner (Chapter 5) and Ray and Reed (Chapter 7). Modernity is thus understood as a field of contestation (or as Habermas puts it, is 'unfulfilled') and consequentially the site of struggles over its meaning and trajectory.

Secondly, it is far from clear that the 'iron cage' reflects a balanced understanding of Weber's thesis. David Chalcraft (Chapter 1) challenges the dominant interpretation of *stalhartes Gehäuse* as 'iron cage'. Rather, he argues, this is a reference in part to the 'steel hard' Puritan personality, but more generally, *Gehäuse* is a dwelling and environment. This refers to the hard shell, or cosmos, of capitalism which defines the terrain upon which organizations develop, a context in which existence is played out under restraint. Viewed as a 'hard shell' of modernity, *stalhartes Gehäuse* is open to both negative and positive interpretations, an empty life or the heritage transmitted from one generation to another.

More generally, one might say that the metaphor of the iron cage has been overstretched.

Further, Clegg criticizes the dominant understanding of Weber's model as a closed system since organizations exist in a state of dynamic interdependency where organic growth and survival require boundary-spanning and adaptation. TINA is a narrow interpretation associated with the idea that Weber is the ancestor of functionalist studies in organizational behaviour. However, Weber did not equate efficiency and bureaucracy in a straightforward way, and was familiar with the Austrian Marginalist School which argued that market efficiency and bureaucracy were actually inimical. At the same time, Weber was more realistic than the Austrian theorists as to the political and cultural dimensions of bureaucracies, which survive not because they are efficient so much as because they are powerful. Indeed, Clegg suggests, Weber is better understood as a cultural rather than as organizational theorist, since organizations exist as a result of shared cultural expectations amongst their members. Organizational behaviour is embedded in cultural practices that presuppose reciprocity, trust and informal relations – which Okun (1981) described as the 'invisible handshake', as opposed to the 'invisible hand' of the market and the 'visible hand' of bureaucracy.

Thirdly, 'rationalization' is not driven by an autonomous and irresistible cultural logic, but is subject to resistance, and might, as with the 'second society' in Soviet-type states, generate social forms antithetical to bureaucratization. Thus the inherent contradictions or limitations of bureaucratic rationalization have implications for the development of forms of thinking and acting which depart from technical-instrumental rationality. From a contemporary perspective, rather more open possibilities have been identified in notions of Giddens' 'radicalized modernity' (1990: 102), Beck's (1992) 'risk society' and Habermas' (1984, 1989) attempt to locate a communicative rationality in certain social movements, especially feminism. This is a theme raised by a number of contributors. John Eldridge (Chapter 3) shows how resistance to bureaucratic rationalization was encountered 'from below' in the early stages of industrialization, from traditional pre-modern cultures and social movements. Ray and Reed (Chapter 7) discuss the dialectic of rationalization and lifeworld resistance in terms of the inherent limitations to bureaucratization in both capitalist and 'socialist' Europe. Analyses such as these suggest that both the trajectory and outcome of bureaucratic rationalization are much more open, contested and unpredictable than more orthodox interpretations of the 'iron cage' thesis allows (Mommsen 1989).

FORMS OF RATIONALITY AND MODALITIES OF SOCIAL ACTION

The central theme here is the question of rationality and its pervasive influence in modern life and indeed, the increasingly problematic nature of the dichotomy between 'traditional' and 'modern' forms of behaviour and organization. Again, the discussion addresses both the relevance of Weber for understanding the contemporary world (e.g. in terms of the 'revival' of traditionalism) and our interpretation of Weber's theory. As Eldridge points out, Weber regarded the *Protestant Ethic* essays as illustrating the only 'superficially clear concept of the rational'. Those who would offer alternatives to the cognitive and organizational power of rational models of social action might actually be assuming a very narrow and inflexible reading of Weber as a prophet of rationalization.

The *Protestant Ethic* essays were probably Weber's most controversial attempt to understand the birth of capitalism, and to define traditional as opposed to rational behaviour. It is well known that he claimed there was an elective affinity between the Protestant ethic and the spirit of capitalism, creating a purposive, technical, instrumental, functional rationality born out of Christian asceticism. The link between Calvinism and modern capitalism is explored by Chalcraft and Eldridge (Chapters 1 and 3). Further, Chalcraft undertakes a textual deconstruction of two editions of *The Protestant Ethic* (the 1904–5 and the 1920 versions) asking: 'where does the meaning of the text lie?' Understanding the organizational principles of the text allows us to view its themes and an inter-weaving of past and present. The main theme of *The Protestant Ethic*, he argues, is not the origin of capitalism, nor the general motif of rationalization, but rather the development of a particular type of personality, which is examined by synchronic comparisons of conceptions of the 'calling' held in different epochs. Hence *ertragen* (to bear) conveys a sense of bearing the psychological burden of Calvinism through *Beruf* (the calling) which enables Weber to make an essentially psychological connection between old Protestantism, Franklin and the spirit of modern capitalism. The intensity of the search for the Kingdom of God passed over into sober economic virtue and in due course its religious roots died out, giving way to utilitarian worldviews. Chalcraft's point is that the text oscillates between the past and the present, and that parallels are made through juxtaposition. He concludes that a main theme in Weber's sociology is an exploration of the relationship between synchronic and diachronic developments, an interpretation which would preclude reading him in terms of a simple transition from 'tradition' to modernity'.

None the less, Weber is often associated with the idea of an endemic tension between 'rational' and 'traditional' forms of social organization, a distinction which, by adopting historical, comparative and analytical approaches, Turner, Albrow and Eldridge call into question. Drawing on E.P. Thompson's *Customs in Common* (1991), Eldridge shows that the birth of capitalism was far from being a victory for 'modern' over 'traditional' ways of acting. Although tradition has often been taken to mean the 'stone wall of habit', it contains the capacity for resistance, disrespect for authority and the capacity for rebellion. Such resistance is far from unreflective, but often invokes the substantive values of justice and solidarity in opposition to the impersonal logic of capitalism. Moreover, plebeian resistance and religious fundamentalism are two classic examples of opposition to rational domination which Weber may have seriously underestimated in his 'disenchantment thesis'.

The rational and affective domains are more interpenetrated than they appear in Weber. The rediscovery of the 'irrational' and its continued impact on contemporary organizational life is explored by Martin Albrow (Chapter 4). He argues that for both individuals and organizations, purpose, cognition and emotion are intertwined. This is an increasingly important part of organizational behaviour in view of the departure from classical forms of hierarchy and the expansion of markets serving non-material, emotional, needs. Albrow addresses four classical areas of organizational analysis – goals, work performance, communication and authority. First, Weber suggests that organizations have fixity of purpose and are governed by calculability, but Albrow argues that goals are less fixed than this supposes and are subject to negotiation. Personal qualities such as imagination, inspiration or creativity become important. Secondly, Weber stressed task performance as an organizational feature, but work situations have emotional content which is not incidental since it structures both performance and actual outcomes. Moreover, his model of bureaucracies as command-action, monocratic hierarchies was derived from the Prussian military. Albrow argues that as the military participation ratio (the proportion of people with experience of military service) has declined in modern societies there has been a further shift away from military metaphors in bureaucratic organization – to the point that advertisements for the military deploy images from civilian management. Albrow also argues that communication flows in organizations are complex, indicating style and ambience and are therefore of more significance than simply an exchange of data. The memo is a 'cool' communication because it invites so many interpretive responses from its recipients. So it is in the social relations of work, not formal bodies, that we see the problematic of organizational emotion. Finally, authority, which is situationally dependent and has an affective dimension, is displaced in Weber to the concept of charisma. The thrust of Albrow's chapter is to develop active and interactive approaches in a broadly Weberian spirit, but to insist that this entails the full acknowledgement of the vital presence of emotions in organizations.

This attention to the micro-dynamics of organizational behaviour opens up another issue (discussed by Ray and Reed): whether the iron cage is as much 'in here' as 'out there'. Since Foucault's (1979) analysis of the micro-physics of institutional power and the encoding of surveillance in routine practices of administration, there has been ample scope for extending Weber's prognosis to the minutiae of organizational life (Gordon 1987). A theme underlying several of the chapters here is whether, in an apparently de-bureaucratizing era, we are witnessing not so much an opening of the iron cage as its more subtle closure.

RATIONALIZATION, GLOBALIZATION AND MODERNITY

This theme concerns the relationship between Weber's political and organizational sociology which, as we noted above, have often been separated. However, as Clegg, Albrow and Ray and Reed argue, this separation is part of the conventional way of incorporating Weber's work within mainstream organization theory. Weber's analysis of domination (*Herrschaft*) provides the irreducible analytical and substantive framework within which his sociology of organizations has to be located and assessed. Once relocated within the framework of his political sociology and political economy, Weber's analysis of bureaucratic rationalization and organization raises fundamental questions concerning the dynamics of politico-economic power and institutional change.

However, in common with most sociologists, Weber identified 'society' with the spatial and organizational boundaries of the nation state, and, as Turner argues, both his concept of citizenship and his personal values involved a commitment to the ethics of *realpolitik* and *staatraison*. Yet in an age of globalization, functions previously performed by the nation state are increasingly being devolved upwards to inter-state bodies and downwards to local agencies – a process Jessop (1992) describes as a 'hollowing out' of the state. These developments raise fundamental questions about the continued relevance of the nation state tradition within contemporary sociological theory. At the same time though, and despite his preoccupation with *realpolitik* and *staatraison*, a global perspective would seem to be a major feature of Weber's comparative sociology.

The underlying tensions in Weber's political sociology between nation state and global perspectives is shown in Figure 1.1. National markets are giving way to internationalized economies in which regions are becoming the central point of intersection between global and local economies. The decline in economic significance of the nation state is complementary to the emergence of transnational corporations, which because of their scope and diversity mark a transition from monocentric order to polycentric fragmentation, and increasing regulation through locally autonomous units. This marks the transition from Hilferding's 'organized' to Lash and Urry's (1987) or Offe's (1985) 'disorganized' capitalism.

The central issue here is rationalization and its contingent effects on the phenomena of globalization and localization. Ray and Reed discuss the implications for Weberian sociology of the collapse of 'Fordist'-style corporatism, reflected in the breakdown both of Western capitalist production regimes based on mass markets, mass production and organization, and Soviet-style command

Nation State	Global Arena
National markets	Internationalized economies
Bureaucracy	'Hollowed out' state
Order	Fragmentation
Monocentric	Polycentric
Control	Autonomy
Organization	Disorganization

Figure 1.1 Nation state and globalization

economies. Are these indicative of the underlying instability of late or post-modern organizational ideologies and structures? Does this indicate a critical transformation or disorganization of the contemporary world system? Perhaps Weber's vision of a rationalized global system is undermined by current structural and cultural transformations that press in the direction of less, rather than more, organized societies.

The creation of global circuits of capital and commodities and a high degree of standardization creates global consumption cultures and communication flows, a process that Ritzer (1992) describes as 'McDonaldization'. Globalization further involves high levels of international mobility, flows of images, commodities, people, and capital through time and space, with the effect of producing a different sort of experience from earlier types of globality. In particular, it is claimed that globalization results in a compression of time and space and radical de-nationalization of space (Harvey 1989). Jessop (1992:17) argues that as a consequence of internationalization states can no longer act as if national economies were closed and their growth dynamic autocentric. Macroeconomic policy instruments lose their efficiency and are being replaced by strategies such as cross-national cooperation, reforming international currency and credit systems, or developing new forms of labour and migration regulation. Despite this, though, the nation state remains the most significant site of struggle between global, supranational and local forces.

One avenue for exploring these tensions would be to examine the struggle between global rationalization and local modes of engagement and commitment that resist the homogenizing impact of global power and culture. In this context, Turner discusses the Islamic fundamentalism in what is also a reassessment of his own thinking about Weber and Islam, compared with his critique of Weber in *Weber and Islam* (1974) or *Capitalism and Class in the Middle East* (1984). This present account further links a Weberian analysis back to the theme of political sociology. Turner suggests that Weber provided two accounts of the lack of capitalist development in Islamic societies. One stressed the cultural inhibitions of Islam (such as the lack of a salvation religion, or *qadi* justice). However, cultural difference is not a sufficient explanation, since according to Weber's own definition of modernity (ascetic discipline, anti-magical beliefs, textually based rationalism, rational procedures for forming legal rules) both Calvinism and Islam are modernist. Of more significance in explaining the pattern of Islamic development, Turner suggests, is Weber's analysis of social stasis, patrimonial bureaucracy, and the absence of a bourgeois class, that is, traditionalism combined with a weak civil society.

This account does indicate greater sympathy with 'internalist' accounts than in Turner's earlier work (especially Turner 1984) which emphasized colonial domination rather than the absence of an entrepreneurial middle class in explaining the underdevelopment of the Levant. None the less, this approach, which examines the intersection of global forces and local forms of political and cultural resistance, might offer a way of taking account of the problematic position of the nation state, whilst reuniting Weber's political sociology and theory of bureaucracy. The local state is thus understood both as caught in a vortex of the world system and as subject to the effects of its particular, institutional and cultural forms. However, rather than view the drift towards more bureaucratically closed forms as the underlying tow of modernity, Turner's account suggests that a testing struggle for democracy and cultural pluralism, in the context of global recession and post-Cold War uncertainties, is still to come. This approach suggests that we can acknowledge the process of globalization while still treating the local polity and civil society as the point of intersection of critical social forces.

SCHOLARSHIP AND POLITICS

Weber's sociology raises basic questions about the relationship between academic analysis, knowledge and political-moral vision. Along with the *Protestant Ethic* debate, the controversy over value-freedom has been one of the longest-standing disputes in twentieth-century sociology. During the decade following the Second World War, Weber was generally acclaimed in Germany as the inspiration of value-free sociology, but this was challenged in 1959 by Wolfgang Mommsen's *Max Weber und die deutscher Politik*, which presented Weber as the ruthless advocate of nationalist *realpolitik* and German imperialism. Herbert Marcuse (1965) went further and argued that Weber's separation of values and science placed sociology in the category of 'irrational values', subjected to the demands of imperialist power politics, a view not unlike that of Georg Lukács in *The Destruction of Reason* (published in 1952). The acerbic dispute that followed, in which Reinhard Bendix defended Weber's position, was to run and run, broadening into the *Positivismusstreit* during the 1960s (Ray 1979). Thirty or so years later we can perhaps take a cooler look at these issues, and the essays in this volume by Turner and by Keith Tribe (Chapters 5 and 6) add to our understanding of the context for Weber's position on scholarship and politics.

Turner argues that Weber's philosophy of science sought to establish scientific grounds on which sociologists could enter political controversy. Tribe points out that this was closely related to debates over the nature of scholarship in the modern university, in a culture increasingly dominated by business values and bureaucratic control. About one-quarter of 'Science as a Vocation' is taken up with university systems in Germany and America. The latter was organized like a modern bureaucracy and thus posed the problem of how scientific and intellectual development might survive pressures to create 'uninventive specialists'. Whilst we might have expected Weber to defend the more traditional, German system, he regarded this as no longer offering a model for the future, and opposed its preoccupation with patronage and status, as well as its subservience to the state. Moreover both systems, American and German, were confronted by different kinds of threats to academic freedom, which Weber emphasizes was a modern rather than a traditional value. The German university had previously been dedicated to training students for the traditional professions of law, medicine and the priesthood, and the concept of a research university, which required academic freedom, was derived from post-bellum America. However, the pursuit of knowledge was threatened not only by the authoritarian state, but also by the tendency, present in both America and Germany, to seek prestige with the business rather than scholarly community, which Weber believed was promoting a new type of mediocrity in the university. Again, as Tribe points out, these issues have a resonance with the status of academic inquiry in British higher education in the late twentieth century, which faces similar contradictions between bureaucratized structures, a commercial orientation, and the pursuit of knowledge.

However, it remains the case that Weber was personally committed to authoritarian citizenship (the tradition of *staatraison* within a global arena of competitive states) which sits somewhat uneasily with his commitment to the Western liberal tradition. Turner, whilst highly critical of the anti-democratic dimension of Weber's political philosophy, suggests that his views on authoritarianism in Russian political culture and anxieties about Islamic values 'are uncannily relevant' to those of the post-Cold War era. Arguing for a sympathetic interpretation of Weber's political sociology, Turner (in company with Eldridge) sees Weber as a powerful critic of bureaucratic socialism as an excessive rationalization of life. Further, despite his limited concept of citizenship guaranteed through a strong state, Turner suggests, Weber's analysis of the conditions for a democratic polity – autonomous urban associations, an ideology of universalism, and rational law-making – provide a basis for addressing contemporary issues of rights. This points towards a rehabilitation of liberalism, which Marxists have too hastily dismissed. Liberalism is not specific to capitalism, is not necessarily anti-social, nor do rights have to be limited to individual form. Defining the conditions for democratic notions of citizenship might involve a positive reappraisal of both liberalism and the progressive aspect of Weber's politics.

THE CLASSICAL TRADITION AND MODERN SOCIOLOGY

The central theme here is the continuing relationship between the classical tradition and modern sociology. Weber's intellectual legacy raises a key question as to whether we should abandon the classical tradition in contemporary sociological discourse, as Giddens (1990) suggests, because it is no longer conceptually equipped to comprehend the dynamics of late/postmodernity, or whether the former can be recovered to provide an appreciation of current institutional transformations. The latter view is closer both to the position of most of the contributors to this volume, and to Giddens' earlier work. None of the contributors here argue for an uncritical Weberianism (if such could be defined) but, as we have seen, in different ways each calls for a nuanced understanding of Weber's legacy and its potential contribution. In particular, Weber's work appears to offer insights into social processes as diverse as the collapse of communism, Islamic neo-revivalism, the differentiation of classical forms of bureaucratic organization, commercialization of the educational system, and problems of commitment and objectivity.

This is possible, in part perhaps because Weber posed wide-ranging questions about the nature of modernity, and in part too because his conceptual scheme displays a kind of methodological ambiguity on crucial theoretical issues, such as individualism–structuralism, materialism–idealism, evolution–contingency, secularism, or the fate of democracy. In a world where uncertainty and risk have become dominant motifs, this conceptual openness seems to address our post-modern anxieties. Yet revitalizing the classical tradition will involve blending the interpretive and structuralist approaches within neo-Weberian sociology so that it is properly equipped to handle the discontinuities of late modernity. In particular, this will involve a challenge to 'vulgar' interpretations, that is, the view of Weber as rationalistic, deterministic, teleological and evolutionary. As Albrow puts it, 'the Weber to whom we return . . . is not the exponent of ideal types and rationalistic methodology' nor the Weber who 'customarily appears in association with bureaucracy' but the historian and interpreter of worldviews, a many-sided Weber of different orientations.

Developing this theme of openness and ambiguity, Ray and Reed argue that against the received or orthodox Weber can be contrasted another, unorthodox Weber. The orthodox Weber is the analyst and prophet of rationalization, the rationalism of *staatraison* and *realpolitik*, rather than the theorist of the non-rational and irrational forms of action, organization and belief. The orthodox Weber views the future in terms of the extension of formal organization, the iron cage of control, rather than an expanding potential for individual freedom and autonomy. The 'other' Weber's *critique* of progressive encroachments on freedom and autonomy resonates with a Foucauldian view of the deep penetration of disciplinary practices into the lifeworld, a critique that itself implies the possibility of resistance and hence points towards a more emancipated future. Against this, the 'orthodox' Weber offers a highly selective and one-sided interpretation, that might have seemed appropriate in an era of organized capitalism and monistic organizations, but today looks rather jaded. The alternative view requires a more open-ended and textured appreciation of his intellectual, moral and ideological legacy than that which has dominated mainstream industrial and organizational sociology.

This more open-ended and textured appreciation of Weber's intellectual, moral and ideological legacy is also likely to facilitate a reconsideration of the relationship between the 'Weberian legacy' and contemporary organizational theory. The chapters in this volume consistently reveal the continued relevance of Weber's theoretical and substantive sociology to the reworking and renewal of social and organizational theory as they struggle to come to terms with the 'fate of modernity'. Contemporary theoretical movements and perspectives as diverse as Critical Theory, poststructuralism, postmodernism, structuration theory, social constructionism, and the 'new institutionalism' in organizational analysis (Powell and DiMaggio 1991) continue to return to Weber as a source of intellectual regeneration. His analysis of the organizational dynamics and trajectory of modernity continues to stimulate the sociological imagination of the social scientific community as it strives to achieve an explanatory leverage on events that seem to undermine the very intellectual and moral foundations of the enlightenment project (Turner 1990).

THE FATE OF MODERNITY

The central theme here is the fate of modernity as read through competing interpretations of Weber's intellectual legacy and moral vision. Weber was committed, as Turner emphasizes, to the emergence of rational law-making as a stable base for procedural rules of adjudication, through which disputes could be collectively resolved by appeal to publicly known norms of procedure rather than *ad hoc* law-making. None the less, Weber himself was pessimistic as to whether democratic politics would resist the pull of bureaucratic domination. This tension is developed in Ray and Reed's chapter, which poses two questions: (i) to what extent do two major organizational transformations, the collapse of communism and the crisis of Fordism, represent a crisis for the Weberian control model? (ii) in view of these, how relevant is the Weberian prognosis of the iron cage, *vis-à-vis* more open, participatory, democratic futures? In the process of this discussion we propose a reading of Weber that is influenced by Habermas' theory of communicative action.

Like other contributors, our aim is to revitalise rather than abandon the Weberian inheritance, and rework it to access and account for the underlying dynamics of and prospects for late modernity. This involves disaggregating rationalization and rationality, to identify quite different processes that often become conflated. A Habermasian reading of Weber enables us to see more clearly that rationalization operates on different and conflicting levels of strategic action (instrumental behaviour in markets and bureaucracies) and communicative action (discursive, open and democratic). This dual conception opens up a vision of an unfinished modernity replete with divergent possibilities, within which the iron cage is but one, and which will anyway encounter limits to the possible extent of rationalization in the form of resistance from the lifeworld.

By way of illustration of this bifurcated rationality, one might contrast two opposed connotations of bureaucratization and rationality. First, there is the kind of rule-following legality to which Turner refers, which is essentially procedural. This might involve formality and correctness, even greyness perhaps, but also guarantees universalism, rights of appeal, organizational balances, and checks against the arbitrary exercise of power. This is likely to be accompanied by professional ethics, notions of collegiality, and enforceable boundaries between spheres of competence, not unlike David Sciulli's (1992) notion of 'societal constitutionalism'. Secondly, there is a Kafkesque irrationality that derives from the unlimited exercise of bureaucratic power, which usually involves cynicism and instrumentality rather than a public service ethos. The personality type this engenders is quite different from the 'soulless' but correct bureaucrat. For example, in Anatoli Rybakov's *Children of the Arbat*, a novel about the Stalin years, one of the central characters, Sharok, having just been offered a post in the NKVD, muses about his future:

> Sharok was created for his job, he was right for it . . . Nobody would be able to wriggle out from Sharok's grasp, or manage to justify themselves. He would not believe in anyone's sincerity – *it was impossible to believe sincerely in this whole business*, and anyone who claimed they did was lying.
>
> (Rybakov 1988: 412, emphasis in original)

While it is quite proper to regard the Soviet experience as validation of Weber's prescient warnings about the destructive potential of bureaucratization, it is equally important not to confuse this experience with either rationalization or bureaucratization *per se*. Against bureaucratic terror can be contrasted formal rationality, as a set of procedures for negotiating difference. From this standpoint, we can question whether the disciplinary society (O'Neil 1986) is inevitable and unstoppable, and whether Weber's prognosis legitimizes this view by making it the only 'realistic' interpretation of the fate of modernity. Our account of the collapse of Soviet-type societies and the crisis of Fordism suggests that an alternative outcome is at least possible.

Of course, we should be realistic. After this appalling century of mass destructiveness, where virtually every revolution has been betrayed, most attempts at cultural subversion have been neutralized, and when two generations have lived under the threat of nuclear annihilation it is hard to summon the self-confidence to call Weber's pessimism unwarranted. Moreover, a pessimistic reading might be reinforced by more recent analyses of the micro-physics of self-regulation which suggest that more unobtrusive, sophisticated and normalizing modes of surveillance and control (see Dandeker 1990), based on the rationalization of the social texture of everyday life, are emerging in the highly dislocated, fragmented and disorganized institutional and organizational forms characteristic of late/ postmodernity.

Even so, there is another, more positive, view of the fate of modernity as an unfinished project, reflected in the writings of Habermas, Giddens or Beck, which focuses on the inherent instability and unpredictability of late modernity and trades, intellectually and morally, on Weber's analysis of the tensions and contradictions embedded in the social fabric of the former and their implications for the dynamics and direction of institutional change. Thus the dialectic of control highlighted by Giddens and others (see Ray and Reed for a more detailed exploration of this concept and its implications) necessarily provides opportunities for more open, participative and communal forms of modernity to emerge and take institutional root. This alternative interpretation of Weber's intellectual legacy, the 'other Weber', focuses on the inherent limitations, failures and unintended consequences of the disciplinary society, while simultaneously emphasizing the reality and significance of resistance, both individual and collective, to more indirect and hidden forms of control. In this context we refer to Zuboff (1988) on the control implications of new technology as an example of this kind of contemporary work. If we take this more optimistic line on Weber and recognize the broader implications of his intellectual legacy and moral vision for contemporary sociology, then prognoses concerning the 'fate of modernity' dominated by conventional visions of 'mindless bureaucrats and soulless experts' need to be balanced against less determinate and more complex interpretations as to the range of possibilities opened up by the dynamism, contingency and uncertainty of modernity and modern organization. At the very least, we need to be much more appreciative of the range of institutional and organizational options made available by modernity and the strategic role of moral values, as well as material interests and political power, in shaping the future development of a post-Weberian world.

REFERENCES

Adorno, T. and Horkheimer M. (1973) *Dialectic of Enlightenment*, trans. E. Cumming, London: New Left Books.
Bauman, Z. (1989) *Modernity and the Holocaust*, Cambridge: Polity Press.
Bauman, Z. (1992) *Intimations of Postmodernity*, London: Routledge.
Beck, U. (1992) *The Risk Society*, London: Sage.
Bell, D. (1973) *The Coming of Post-Industrial Society: A Venture in Social Forecasting*, New York: Basic Books.
Crook, S., Pakulski, J. and Waters, M. (1992) *Postmodernization: Change in Advanced Societies*, London: Sage.
Dandeker, C. (1990) *Surveillance, Power and Modernity*, Cambridge: Polity Press.
Foucault, M. (1979) *Discipline and Punish: The Birth of the Prison*, Harmondsworth: Penguin.
Fukuyama, F. (1992) *The End of History and the Last Man*, New York: Free Press.
Giddens, A. (1990) *The Consequences of Modernity*, Cambridge: Polity Press.
Gordon, M. (1987) 'The Soul of the Citizen: Max Weber and Michel Foucault and Rationality in Government', in S. Whimster and S. Lash (eds) *Max Weber, Rationality and Modernity*, London: Allen and Unwin.
Habermas, J. (1984) *The Theory of Communicative Action*, vol. 1, London: Heinemann.
Habermas, J. (1989) *The Theory of Communicative Action*, vol. 2, Cambridge: Polity Press.
Harvey, D. (1989) *The Condition of Postmodernity*, Oxford: Blackwell.
Jessop, B. (1992) *From the Keynesian Welfare to the Schumpeterian Workfare State*, University of Lancaster Regionalism Group Working Paper 45.
Kerr, C., Dunlop, J. T., Harrison, F. and Myers, C. A. (1960) *Industrialism and Industrial Man*, Cambridge Mass.: Harvard University Press.
Lash, S. and Urry, J. (1987) *The End of Organized Capitalism*, Cambridge: Polity Press.
Lukács, G. (1980) *The Destruction of Reason*, trans. P. Palmer, London: Merlin Press.
Marcuse, H. (1965) 'Industrialisation and Capitalism', *New Left Review*, 30: 3–17.
Mommsen, W. (1959) *Max Weber und die deutscher Politik*, Tübingen: J.C.B. Mohr.
Mommsen, W. (1989) *The Political and Social Theory of Max Weber*, Cambridge: Polity Press.

Offe, C. (1985) *Disorganized Capitalism*, Cambridge: Polity Press.

Okun, A. (1981) *Prices and Quantities – A Macroeconomic Analysis*, Oxford: Blackwell.

O'Neil, J. (1986) 'The Disciplinary Society', *British Journal of Sociology*, 37(1):42–60.

Parsons, T. (1966) *Societies: Evolutionary and Comparative Perspectives*, Englewood Cliffs NJ: Prentice-Hall.

Powell, W.W. and DiMaggio, P.J. (1991) *The New Institutionalism in Organizational Analysis*, Chicago: University of Chicago Press.

Pugh, D. and Hickson, D. (1976) *Organization Structure in its Context: the Aston Programme* I, Farnborough: Saxon House.

Ray, L. J. (1979) 'Critical Theory and Positivism: Popper and the Frankfurt School', *Philosophy of the Social Sciences*, 9(2): 147–73.

Ritzer, G. (1992) *The McDonaldization of Society*, Beverly Hills, CA: Sage.

Roth, G. and Bendix, R. (1959) 'Max Webers Einfluss auf die Amerikanische Soziologie' *Kölner Zeitschrift für Soziologie und Sozialpsychologie*, 11.

Rybakov, A. (1988) *Children of the Arbat*, London: Sphere.

Sciulli, D. (1992) *Theory of Societal Constitutionalism. Foundations of a non-Marxist Critical Theory*, Cambridge: Cambridge University Press.

Turner, B.S. (1974) *Weber and Islam*, London: Routledge and Kegan Paul.

Turner, B.S. (1984) *Capitalism and Class in the Middle East* London: Heinemann Educational Books.

Turner, B.S. (1990) *Theories of Modernity and Postmodernity*, London: Sage.

Weber, M. (1978) *Economy and Society*, 2 vols, London: University of California Press.

Zuboff, S. (1988) *In the Age of the Smart Machine: the Future of Work and Power*, London: Heinemann.

Chapter 1

Bringing the text back in: on ways of reading the iron cage metaphor in the two editions of *The Protestant Ethic*

David Chalcraft

INTRODUCTION*

One of the central concerns of the essays in this volume is to seek to uncover in Weber's writings forgotten or previously neglected aspects of his analysis of aspects of modernity which may serve to illuminate contemporary social processes and thereby inform current sociological analysis. As such, the essays in this volume might be described as experiments in, and contributions to, Weberian sociology. The *sine qua non* of such exercises in Weberian sociology, in my view, is an understanding of Weber texts. In this chapter I seek to approach Weber's writings less from a presentist concern with undertaking Weberian sociology than from the other direction: that is, beginning with the texts themselves and working towards a Weberian perspective (Seidman 1983: 281–97). My starting point is not in Weberian sociology, but, for want of a better term, in Weberology, and the former must needs be based on the latter if the texts are to speak to us in our historical situation. The intention is not to read into Weber answers to our own dilemmas (eisegesis), but to read out of Weber's texts questions, concepts and perspectives which emerge from an open dialogue with his writings, predicated on an approach which is willing to have its pre-judgements and pre-understandings transformed in the process of reading a classical text (exegesis) (Thiselton 1992: 31–54; Gadamer 1979: 238ff). Such an openness to the transforming power of the text is necessary with regard to the understanding of the 'iron cage' metaphor which is now so familiar that our appreciation of its meaning has become ritualized. The 'iron cage' metaphor has become synonymous with Weber's analysis and assessment of modernity, in particular, with his understanding of the role of rationality in modern life, and of the evils of bureaucratization. In contemporary sociology commentators ritually refer to the 'iron cage of bureaucracy'; we need to make strange again what has become so habitual.

The image of existence within a cage with iron bars, which determines existence so that we live out our lives coerced by an external and inescapable prison, is perhaps the most frequent picture that is conjured up by this metaphor.

This chapter seeks to address whether this is what Weber had in mind when he used this metaphor at the close of the *Protestant Ethic* (*PE*).

Starting from within Weberology, my central question is not: is Weber's conception of the 'iron cage' more or less accurate as a description of modernity, and is it more or less useful in directing our own researches? Rather, my central question is: how can we understand what Weber was seeking to communicate and by what means can a postulated interpretation be defended? In what follows, therefore, I focus on the meaning of the 'iron cage', but in order to defend a particular interpretation I foreground the processes of arriving at any kind of understanding of Weber's writings. In the discussion of a range of interpretative options I argue that the 'iron cage' metaphor needs to be placed within its textual context and this requires paying attention to various linguistic and organizational principles in the *PE*. Further, I make reference to the fact of the two editions of the *PE*, since this is the textual reality with which we now need to engage if we are seeking to arrive at understandings of Weber's text:[1] in other words, the existence of two editions raises the *possibility* that there is more than one meaning to the *PE* simply on the basis of there being two versions. In this sense, the meaning of the 'iron cage' metaphor may alter if the key to its meaning is the intratextual relations within the *PE* and if those relations alter because of Weber's revisions to the text.

Hence, my main concern here is with understanding Weber. Now all of this is of significance for contemporary sociology since the conclusions reached as to what Weber was attempting to communicate will inform Weberian sociology and any attempt to extend, apply or criticize Weber's ideas in the analysis of modernity and the analysis of the prospects for individual autonomy in a bureaucratic world. The chapter seeks to unravel certain linguistic and organizational principles in the two editions of the *PE* to arrive at an understanding of what Weber was seeking to convey about the nature of life in modern capitalism, since this is the essential prerequisite for any approach that wants to label itself Weberian.

An engagement with the organizational principles of the *PE* allows us to witness the central themes in the work and the ways in which these may be undermined in the second edition. What emerges from the analysis is the way in which the *PE* is crafted to highlight the nature of the modern capitalist order. Weber's attempt to understand 'the reality in which we move' (Weber 1949: 72), is predicated on viewing the past from the perspective of the present and the present from the perspective of the past. The juxtaposition of past and present – in an effort to specify what is continuous and discontinuous between various cultural epochs – is the fundamental organizational principle of the *PE*. For Weber, then, a characteristic feature of modern culture is the intertwining of various inheritances from the past. Modern persons need to be emancipated from some of these legacies (e.g. traditionalism), whereas others need to be inculcated if one is to survive in modern capitalism. But this survival in capitalism cannot simply be reduced, for Weber, to economic existence and while there is a direct link between notions of the calling in old Protestantism, in Franklin and in the modern order, which means that the modern person has to work in one sphere, a variety of lifestyles (as in the past, so in the present) continue to exist: the point is that increasingly these lifestyles are maintained, and define themselves in relation to the 'iron cage' of modern material culture.

To ignore the linguistic and organizational principles of the text – the features which direct us to the identification of theme – would be to reduce the *PE* to a set of propositions about the past, whereas in fact it is also, and perhaps predominantly, a cultural exploration of what it means to live in the modern capitalist order. One of the central questions that needs to be addressed, therefore, in the interpretation of the *PE*, given the existence of two editions, is whether the meaning of the text alters in the process of Weber's revisions (Hennis 1988: 22–61; Tenbruck 1989).

Weber's writings as texts and interpreters as readers

Before any systematic conclusions can be reached concerning the significance of the textual variants for the understanding of the two editions of the *PE*, it is necessary to critically examine where we consider meaning to reside in Weber's work(s). One way of entering into such a discussion is to pose the following type of question: what factors do we appeal to in our engagement with Weber's writings to support interpretations? For example, is the key to the meaning of Weber's writings the texts themselves and how we consider them to 'work'? Or, is the key to be found in the reader's questions, locations (historical and institutional) and experience of engaging with Weber's texts? Then again, does the meaning of the *PE* reside in the relationship between this text and Weber's other writings and the relationship of Weber's work to his sources (both academic and literary)? Further, what role should be accorded to the extra-textual contexts of the cultural and historical location of the text? Does the meaning of the *PE* depend on the author's intentions and what is the relationship between the text and Weber's personal experiences and values which constitute his motives and worldview? Finally, in the light of two editions, is the meaning of the *PE* now to be located in the interface of these editions: an encounter of a third kind since the understanding of one or the other cannot be achieved independently of, or in innocence of, the other?[2]

These questions are of significance for assessing the ways in which textual changes may affect the meaning of the *PE*. For example, we need to ask: what types of textual change or change in context would actually constitute a change in meaning rather than merely suggesting ways in which Weber's development and relation to his context can be understood? Is the meaning of the *PE* affected by changing circumstances of composition, context, author's intentions and author's biography or by alterations in how the text 'works'? If we accept that the way the text works is a central part of the uncovering of the meaning of the *PE* how do we reach such an understanding of how the text does actually 'work'? Is argument about how a text 'works' to be located in the recovery of an author's intention or in the interaction of the reader with the text? If meaning is related to the active reader who is engaged with the text, is it only possible to describe this as an exercise in subjectivity or are there controls which keep the reader's interpretations within reasonable bounds? While we may accept that there will never be a correct interpretation – in terms of final, all-encompassing, non-corrigible interpretations – we tend to hold that some interpretations are more correct than others: the task is to seek to elaborate criteria by which 'more correct' interpretations can be judged.

These hermeneutical questions may seem to be more apposite to literary, legal and theological texts but these issues are important for Weber studies for the following reasons. First, Weber's writings are texts. By this I mean simply that they are linguistic communications in written form. If we want to know what Weber said we need to read what he wrote. To acknowledge that Weber's works are texts means that his thought does not exist independently of the form in which it is presented nor the language used for its articulation. Secondly, if the former is unlikely to be accepted without debate, it is certainly obvious that the fact of two or more editions/versions of a particular work is, by definition, a textual problem. Since this is the case, philological, textual and literary criticism is of more than peripheral interest.[3] Thirdly, if engagement with Weber is first and foremost a reading of what he wrote, theories of meaning creation and the diversity of reasons for reading Weber need to be foregrounded.

In what follows, rather than provide a theoretical discussion of hermeneutical issues,[4] I focus on the various contexts of the two editions of the *PE* in an attempt to illustrate the ways in which various alterations in the text and context interweave to raise complex interpretative issues. I begin with a brief examination of the extra-textual dimension of author's biography and the question of intentions. In the second part of the chapter I turn to consider the intratextual context of the *PE*: namely, the linguistic and organizational principles of the text. I dwell on this aspect of the discussion since it brings the text into central focus and is generally where I consider meaning to reside. I seek to provide an introduction to various organizational principles of the text and in the process propose a new translation for 'iron cage/*stahlhartes Gehäuse*' which illustrates the role of linguistic criticism in determining Weber's meanings. Further, the discussion of this issue leads us to the heart of Weber's analysis of the fate of the individual in modernity. Finally, I turn to consider the intertextual context of Weber's use of sources.[5]

In each of the discussions what I am seeking to put across is that the intratextual dimension is central to the creation of the meaning of the *PE*, and while the author's intentions, sources and other contexts have a role to play in interpretation, and are of course not totally unrelated to the meaning of the two editions, and hence for the understanding of the 'iron cage' metaphor, it is the former context which must be given priority: it is the point of departure and the final court of appeal in any interpretation. In this light the other contexts would serve as controls for the reconstructions proposed on the basis of the engagement with the text itself.

THE TEXT AND ITS CONTEXTS

The extra-textual context: author's biography and intentions

Biographical studies have an uneasy status in Weber research. On the one hand there is a fascination with Weber's life and loves which shows no signs of abating. On the other hand, there is a resistance to assessing Weber's work in the light of his life. The analysis of the *PE* from a biographical perspective is a case in point. Perhaps more than any other of his writings the *PE* 'is connected with the deepest roots of his personality' (Marianne Weber 1975: 335) and bears its stamp, and yet such a relation to his personal life, it is argued, should be restricted to questions of genesis. For example, Poggi defends the biographical introduction to his study of the *PE* in the following way: 'I raise these matters at the beginning of the discussion because by and large, in my view, it is here that belong questions pertaining to the genesis of a text – not because I attribute to such matters a direct and substantial bearing on the *elucidation of that text*, much less on the validity of its content' (Poggi 1983: 1, my italics).

However, it does seem that Weber was deeply involved with the questions he addressed in the *PE* and it seems possible to delimit the range of what the *PE* can be said to be about, and what his attitude to the culture of the calling in modernity was, from knowledge of that personal interest and his biography. As is well known, Weber wrote the *PE* in the context of his struggle with his mental/ physical incapacity. One side of the experience of this illness was the moral dilemma it placed Weber under. This can be gathered quite clearly from the following letter written by Marianne Weber to Helene Weber (his mother) in 1902:

> In the meantime he has again expressed himself about what torments him most. It is always the same thing: the psychological pressure of the 'unworthy situation' in which he draws a salary and will not be able to accomplish anything in the foreseeable future, combined with the feeling that to all of us – you, I, everyone – only a person with a vocation (*Berufsmensch*) counts fully.

(Marianne Weber, 1975: 261)

What this would suggest is not that the strains and stresses of the need to be a *Berufsmensch* caused his breakdown, but that the difficulty of dealing with that breakdown was heightened by the culture of the calling he encountered. The *PE* can be read on this level as an investigation into the question of where this idea of the calling stemmed from and why it held such a coercive moral power. His insights into the Calvinist personality and the way in which Calvinists overcame their salvation anxiety through work and commitment to duty stem from this personal self-searching. If it had not been for the breakdown and Weber's own analysis of the experience of illness, this reconstruction of the ascetic personality would conceivably be quite different. Equally, Weber's subsequent development, reverting to travel in between bouts of intense scholarly activity, political involvement and erotic relationships (cf. Chalcraft 1993), indicates that the assessment of the need to be a *Berufsmensch* and its attendant meanings cannot be reduced to a simple formula.

Biographical information therefore cannot be restricted merely to questions of genesis, since Weber's motivation, as well as the things he saw, and the things he could not see, seems to have a close relation to the text and the arguments made. An important point to keep in mind is the way in which the life and the work are currently reconstructed reciprocally. The evidence for Weber's life is itself a series of texts which need to be interpreted just as the *PE* itself is a text (Crossman 1980). We must be wary of reading Weber's life in such a way that it supports a reading of the *PE* which we have possibly arrived at on the basis of a reconstruction of the biography, which is itself based, perhaps unconsciously, on the *PE* or a particular understanding of its role in Weber's life. A pressing concern in contemporary Weber studies is the examination of alternative textual and pictorial sources for Weber's life, the careful comparison of Marianne's citation of letters against the original typescripts, an analysis of the biography itself and other reconstructions, and theoretical investigation of the general relation between a life and a work.[6] Nevertheless, the biographical dimensions of the text illustrate that Weber's concern was with the modern epoch; that is to say, analysis of his own reality and experience, his own fate and inheritance, mirrored the cultural concerns of his class and epoch and illuminated them.

Author's intentions

The question of author's intentions is a vexed one in interpretative theory particularly in the light of reader-response theory and deconstructionism. However, a number of observations can be made without entering into the debate in too much depth (cf. LaCapra, 1983: 36–9; Thiselton 1992; Crossman 1980; Fish 1980; Skinner 1988: 29–67; 68–78). We may feel that we can uncover intentional statements in Weber's texts and letters, but the question is whether these statements restrict what the text can be said to be about. We tend to feel that if we can locate intentional statements, and support our interpretations on their basis, that our conclusions are sounder. However, if it is readers engaging with texts who construct meanings, then to speak of author's intentions is actually to falsely dress up a reader's response as an uncovering of the author's intentions. Nevertheless, since it is the author who wrote the text – chose the language and the form of the text from available alternatives (although there may be constraints here) – fidelity to what the text seems to do cannot always be seen as totally unrelated to the author's activity.

Two dimensions of this question of author's intentions need to be distinguished. The testing of author's intention against the text; and the uncovering of possible intentions from the text itself. With respect to the former, our relation to author's intention should not be characterized by too much deference: if the text does not seem to convey those intentions or if other meanings are conveyed, the text cannot mean what the author explicitly says he/she intended but what we take it to mean on the basis of a careful review of the evidence and honest engagement with the text. In short, it is the text which is the data against which supposed intentions are to be judged.

With respect to the latter dimension, if it is the text which is the source for the elucidation of the intentions themselves we have evidence for intentions which are not explicitly stated by the author, but which she/he may have had. The only control for such a construction not becoming fanciful and telling us more about the reader than the author and their text, is that the interpretation offered does not wilfully ignore the historical setting, nor the philological dimension of the text, and is not made without careful consideration of what is known about the author. Above all, the reconstruction needs to point as clearly as possible to what features of the text suggest such a reading.

For example, Weber states at the close of the *PE* what he felt he had demonstrated in the work (in which 'modern' is added in the second edition):

> One of the fundamental elements of the spirit of *modern* capitalism, and not only of that but of all modern culture: rational conduct on the basis of the idea of the calling, was born (*geboren*) – this is what this discussion has sought to demonstrate – from the spirit of Christian asceticism.
>
> (*PE* 1930: 180; *PE* 1920: 202)

This passage functions as a summarizing intentional statement, and to ignore it in determining what the *PE* can be said to be about would be to ignore the evidence (cf. Hennis 1988: 26ff.). However, there are problems with taking this statement at face value. For example, the statement does not tell us how Weber actually felt he had demonstrated the 'birth' of rational conduct from asceticism: on the basis, for example, of a synchronic series of snapshots which compare and contrast the Protestant ethic and the spirit of capitalism; on the basis of a diachronic account of a series of links in a causal chain; or on the basis of a concurrent relationship of mutual reinforcement between carriers of the ethic and carriers of the spirit. The unravelling of these options, and the degree of their presence in the two editions of the *PE*, revolves around careful consideration of the text and determination of the meaning of the use of the notion of elective affinities (*Wahlverwandtschaften*) in the work.[7] Secondly, this is not the only intentional statement in the work itself. For example, in the second edition Weber is at great pains to emphasize the importance of the psychological sanction and that this factor is 'the point of the whole essay' (*PE* 1930, 197; *PE* 1920: 40).[8] Finally, the statement does not indicate why Weber considered it interesting to address this question. Did it derive from historical curiosity; from a concern with the fate of humankind in modernity; with explaining why Protestants were predominant in modern German capitalist enterprises, and so on? Each of these questions direct us to the text to find answers. The evidence of the text needs to be checked against other items of evidence gleaned from a variety of contexts, but the final court of appeal would be the text itself.

The intratextual context: linguistic and organizational principles of the *PE*

By the intratextual context I mean that the immediate context for interpreting the linguistic elements in the text is their relationship to other linguistic elements in the text itself. The meaning of a text is based on the relationship between the elements. This is not to say that we can ignore the historical linguistic context – that is, we recognize that words change their meanings, and research into particular words requires paying attention to historical-philological issues. But even here it could be argued that it is Weber's use of these words in the text itself which is the key to what he intended to convey by them or what, from a reader's perspective, delimits the range of possible meanings. Taking Weber's work seriously as a text means that we need to become attuned to the use of language and the ways in which the linguistic features of the text constitute a coherent sequence of words, sentences, paragraphs, sections and chapters which communicate meaning. In what follows I seek to illustrate from a number of passages what meanings are suggested by Weber's use of language and how this usage is linked into the structure of the work. It is due to the similarity of language between various passages that comparisons are suggested and this draws the reader's attention to particular features of the text and highlights the themes discussed. In this manner, what Weber was seeking to communicate through the 'iron cage' metaphor is illuminated by appreciating the linkages between this metaphor and the themes of the work identified.

Herrschaft, Ertragen and Gehäuse: dominance, compulsion and the contexts for meaningful existence

Passage 1

Let us begin with the following passage which occurs in the opening paragraph of the *PE* in the German texts. (In all my quotations from the texts, those elements which are underlined are new to the second edition. I give Parsons' translation of the *PE*, providing in parentheses the original German: this should not be taken to mean that I necessarily accept his renderings of particular words and concepts, e.g. *Herrschaft* (cf. Murvar 1964: 375; Cohen *et al*. 1975: 237–9; Hinkle 1986). Rather, I have provided the German to highlight the features of the text I wish to draw attention to.)

> The emancipation from economic traditionalism appears, no doubt, to be a factor which would greatly strengthen the tendency to doubt the sanctity of the

religious tradition, as all traditional authorities. But it is necessary to note, what has often been forgotten, that the Reformation meant not the elimination of the Church's control (*Herrschaft*) over everyday life, but rather the substitution of a new form of control for a previous one. It meant the repudiation of a control (*Herrschaft*) which was very lax, at that time scarcely perceptible in practice, and hardly more than formal, in favour of a regulation of the whole of conduct (*Reglementierung der ganzen Lebensführung*) which, penetrating to all departments of private and public life (*alle Sphären des hauslichen und öffentlichen Lebens*), was infinitely burdensome (*unendlich lästige*) and earnestly enforced. The rule (*Herrschaft*) of the Catholic Church 'punishing the heretic, but indulgent to the sinner', as it was in the past even more than today, is now tolerated (*ertragen*) by peoples of thoroughly modern economic character, <u>and was borne (*ertrugen*) by the richest and economically advanced peoples on earth at about the turn of the fifteenth century</u>. The rule (*Herrschaft*) of Calvinism, on the other hand, as it was enforced (*selbst in Kraft stand*) in the sixteenth century in Geneva and Scotland, at the turn of the sixteenth and seventeenth centuries in large parts of the Netherlands, in the seventeenth in New England, and for a time in England itself, would be for us the most absolutely unbearable (*unerträglichste*) form of ecclesiastical control (*Kontrolle*) of the individual which could possibly exist. <u>That was exactly what large numbers of the old commercial aristocracy of those times, in Geneva, as well as in Holland and England, felt about it</u>. And what the reformers complained of in those areas of high economic development was not too much supervision of life (*Beherrschung des Lebens*) on the part of the church, but too little. Now how does it happen that at that time those countries which were most advanced economically, and within them the rising bourgeois *middle* classes, not only failed to resist this <u>unexampled</u> tyranny of Puritanism (*puritanische Tyrannei*), but even developed a heroism in its defence?

(*PE* 1930: 36–7; *PE* 1920: 20; cf. *PE* 1904: 3)

The following observations can be made about this passage. First, the frequent use of the noun *Herrschaft* and other related nouns and verbs conveying the conception of the Calvinist rule and control of everyday life in contrast to the Catholic, suggests a conscious crafting of the passage. Secondly, the words used to describe the tolerance of the system of Calvinist domination over all spheres of existence have significance: the adjective *lästige* (tiresome, irksome, aggravating) and the verb *ertragen*, which occurs some three times. This particular verb is well chosen to convey the sense of the psychological burden caused by the dominance of Calvinism. Weber does not use the verb *tragen* (to carry) in these instances but the verb *ertragen*. The former does relate to the bearing of (physical) burden, but not to the psychological sense of the latter, which 'stresses the patience and perseverance with which particularly trying evils are borne' (Farrell 1977: 40).

It is precisely this verb that Weber uses to introduce the discussion of the psychological consequences of Calvinistic doctrine in Chapter 4. At that juncture he writes: 'For us, the decisive problem is: How was this doctrine borne (*wie wurde diese Lehre ertragen*) in an age in which the after-life was not only more important, but in many ways more certain than all the interests of life in this world?' (*PE*, 1930: 109–10; *PE* 1920: 102–3). Further, the first added sentence also contains a form of the verb *ertragen* which appeared in the original showing a continuity of thought and giving the impression of a seamless text. Finally, it is to be noted how the text oscillates between past and present periods in discussing the subject and how these parallels and comparisons are made fuller through additions, as well as indicating that not all persons are affected equally by a system of ideas and structures. This – the juxtaposition of historical periods and the reordering of chronological time in the narrative – is a feature of the *PE* as a whole and is linked to the macro structure of the work, as will be seen below. The past is viewed from the perspective of the present and the present from the past, allowing what is distinctive to each period to emerge in the course of the discussion. This, of course, is not fully comprehended until the end of the work, but once it is realized earlier passages can be seen as anticipating the conclusion and as having a particular function in the text as a whole.

All of this takes place in the first chapter, whose chief function is to isolate which features of Protestantism and Catholicism should be studied in depth if 'any inner affinity (*innere Verwandtschaft*) is to be found between certain aspects of the old Protestant spirit and modern capitalist culture (*modern kapitalistische Kultur*)' (*PE* 1930: 45; *PE* 1920: 29). This indicates that Weber's central interest is in modern capitalist culture and that his understanding of it will be informed by investigating its linkages to old Protestantism and, in the process, what is distinctive to the latter will also emerge in contrast to the former.

Passage 2

In Chapter 2 of the *PE* the descriptions of modern capitalism as a dominant system which overpowers individuals and compels them into certain types of attitude and action are similar to these descriptions of the rule of Calvinism introduced in Chapter 1 and explored in depth in Chapter 4. As will be seen, this description of modern capitalism anticipates the treatment of the same theme found at the close of the *PE*. But there, the Puritan way of life, albeit briefly, is compared with the way of life in the system of modern capitalism. In other words, while the passage in Chapter 1 sets up the dominance of Calvinism, and Chapter 2 the dominance of capitalism, the final passage under consideration, from Chapter 5, places them side by side – a resolution of the two previous treatments which serves to highlight similarities and differences between the two systems. In this way the basic theoretical framework of the *PE* comes to light: namely, that different institutionalized belief systems/ways of living provide the framework for the analysis of conceptions of the calling held during particular epochs and, in turn, emphasize the fate of the individual in the 'iron cage'.

To turn to the passage in Chapter 2. After the establishment of the calling – the devotion to labour and to the making of money – as the 'Alpha and Omega' of Franklin's ethic, Weber offers some observations on the nature of modern capitalism and the ethical conceptions held by the majority of the population:

> The capitalist economy (*Wirtschaftsordnung*) of the present day is an immense cosmos (*ungeheurer Kosmos*) into which the individual is born (*hineingeboren wird*), and which presents itself to him, at least as an individual, as an unalterable order of things (*als faktisch unabänderliches Gehäuse*) in which he must live. It forces (*zwingt*) the individual, in so far as he is involved in the system of market relationships, to conform to capitalistic rules (*Normen*) of action. The manufacturer who in the long run acts counter to these norms, will just as inevitably be eliminated from the economic scene as the worker who cannot or will not adapt himself to them will be thrown into the streets without a job.
>
> (*PE* 1930: 54–5; *PE* 1920: 37; cf. Durkheim 1982: 51)

The presence of *Gehäuse*, and the idea of the unalterable and unavoidable/inevitable fate of the individual born into this system, described as an immense cosmos which forces the individual into certain types of activity if he/she is to survive economically, relate this passage to the closing sections of the *PE*, as will be seen. In the edition of 1904 there is a footnote to this discussion to which we will return below. For the moment it is important to note that the very next sentence in the main text continues with the theme of the dominance of capitalism. Weber describes this dominance through *Herrschaft* and points out that it selects persons in accordance with its needs (*deren er bedarf*) (*PE* 1930: 55; *PE* 1920: 37). Persons of other dispositions – who will or can not adapt to its requirements – we learn a little later, it cannot use (*nicht brauchen*) (*PE* 1930: 57; *PE* 1920: 42).

Passage 3

If we now turn to the close of the *PE* and examine the language used there, it can be seen how it is reminiscent of the passages discussed above. In a passage which is probably the most famous in the *PE*, containing as it does the 'iron cage' metaphor, Weber expresses himself as follows:

> The Puritan wanted to work in a calling; we are forced to do so (*wir mussen es sein*). For when asceticism was carried out (*übertragen*) of the monastic cells into everyday life, and began to dominate (*beherrschen*) worldly morality, it did its part in building (*erbauen*) the tremendous cosmos (*mächtigen Kosmos*) of the modern economic order. This order is now bound to the technical and economic conditions of machine production (*mechanish-maschineller Produktion*) which today determine (*bestimmt*) the lives of all the individuals

who are born (*hineingeboren werden*) into this mechanism (*Triebwerk*), not only those directly concerned with economic acquisition, with irresistible force (*mit überwältigendem Zwange*). Perhaps it will so determine (*bestimmen*) them until the last ton of fossilized coal is burnt. In Baxter's view the care for external goods should lie on the shoulders of the 'saint like a light cloak (*ein dünner Mantel*) which can be thrown aside at any moment'. But fate (*Verhängnis*) decreed that the cloak should become an iron cage (*ein stahlhartes Gehäuse*). Since asceticism undertook to remodel (*umzubauen*) the world and to work out its ideals in the world, material goods have gained an increasing and finally inexorable power (*unentrinnbare Macht*) over the lives of men as at no previous period in history. Today the spirit of asceticism – whether finally, who knows? – has escaped from the cage (*aus diesem Gehäuse entwichen*). But victorious capitalism, since it rests on mechanical (*mechanische*) foundations, needs its support no longer. The rosy blush of its laughing heir, the Enlightenment, seems to be irretrievably fading and the idea of duty in one's calling (*Berufspflicht*) prowls (*geht*) about in our lives like the ghost (*Gespenst*) of dead religious beliefs.

(*PE* 1930: 181–2; *PE* 1920: 203–4; cf. *PE* 1905: 108)[9]

Here we find the dominance of Calvinism replaced by the dominance of capitalism, and a description of the way in which asceticism itself came to dominate worldly morality which was part of this change from one institutionalized system to another. The steel hard (*stahlhartes*) Puritan personality (e.g. *PE* 1920: 105) moulded by the Calvinistic doctrines and their consequences does its part in creating the tremendous cosmos of the economic order, also referred to as the 'iron cage' (*stahlhartes Gehäuse*) of material goods. The sense of compulsion is clearly conveyed (*mussen, bestimmen*) as well as the inevitability and fate/ calamity (*Verhängnis*) of what has occurred. It is into this *Gehäuse* that individuals are born. It is this *Gehäuse* which raises the problem of meaningful and ethical existence in the modern world just as Calvinist doctrine posed a problem for those motivated by the search for certainty of salvation captured in the question: 'What must I do to be saved?'

Weber makes clear in the *PE* that the modern individual is not motivated by religious questions (unlike the Puritan), nor by a commitment to a naturally revealed ethical system (unlike Franklin), but by the struggle for economic existence: the calling has become a necessity. It is precisely these similarities and differences that the linguistic and organizational principles of the *PE* convey. The steel-hard Puritan personality which is created by Calvinism has a hand in the creation of the steel-hard reality of modern capitalism in which modern personalities are moulded and developed, or at least provides the context in which any formation of personality must take place. For these reasons the exact sense that Weber is seeking to communicate through the 'iron cage' metaphor for the degree of autonomy that exists for the individual in modernity – the nature of the personalities that can be developed – takes on major significance.[10]

The omitted footnote

It is at this point that we can return to the omitted footnote mentioned previously. When this is admitted back into the text two things emerge. First, that the omitted passage, viewed in its context, brings out further the compulsion and inescapability of capitalism (and, in turn, of socialism) which further connects the passage as a whole with the close of the *PE*, at the same time as the military analogy (the barracks) reminds us of the regulation (*Regelmentierung*) of life mentioned in the first passage which has a military flavour. And, secondly, given the similarity in language and theme, we have further evidence, alongside the earlier occurrence of *Gehäuse* (and *Kosmos*), for discussing the semantic source, and hence the meaning, of the 'iron cage' metaphor itself. It is this latter point which is of most interest to us here.

In 1904 Weber wrote in the footnote:

> Wenn man den auf sozialdemokratischen Parteitagen gefallenen Satz: 'wer nicht partiert, fliegt "hinaus", als "kasernenton" bezeichnet hat, so ist das ein arges Missverstandnis: aus der Kaserne fliegt der Renitente keineswegs 'hinaus', sondern erst recht 'hinein' – in den Arrestzelle nämlich. Sondern es ist des öekonomische Lebensschicksal des modernen Arbeiters, wie er es auf Schritt und Tritt erlebt, welches es in der Partei wiederfindet und erträgt: die Disziplin in der Partei ist Widerspiegelung der Disziplin in der Fabrik.
>
> *(PE* 1904: 18, note 1)[11]

The reference to the fate of the modern worker, the tolerance (*ertragen*) of the burden of the discipline of the Social Democratic Party, which is an exact reflection of the discipline and dominance of the factory, recall the images we have pinpointed in the passages previously discussed. The 'iron cage' is hinted at to the extent that there is no escape from the discipline demanded by capitalism: the person who wishes to escape/flee from the barracks (capitalism) does not accomplish this. On the contrary, any attempt to escape the barracks results in a greater imprisonment: a literal and factual one in the arrest-cell of the barracks itself.

What Weber says here is of interest for the reconstruction of his views about socialism, and the degree to which he held that this social formation, or the Social Democratic Party which sought to promote it in Wilhelmine society, would be free of bureaucratic control and discipline. In this sense the promise of social revolutionary politics is not any kind of solution which would enable an escape from the consequences of rationalization and organizational processes. What Weber expresses in this passage agrees with his historical assessment of socialism as portrayed in his speech, *Der Sozialismus* (For the General Information of Austrian Offices in Vienna) of 1918 (Eldridge 1971: 191–219), but the fact that the footnote is dropped from the second edition of the *PE* may reflect not only the fact that Weber had presented his views of the Social Democratic movement elsewhere but also the fact that after the First World War he appeared to be less critical of the party (Beetham 1985: 176).[12]

I am drawing attention to this passage not to contrast Weber's assessments of life in the 'iron cage' of capitalism with that in the 'iron cage' of socialism, but rather to try and prise open what image Weber was seeking to convey; that is, the description of the person moving from the barracks into an arrest-cell within the barracks is an image which may or may not relate to the somewhat similar image of the iron cage at the close of the *PE*. To what extent, therefore, can the iron cage of the capitalist order be thought of as a barracks or an arrest-cell, which, at first sight, seems to be similar to the notion of a constraining structure, or even a structure with iron bars: the image suggested by the iron cage? Stephen Kent has argued that a more appropriate translation than 'iron cage' for the *stahlhartes Gehäuse* is 'a casing as hard as steel' (Kent 1983). In this sense, is the *Arrestzelle* in the omitted footnote an equivalent image to the 'housing as hard as steel' referred to at the close of the *PE*? Indeed, is Kent's suggested translation for the *stahlhartes Gehäuse* adequate to convey Weber's meaning?

Translating the 'iron cage' metaphor

In order to answer these questions we need to examine all of the linguistic elements identified above and review Kent's suggestion in the light of them. Kent bases his argument on the fact that 'iron cage' stems from Parsons who traced the image back to Bunyan, whereas Weber is more influenced by Goethe and Nietzsche than by Bunyan, and there is, besides, little philological evidence to support Parsons' rendering.[13] Kent also argues that there is a high degree of reference to mechanical aspects of capitalism in the closing passages of the *PE* for which a translation referring to the steel casings of objects would seem appropriate. However, we can question whether this translation fits with other philological features of the passages under consideration. In particular, we need to ask whether 'steel casing' can correspond to a 'light cloak'; whether the verbs for 'escape' suggest escape from a cage, casing, barracks, prison or some other constraining device; whether 'casing' is plastic enough to be extended to include the idea of *Kosmos*, which is also used by Weber to describe the nature of capitalism and, finally, whether we can find a translation that would fit each use of *Gehäuse* adequately.

It is undoubted that *Gehäuse* conveys the idea of containment. Originally, the word was a collective for house/dwelling. It subsequently became restricted to the idea of containment for lifeless objects (Paul 1966: 233–4; Drosdowski 1989: 224). For example, Goethe used it as a synonym for containers such as saddle-bags (*Mantelsäcke*), suitcases and other leather articles. In modern German *Gehäuse* is used to refer to the casings/cabinets for a number of unrelated objects. For example, as the casing for a clock (*Uhrengehäuse*), the cabinet for a loud-speaker, the housing for a pump (*Brunnengehäuse*) and so on. However, Schiller could use the word as a poetic expression for the body, which contains the spirit of a person (Paul 1966: 233–4). While Weber's assessment of the type of life lived in the *Gehäuse* – as lifeless to the extent that it can be without meaning – it is also true that Weber envisages the individual as living within this *Gehäuse*: it is into this *Gehäuse* that the individual is born and in which he or she must live their life. Thus, Weber is thinking less of a container for lifeless objects and more of a context in which existence is played out under restraint; of a dwelling and constraining environment. In this sense, a prison or detention cell in a barracks might be envisaged. However, for the reasons given below, a prison does not seem to fit the uses of *Gehäuse* in the contexts in which they occur – they could not be translated as 'prison'.

What seems more likely is something along the lines of a hard shell. For example, a *Schneckengehäuse* is the shell of a snail. The shell of a snail is comparatively hard and is the 'house' within which it lives and moves. It provides the context for the snail's existence but must be carried round. The shell is a burden which constrains its movement, but existence outside of the shell is inconceivable. The shell is the covering for the snail, its shelter and context, but also its constraint. I suggest that this is what Weber had in mind. Not, to be sure, in the strict sense of comparing modern persons to a snail (!), but in the sense of the shell in which modern people must live and breathe and which they carry with them wherever they go. Although it provides the context for existence it is not simply outside of the individual but is part and parcel of their very existence. Indeed, in art and literature the snail with its shell can symbolize 'one's personality, which one carries about everywhere and cannot leave behind' (de Vries 1974: 430). In this sense, Weber's use of the idea of the shell is related to his interest in the nature of the modern personality required by modern capitalism and the degree to which differing lifestyles can be cultivated within the system of capitalism. I will return to this point. For the moment it needs to be mentioned that *Schneckengehäuse* is still used in modern German to refer to the shell of a snail and was also current in Weber's day (Mauret-Saunders 1910).

One problem with the 'iron cage' translation is the way in which it functions as a transformation of the 'light cloak'. The light cloak is transformed, by necessity and fate, into an iron cage. It seems more likely that a light cloak would be transformed into a heavy cloak of the nature of steel. That is, if we were to continue with the clothing dimension of the metaphor something like a strait-jacket would appear more appropriate. In German a strait-jacket is a *Zwangsjacke* which would cohere quite nicely with the verbs for compulsion (e.g. *zwingen*) and the nouns for force (e.g. *Zwang*) used in the passages discussed. What is more, a *Zwangsjacke* has a psychological resonance since it relates to the constraint of someone who is either violent or mentally ill. This might appeal to those commentators who wish to see some relationship between Weber's breakdown and his experiences prior to writing the *PE*. Just as the barracks analogy could draw on Weber's experience of national service, the *Zwangsjacke* could draw on Weber's knowledge of psychotherapy and practices in various sanatoria. That is, when Weber was looking for ways to express his ideas these two contexts may have provided him with vocabulary.[14]

But support for such a translation is slight. First, if Weber meant this he could have used *Zwangsjacke*, which he obviously did not. Secondly, the verb used for 'escape' from the *Gehäuse* in the passage (*entweichen*) does not relate to the freeing of oneself from such a device (see below). Thirdly, it would constitute a misunderstanding of Weber's figures of speech. It is the care for material goods which is first like a light cloak and then, subsequently, like a *stahlhartes Gehäuse*. Thus, 'light cloak' and *stahlhartes Gehäuse* are two separate similes for the role of material goods in a person's life and the two need not have a logical relationship to each other. Nevertheless, what the similes have in common is the factor of a covering of the person: one more or less malleable, the other, on the contrary, rigid like steel. This is the heart of their metaphorical relationship. Weber's use of the noun *Kosmos* needs now to be considered in this connection. In the passages in Chapters 2 and 5 *Kosmos* relates to the constraining and powerful nature of capitalism which the individual encounters, but Weber seems to have in mind here more the idea of a world order than the specific micro world of individuals. In this sense, *Gehäuse*, which also appears in the passage in Chapter 2, is a covering, inasmuch as the cosmos is the canopy of all activity. This passage, and the use of *Gehäuse*, has a relationship to the 'iron cage' passage in Chapter 5, since both uses relate to the notion of a covering, so it is possible to apply the idea of shell here by extension.

Parsons' rendering of *Gehäuse* in the passage in Chapter 2 as 'order of things' conveys the sense of the universality of capitalism Weber is indicating. It is the environment in which world economic activity takes place. But to come down to the individual level this *Gehäuse* is not a prison or some strait-jacket, rather it is the shell as hard as steel in which existence is played out. But within this shell the individual must live and develop a personality, a personality that constitutes the shell that the individual carries around with them wherever they go. Hence, we can say that when the passages are brought into relationship to each other – which is justified by their similarity of theme and language – Weber has in mind in both uses of *Gehäuse* the shell/living space in which human activity and valuing takes place: one refers to the universal world order of capitalism, the other to the more micro order of individual social worlds. And, of course, the two are interrelated: the individual is born into the great world order of capitalism but experiences it on the individual level. The shell as hard as steel constitutes the macro environment in which the individual develops their own shell of existence. The former determines the possibilities of the structuring of the latter and the more the steel shell of capitalism is felt on the individual level the less autonomy there is for the development of alternative lifestyles in the system. A casing as hard as steel could not apply to the *Kosmos* idea and neither does it conjure up the context in which people live.

The verbs for escape in the passage in Chapter 5 now need to be considered. If Weber had the idea of a strait-jacket in mind the construction to express escape from this would be *Sich befreien* (Farrell 1977: 108). If Weber had a prison or cage more in mind here, such as the arrest-cell of the barracks mentioned in the omitted footnote, verbs relating to escape such as *ausbrechen* or *fliehen* would be more appropriate (Farrell 1977: 108). Indeed, Weber used the verb *fliehen* in the omitted footnote. Thus, while Weber can express the experience of capitalism as living in a barracks, and we can see how easily such a conception follows from the ideas he is conveying on a macro level, this sense does not seem to be the appropriate one for the uses of *Gehäuse* in the passages studied since the verbs used are not *fliehen*, and *Gehäuse* seems more related to cosmos and shell than casing or prison. Nevertheless, translating *Gehäuse* as shell, as well as maintaining the micro and macro dimension in Weber's sociology, also maintains the constraining and coercive nature of capitalism communicated in the text.

In the final passage the words for escape are the negative *unentrinnbare* (inescapable) and *entweichen*. The adjective *unentrinnbare* comes from the verb *entrinnen*. According to Farrell, *entrinnen* is an 'elevated term and used figuratively', usually in speaking of escape from particular dangers (1977: 109). *Entweichen*, on the other hand, appears to be more precise since it is often used to describe the slow seepage of gas from its container: that is, 'it is the normal term in reference to gas'. In this sense, the verb would appear to support Kent's idea of a casing as a translation for *Gehäuse*. However, this usage is an application of the more generic meaning of *entweichen*; namely, 'to escape silently, stealthily' (Farrell 1977: 108). Hence Weber is perhaps describing less the escape from a particular type of constraint and more the nature of the escape itself: slowly, stealthily and without notice. Yet, on the evidence of the Mauret Saunders dictionary of 1910, *entrinnen* and *entweichen* could be seen as general and colourless verbs for escape. As such, the verbs Weber uses cannot be used to determine precisely what he had in mind, but they can be used to determine what he did not mean. In other words, the verbs used cannot be taken as evidence against the translation of 'shell' for *Gehäuse* but they do seem to suggest that casing and prison/barracks/cage are inappropriate in this context.

Summary

What the comparison of the three passages (and the omitted footnote) in the *PE* undertaken above shows is that the themes discussed are similar and that this is brought to the reader's attention, as well as being confirmed, by the similarity in the language used. What is more, this feature of the text enabled the examination of what Weber may have been seeking to convey by the 'iron cage' metaphor. It has been argued that a more appropriate translation of *ein stahlhartes Gehäuse* than 'iron cage' or 'a casing as hard as steel' is 'a steel shell/a shell as hard as steel'. This translation has been defended on the basis of the comparison of the passages, and by paying attention to historical philological issues. The exercise is an example which confirms that no linguistic element in the *PE* can be viewed in isolation from another. But, at the same time, the proposed translation coheres with the themes of the *PE* as a whole, to which our attention is drawn by the passages studied, and by other features of the text, some of which are further elaborated below. That is to say, the translation maintains the notion of the constraining macro nature of capitalism at the same time as maintaining Weber's interest in the types of personality demanded by capitalism. Moreover, it relates to the closing passages of the *PE* taken as a whole in so far as a degree of choice appears to be possible for persons within the macro 'shell as hard as steel' which is the capitalist system.[15]

For example, while it is undoubted that for all modern persons the way of life to be adopted is determined in relation to the steel shell of the capitalist order, a degree of variety is possible. For some, especially those who have been exposed to a Protestant ascetic educative influence (like the Pietists; *PE* 1930: 62–3) adapting to the system is relatively easy since they have the requisite personality, which, of course, explains why they are predominant (*PE* 1930: 35); for others, adaptation is less easy and 'the idea of duty in a calling stalks around in their lives like the ghost of dead religious beliefs'. Again, for still others, while their lives are affected by the steel shell of capitalism they refuse to adapt and forgo whatever benefits, usually material rewards, the shelter of the shell provides (*PE* 1930: 56; 60). Their situation is similar to those who escape from the steel shell altogether – escape is possible, and their ways of life are different, but they exist outside the shell. And, finally, there are those 'last men' who are satisfied with the comforts they have acquired, thinking this is all that life has to offer.[16]

In other words, the steel shell of the capitalist order determines the choices that people will make as to how they will order their lives and what they will value, but the personality they will develop, the shell they will carry around on their backs, is capable of differing constructions. They can choose not to conform and face the consequences. While the Puritan wanted to work in a calling, and we have to *if* we want to be successful in the economic struggle for existence, our approach to that will depend on our own choices. Each, we could say, must decide and obey the demon who holds the fibre of their very lives (Weber 1948: 156).

For these reasons, I would argue, the translation of *ein stahlhartes Gehäuse* as a 'steel shell' is superior to 'iron cage' since the latter conveys a macro structure and relates only to the external coercive nature of the capitalist system. Weber's concern with ways of life and with what manner of life can be adopted in modernity is therefore lost sight of (cf. Hennis 1988; Turner 1992). In this way, some of the central themes of the *PE* are forgotten. And, finally, of course, the philological evidence for 'iron cage' is less than slight. What the implications are for Weberian sociology I will mention in my concluding comments below.

Intratextual context II: the Franklin Bridge and the structure of the narrative

The above argument is predicated on the similarity in language and theme of the passages discussed. That is, these similarities suggest a conscious structuring of the narrative, and it follows that if, in the second edition, the way the text works has been altered then this may have implications for the identification of theme on this basis. In what follows, therefore, I focus on one unaltered passage which appears to be a further articulation of the ordering of the text illustrated above, and then, in the final part, I turn to consider a passage that has been dramatically altered in the second edition. The question there will be: to what extent does this alteration suggest a change in meaning and, if so, does that change affect the foregoing argument?

At no point in the *PE* does Weber state that his aim is to compare and contrast past and present conceptions of the calling in an effort to specify what is continuous and discontinuous in ideas of the calling held in old Protestantism, by Franklin, and in the modern order of capitalism and thereby to elaborate the nature of ways of life in the steel shell of modern capitalism. However, a close concentration on the macro and micro levels of the text reveals that this is conceivably what Weber does: the way the text works is to communicate such a structure in the work. We have seen above how the use of language suggests a greater macro ordering of the text. The text can also be seen as structured in such a way to indicate relationships: anticipating and recalling and suggesting temporal linkages and comparisons. One instance of this in the text on the micro level (which mirrors the organization of the *PE* as a whole) is in the context of the discussion of Franklin's specific attitude to making money and living ethically: namely, the first discussion in the *PE* of the idea of the calling. Weber has just elaborated Franklin's attitude to making money as a duty and continues as follows:

> This reversal of what we should call the natural relationship, so irrational from a naive point of view, is evidently as definitely a leading principle of capitalism as it is foreign to all peoples not under capitalistic influence. At the same time it expresses a type of feeling which is closely connected with certain religious ideas. If we thus ask, why should 'money be made out of men', Benjamin Franklin himself, although he was a colourless deist, answers in his autobiography with a quotation from the Bible, which his strict Calvinist father drummed into him again and again in his youth: Seest thou a man diligent in his business (*Beruf*)? He shall stand before kings (Prov.22.29). The earning of money within the modern economic order is, so long as it is done legally, the result and the expression of virtue and proficiency in a calling: and this virtue and proficiency are, as it is now not difficult to see, the real Alpha and Omega of Franklin's ethic, as expressed in the passages we have quoted, as well as in all his works without exception'.
>
> (*PE* 1930: 53–4)[17]

The feature of the above passage I wish to draw attention to is the way in which Franklin is used as a bridge between two epochs/temporal conceptions of the calling. Weber begins with a general overview of the character of modern capitalism. Then he shows the linkage back with Puritan ideas, although Franklin is described as a colourless deist, suggesting the transformation of the religious motivation for the calling in Franklin's ethic. Franklin's ethic is then connected to work-ethics in the modern order. And each of these discussions is then used to reaffirm the distinctive nature of Franklin's attitudes to work and money as an ethical duty. Hence, old Protestantism, Franklin and the modern order are connected in this brief passage and affinities between them are suggested at the same time as we are made very much aware that they cannot be seen as equivalent to each other. What occurs here is a microcosm of the text as a whole. The way the *PE* progresses chapter by chapter corresponds with these three stages, with religion introduced but held in abeyance until Chapters 3 and 4, whereupon the narrative begins to work its way back to the modern order, ending up with describing the steel shell of modern capitalism, once the Calvinist conception of the calling has been examined in depth and related to rational conduct in all spheres of life.

Thus, while the three passages focused on previously show an interrelationship in language and theme which suggests the theoretical and contextual framework for the discussion of the calling in that they set up the fact that in different institutional settings different conceptions of the calling are demanded more than others, this passage shows the historical linkage between conceptions of the calling. The three stages indicated in the passages I discussed are here found in one passage. Hence all the passages serve to reinforce the reading of the organizational principles of the text argued for here. Of course, the sequence of exposition I have related is not necessarily a record of how these relationships were first suggested to me: this reading of the *PE*, as is any reading, is an example of the hermeneutical circle – once one has, so to speak, gone round the circle a number of times, reading and rereading the work, so it is difficult to locate precisely where the original point of departure is to be found.[18]

All these passages tend to agree with the intentional statement we analysed above and tend to suggest that the idea of 'birth' mentioned there is more in terms of a comparative causal link (a series of synchronic snapshots) than a dynamic causal sequence which will be articulated in detail throughout the text. What is more, these passages are unaltered in the second edition, which suggests that if the meaning of the *PE* is to be located in this intratextual context, that here, at least on the basis of the passages discussed, the meaning does not change: the narrative structure – the organizational and linguistic principles in the text – remain intact and the reading of the 'iron cage' metaphor does not need to be revised. However, if we now turn to consider another passage under the heading of the intertextual context we can see how a more dynamic dimension is emphasized in the second edition of the *PE*, to fill the gaps, so to speak, between the comparative analysis of conceptions of the calling.

The intertextual context

In the second edition of the *PE* there are a group of variants that relate to new sources which appear to share a common purpose. Namely, to provide evidence that contemporary witnesses observed the relationships between piety and business sense Weber presupposes. If the relationship was obvious to contemporaries, Weber asks in the second edition, why then do modern commentators deny it? (*PE* 1930: 191, note 23; 280, note 96). In this respect all the references to Sir William Petty, for example, are new to the second edition (e.g. *PE* 1930: 43; 179; 279, note 93). Related to these additions are those which add further illustration of English social history during the seventeenth century. Weber here uses the work of Levy (1912), Unwin (1904), Leonard (1900) and Sir Maurice Ashley. The work of Maurice Ashley may indeed be the main source for the other authorities cited in the text. Weber acknowledges a letter from Ashley from 1913 which pointed out a quotation from Wesley that would support his case, of which, he confesses, he previously was unaware (*PE* 1930: 280, note 95). Ashley's letter, apparently, expressed support for Weber's arguments (*PE* 1930: 280, note 96) and an examination of Ashley's writing from this time (Ashley 1913, 1914) illustrates his indebtedness to Weber, and confirms that Weber may have acquired knowledge of these other works from him, but not the exact wording of the Wesley extract.

The additions made to the second edition which stem from these sources generally do not affect the arguments made (*PE*, 1930: 279–82). Rather, they function more by way of illustration and further documentation of previously argued points about, for example, the attitudes of Cromwell, Prynne and Parker to monopolies and commercial life (*PE* 1930: 179–80; 213, note 12), the antagonism between the squirearchy and the middle and lower classes in Puritan England (*PE* 1930: 217, note 31), Puritan attitudes to the maypole (*PE* 1930: 168) and such like. The quotation from Wesley, on the other hand, has a more dramatic role in the text, even though it does appear to bring into central focus elements in the text which appeared previously. These elements are now stressed to such an extent in the second edition that a change in meaning can possibly be located here in so far as the stress on a dynamic sequence of change stands in some tension with the organizational principles of the *PE* discussed above.

John Wesley in the second edition of the PE

The long quotation from Wesley appears in Chapter 5 in the second edition in the context of Weber's discussion of the secularizing influence of wealth. Since the quotation serves to further emphasize this general social process (which had characterized the history of monastic communities in the past) it tends to confirm that this is what Weber was originally intending to communicate. This addition, however, serves to elevate the point to the extent that reading the second edition at this juncture is strikingly different from the experience of the first.

The passage is as follows:

> The great revival of Methodism, which preceded the expansion of English industry toward the end of the eighteenth century, may well be compared with such a monastic reform. We may hence quote a passage here from John Wesley himself which might well serve as a motto for everything which has

been said above. For it shows that the leaders of these ascetic movements
understood the seemingly paradoxical relationships which we have here analysed perfectly well, and in the same sense that we have given them.

Weber then goes on to quote a long passage from Wesley, which can be summed
up in the following sentence from Wesley:

For religion must necessarily produce both industry and frugality, and these
cannot but produce riches. But as riches increase, so will pride, anger, and love
of the world in all its branches.

Weber completes the quotation, and then paraphrases Wesley, finally adding his
own comments before returning to the wording of the first edition, as follows:

We ought not to prevent people from being diligent and frugal; we must exhort
all Christians to gain all they can, and to save all they can; that is, in effect, to
grow rich'. There follows the advice that those who gain all they can and save
all they can should also give all they can, so that they will grow in grace and
lay up a treasure in heaven – it is clear that Wesley here expresses, even in
detail, just what we have been trying to point out.
    As Wesley says here, the full economic effect of those great religious
movements, whose significance for economic development lay above all in
their ascetic educative influence, generally came about only after the peak of
the purely religious enthusiasm was past. Then the intensity for the search for
the Kingdom of God commenced gradually to pass over into sober economic
virtue; the religious roots died out slowly, giving way to utilitarian worldliness.
                    (*PE* 1930: 175–6; *PE* 1920: 196–7; cf. *PE* 1905: 104)

These additions raise the question of author's intentions and the role of the reader
in reconstructing the meaning of the *PE*. For instance, once this addition is
acknowledged it becomes obvious that the secularizing influence of wealth, the
dying out of the religious roots of the calling and the transformation into utilitarianism were features of the original argument as seen in the passage cited
above and in other places in the first edition (e.g. *PE* 1930: 177). The question is
whether the reader would have spotted these features, or at least concentrated on
them to the extent that is now the case in the light of the addition. Here we have
an example of the way in which the meanings of the two editions appear to be
inseparable from each other once they are brought into a comparative relationship.

If Weber was merely pulling out what was originally present we need to ask
why the change was made at all. It seems to have been made to highlight this
feature of the text, which suggests that this had either been overlooked by
Weber's critics or that he felt that his argument had been misunderstood on this
point. But it does not follow that Weber wanted to make a statement that
conveyed the dynamic causal features of his account: rather, he simply wanted to
add the evidence of a contemporary source, as is the case with the other variants
to which it appears to be related. Indeed, in the first added footnote to the second

edition as a whole, Weber claims that he has not altered any sentence which contained any essential point (*PE* 1930: 187). Do we then presume that this is not an essential point or that Weber has not expressed anything new through the addition?

Whatever his intentions may have been – and note the way in which we must guess at them – the question remains as to whether all this makes a difference to us. To be sure, the text of the second edition at this point is different and the experience of reading it is also different from an engagement with the first. The question is: has the meaning changed? From Weber's perspective it would appear that the meaning had not changed. But for the reader, especially on the basis of the structure of the work we have identified above, the situation is surely different. The reader is now provided with a firm and powerful statement about the effect of wealth on the religious ethic and provided with a clearer under-standing of the causal processes which may have led from the old Protestant ethic to the ethic of Franklin and the conception of the calling held in modern capitalistic culture. These are concerns which, retrospectively in the light of the second edition, were present in the first edition, but now in the second cannot be ignored and stand in a degree of tension with the more comparative analysis of conceptions of the calling which is conveyed by the organization of the text in both editions.

When these additions are coupled with the growing stress on the psychological sanction, the changes of tense (especially in Chapter 5), and the 'disenchantment' additions found in the second edition (e.g. *PE* 1930: 105, 109, 147), all of which require a separate study in themselves, the situation suggests that the original organization of the narrative may have begun to be undermined in the second edition, although, paradoxically, central features of it remain and are even rein-forced. Thus, if the 'iron cage' metaphor has been interpreted on the basis of the organizational principles identified in the narrative, as it has been above, the fact that other principles can also be identified, especially in the second edition, means that while we need not revise our understanding of the 'iron cage' argued for above, we do need to appreciate that the centrality of Weber's concern with ways of life in modern capitalistic culture is somewhat reduced in the second edition, and might now need to be placed alongside other central themes.

SUMMARIZING CONCLUSION

I have tried to show, through a preliminary discussion of method in Weber studies, that a fundamental question that any reader of Weber must ask is: where does meaning reside in Weber's work? I have sought to argue that, in the final analysis, it is the text itself which must be taken seriously and which is the point of departure and the final court of appeal – but by no means the only relevant body of evidence – for the production and defence of any reading of Weber's work. By focusing on the texts of the two editions of the *PE* I emphasized certain linguistic and organizational principles of the text as being the key to the reading of the work. I argued that the *PE* is structured in such a way as to highlight the nature of life in modern capitalistic culture. Weber achieves this by past and present comparisons, and we are invited to make such comparisons through the way the narrative is structured on the micro and macro levels. My analysis suggests that the main theme of the *PE* is not the origins of capitalism, nor the general theme of rationalization, but rather the development of particular types of personality, which are examined by synchronic comparisons of conceptions of the calling dominant in particular epochs. Further, these comparisons are undertaken in an effort to understand the nature of, and the possibilities for, ways of life in modern capitalism. It is here that the translation of *ein stahlhartes Gehäuse* takes on significance. The translation of this phrase as a 'steel shell' was shown to have a firmer linguistic, theoretical and thematic basis than 'iron cage', and illustrates the method of the essay as a whole. This takes us to the heart of Weber's characterology of modern capitalist culture. Weber's concern was to express both the increasingly constraining nature of capitalistic culture and the extent to which modern persons could develop ways of living within that overarching structure. While ways of life (*Lebensführungen*) are always established in relation to the steel shell of capitalistic organization, the range of possible adaptations to the system has a degree of flexibility. One can, for example, elect not to value working in a calling; to elect not to value success in the economic struggle for existence. Finally, I have suggested that the synchronic treatment of conceptions of the calling in the first edition of the *PE* sits somewhat uncomfortably with the more diachronic nature of the second edition. The extent to which this diachronic feature of the work undermines Weber's predominant concern with the modern capitalist order in the first edition, and constitutes an alteration in meaning, is a question to which attention can now be turned. However, the fact that, at the same time, the original organizational principles of the text remain intact in the second edition suggests that our reading of the 'iron cage' does not need to be revised; only that when both editions are taken into consideration there is more than one central preoccupation in the *PE*.

For the moment, the implications for Weberian sociological approaches to modernity are obvious. Alongside the more common concentration on the constraining power of capitalism, and the inner logic of the spread of rationalization and bureaucracy, equal attention needs to be paid to the variety of human experience and valuing, the development of alternative personalities, within the steel shell of capitalism. Our attention should also be directed to the personalities that are created within capitalistic culture, and focus on the nature of those shells which people carry around with them wherever they go in the steel shell of capitalist culture, and which constitute the meaningful context of a person's existence. A Weberian sociology should seek to uncover the full range of social reality and capture the kaleidoscope of human experience and the ways in which people construct meanings within their micro social worlds, which, as we have seen, takes place within the macro steel shell of modern capitalist culture.

NOTES

* I would like to acknowledge the importance of the comments and ideas of numerous students who have taken Sociological Theory I with me at Oxford Brookes University and who have made me think again and again about the meaning of the *PE*. If they have learnt as much from me as I have from them, teaching does have its rewards. I would also like to thank Larry Ray and Mike Reed for their comments on previous drafts of this chapter. The shortcomings of this piece are nobody's fault but mine.

1 The first essay of the *PE*, which corresponds to Chapters 1–3 of the second edition, was published in the *Archiv für Sozialwissenschaft und Sozialpolitik* in 1904 (Weber 1904). The second essay, corresponding to Chapters 4 and 5 of the second edition, written after Weber's trip to America, was published in the same journal in 1905 (Weber 1905). The second edition can be found in the first volume of the *Gesammelte Aufsätze zur Religionssoziologie* published in 1920 (Weber 1920), and this text forms the basis for Parsons' translation of 1930 (Weber, 1930). In my citation of the sources I use *PE* 1904, *PE* 1905, *PE* 1920 and *PE* 1930 to refer to these texts.

2 In his writings Jerome McGann reflects on this situation which shows a shift in editorial theory (McGann 1983, 1985: 69–89; cf. Zeller 1975a, 1975b; Tanselle, 1990: 27–71; 186–9). Basically, it involves a shift away from the production of authoritative texts which reflect author's final intentions to an appreciation of the fact that different editions/versions reflect different intentions at different times. The result has been the production of genetic texts which allow for the reconstruction of the earlier editions on the basis of the critical edition of the later text. This is precisely the editorial theory adopted by the editors of the Weber *Gesamtausgabe* (Schluchter 1981). The unintended consequence of this policy might be the appreciation of instability in the meaning of Weber's texts.

3 What is more the *PE* is not the only text which has a number of different versions or a complex textual history. The same is true of the majority of Weber's texts: for example, the China and India studies, the Sects essays, the *Einleitung*, the *Zwischenbetrachtung*, *The Agrarian Sociology of the Ancient Civilisations*, and, above all, *Economy and Society*.

4 For discussions of the hermeneutical issues involved see, for example, Newton 1990; Bonnycastle 1991; Thiselton 1992; LaCapra 1983: 23–71.

5 There are two aspects of the intertextual context – essential for a comprehensive exegesis of the *PE* – which, for reasons of space, cannot be entered into here: the relationship between the *PE* and Weber's other writings (especially the Sects essays, the *Economic Ethics of the World Religions* series and the *Psychophysics of Industrial Labour*, Weber 1909); and, secondly, a whole range of intertextual affinities between Weber's writings and a host of literary sources popular in Weber's day to which he alludes directly or indirectly (including Goethe, Ibsen, Tolstoy, Keller, George, to name but a few examples; cf. Chalcraft 1993; Scaff 1989, Goldman 1988, Lepenies 1988, Albrow 1990).

6 In a recent study (Chalcraft 1993) I reflect on the relationship between the production of the second edition of the *PE* and Weber's personal life, by focusing on the addition to the text of Siegmund's reply to the herald of death from Wagner's opera *Die Walküre* (*PE* 1930: 107–8). The reader is referred to this for further references on the study of Weber's life.

7 That is to say, Goethe's novel of the same name, from which Weber seems to have taken over this notion (Goethe 1809/1971) can be taken to support these interpretations. An 'elective affinity' can relate to the determination of 'spiritual parenthood' on the basis of the characteristics of the 'child' (Goethe 1809/1971: 220–1; Garland and Garland 1986: 951); equally, it can describe the process whereby various elements in

reality become dissociated from their original combinations to recombine with others to which they are more suited and which, in the process, support one another (Goethe 1809/1971: 46–57; cf. Goethe 1980). In such a situation which element is the dependent, and which the independent, variable is not a sensible question to ask. While both these conceptions are present in the *PE* the question remains as to which is uppermost, and in which edition. In particular, as will be seen below, the details which stand between the 'conception' and the 'birth' of the spirit of capitalism, and in turn, modernity, are 'filled out' in the second edition and related to world-historical processes. It does not appear to be fanciful to connect the *PE* with Goethe's novel. On the contrary, many of the images which seek to explain the relationship between the Protestant ethic and the spirit of capitalism have familial content. For example, Weber speaks of the Puritan outlook standing at the 'cradle of modern economic man'(*PE* 1930: 174), and what Protestant asceticism contributes to the growth of modernity is described as a 'bequest' (*PE* 1930: 176). Further, the notion of fate (*PE* 1930: 172, 181), the unintended consequences of social action and the themes of renunciation and denial are equally traceable in Goethe's *Elective Affinities*, as they are in the other works Weber cites from the pen of Goethe: *Faust*, and *Wilhelm Meister* (*PE* 1930: 180–1). We most certainly need, alongside a critical, annotated, English edition of the *PE*, a study of Weber analogous to Prawer's excellent, and fascinating, *Karl Marx and World Literature* (Prawer 1976).

8 It is noteworthy, from the perspective of the organization of the text (see below) that Weber here acknowledges that the introduction of the idea of the psychological sanction at this juncture is to break the sequence of the original narrative.

9 While the phrase from Baxter is given in speech marks, this is not an exact quotation from *The Saints' Everlasting Rest* (1651). Baxter wrote: 'I advise thee, Christian, who hast tasted the pleasures of a heavenly life, if ever thou would taste them more, avoid this devouring gulf of an earthly mind. If once thou come to this, that 'thou wilt be rich' thou fallest into temptation and a snare, and into many foolish and hurtful lusts. *Keep these things loose about thee like thy upper garments, that thou mayest lay them by whenever there is need*; but let God and glory be next thy heart' (Baxter, 1651/1978: 309–10, my italics).

10 When I refer to 'personality' I have in mind the use Weber gave it in the *PE*: the ability to act, rationally and methodically, on one's constant motives (*PE* 1930: 119).

11 The passage can be translated, somewhat literally, as follows: 'If one calls the comment heard at Social Democratic Party conferences – that, 'who does not participate, flees out' – barrack room language, it is a serious misunderstanding. The renegade in no way escapes from the barracks, but rather goes 'straight in' – namely, into the arrest cell. Indeed, what the modern worker experiences with every step he takes, and which he rediscovers and bears in the party, is his economic fate: the discipline in the party is the mirror image of the discipline in the factory' (my translation). I wish to acknowledge here the useful conversation I had with Sara Schaefer, one of my sociology students, about the meaning of this passage.

12 Further information on Weber's relationship to the Social Democratic Party, and his attitudes to socialism, can be found in Mommsen 1984; 1989: 74–86, 87–105 and Beetham 1985. The essays by Eldridge, Turner, and Ray and Reed in this volume also discuss these relationships.

13 It is important to keep in mind, as Kent (1983) points out, that any search for the source of Weber's image should not take 'iron cage' as the point of departure. To take an example (one not used by Kent himself) one might think that Weber had taken over the idea from the Grimm Brothers, in so far as Wilhelm Grimm wrote to his brother Jacob, on 28 May 1809, of a dream he had, during which he ascends (like Goethe) a mountain in Switzerland and encounters a body in a 'wire cage/iron cage' which turns

out to be his brother. The passage in question reads as follows: 'Suddenly, I was somewhere else, on the way to a high mountain. Now you know that on the St Gothard in Switzerland there is a wire cage where they put people who have perished in the cold . . . I then stood in front of a wired cavern, and in it you sat' (Michaelis-Jena 1970: 40). However, a glance at the original German of the letter shows that the formulation is hardly related to Weber's *ein stahlhartes Gehäuse* after all. Rather, one finds: *vergittertes Behaelter* and *vergitterten Höhle* respectively (Grimm and Hinrichs 1963: 105). The same is the case in the story of *Der Eisenhans*, where the wild man who is responsible for the disappearance of numerous huntsmen is finally captured and kept secure in an 'iron cage' (*eisernen Käfig*) (Grimm and Grimm 1980: 234; cf. Grimm and Grimm 1982: 264).

14 In Thomas Mann's *Magic Mountain*, the routine of life in the sanatorium is described in similar military terms (e.g. Mann 1924/1952: 146). Indeed, the whole of German society is likened to a barracks by Dr Krokowski: 'Unser liebes Deutschland ist eine grosse Kaserne, gewiss' (ibid.: 207). For Weber's experiences of military service see Marianne Weber (1975: 70–8). In Wilhelmine Germany the spread of military language into everyday life was commonplace (Wells 1985: 377–82).

15 The translation 'steel shell' also maintains the positive and negative assessments of modernity which exist side by side at the close of the *PE*. In a negative sense a shell can symbolize a body 'discarded by a soul; tenements emptied of life' (de Vries 1974: 419). On the other hand, a shell can symbolize the 'prosperity of one generation rising out of the death of another' (ibid.).

16 That there is an allusion to Nietzsche's *Thus Spake Zarathustra* at the close of the *PE* has only recently begun to be appreciated. We were sent on the wrong track track by Parsons' misleading translation of 'lätzen Menschen' as 'last stage', rather than the actual 'last men' (cf. Nietzsche 1957: 8–10; Kent 1983; Hennis 1988: 146–62).

17 Although both English and German Bibles (e.g. Luther's) translate the Hebrew of Proverbs here with 'business' or even 'work' (RSV), in the original German of the *PE* Weber quotes a version of the verse which translates it as *Beruf* and not *Geschäft* (business). As such, Parsons' translation of *Weber* is not correct, and the construction of the whole passage, and its role in the argument, is therefore not appreciated in the English. Moreover, in Franklin's *Autobiography* the version he used had 'calling' and not 'business' (Franklin 1986: 88).

18 The notion of the hermeneutical circle goes back to Schleiermacher, was subsequently taken up by Heidegger and Gadamer (1979) and has become a central part of hermeneutical theory (Thiselton 1992; Palmer 1969; Warnke 1987; Newton 1990: 40–58). It refers to the process of dialogue between the historically situated reader and the historically situated text. The reader approaches the text with particular prejudices and questions, but if progress in understanding is to occur the reader must also be open to be questioned by the text. As the process of question and answer continues the horizons of the reader are expanded. However, the process of understanding is never a final one. For example, in order to understand a part of a work the reader must project some pre-understanding of the whole, but the understanding of that whole will be transformed by the understanding reached of the part, and so on. As Schleiermacher said, 'every reading puts us in a better position to understand' (Thiselton 1992: 221). It is precisely this principle of what occurs in interpretation that needs to be acknowledged by commentators who wish to find a thematic unity in Weber's writing.

REFERENCES

Albrow, M. (1990) *Max Weber's Construction of Social Theory*. London: Macmillan.

Ashley, M. (1913) *Birmingham, Industry and Commerce* (Handbook). London: British Association for the Advance of Science.

Ashley, M. (1914) *The Economic Organization of England*. London.

Baxter, R. (1651/1978) *The Saints' Everlasting Rest*. Welwyn: Evangelical Press.

Beetham, D. (1985) *Max Weber and the Theory of Modern Politics*. Cambridge: Polity Press.

Bonnycastle, S. (1991) *In Search of Authority: An Introductory Guide to Literary Theory*. Lewiston, NY: Broadview Press.

Chalcraft, D.J. (1993) 'Weber, Wagner and Thoughts of Death', *Sociology*, 27, 3: 433–49.

Cohen, J., Hazelrigg, L. and Pope, W. (1975) 'De-Parsonizing Weber: A Critique of Parsons' Interpretation of Weber's Sociology', *American Sociological Review*, 40: 229–41.

Crossman, R. (1980) 'Do Readers Make Meaning? in Suleiman, S.R. and Crossman, I. (eds) *The Reader in the Text*. Princeton, New Jersey: Princeton University Press.

De Vries, A. (1974) *Dictionary of Symbols and Imagery*. Amsterdam and London: North Holland.

Drosdowski, G. (1989) *Duden: Etymologie Herkunftswörterbuch der deutschen Sprache*. Mannheim: Duden Verlag.

Durkheim, E. (1895/1982) *The Rules of Sociological Method*. Halls, W.D. (trans.), Lukes, S. (ed.) London: Macmillan.

Eldridge, J.E.T. (ed.) (1971) *Max Weber: The Interpretation of Social Reality*. London: Thomas Nelson.

Farrell, R.B. (1977) *A Dictionary of German Synonyms*, third edition. Cambridge: Cambridge University Press.

Fish, S. (1980) *Is There a Text in this Class? The Authority of Interpretative Communities*. Cambridge, Mass: Harvard University Press.

Franklin, B. (1986) *The Autobiography and Other Writings*. Harmondsworth: Penguin Books.

Gadamer, H.G. (1979) *Truth and Method*, second edition. London: Sheed and Ward.

Garland, H. and Garland, M. (1986) *The Oxford Companion to German Literature*, second edition. Oxford: Oxford University Press.

Goethe, J.W. von (1809/1971) *Elective Affinities*. Harmondsworth: Penguin Books.

Goethe, J.W. von (1980) *Die Wahlverwandtschaften*. Munich: Deutscher Taschenbuch Verlag.

Goldman, H. (1988) *Max Weber and Thomas Mann: The Calling and the Shaping of the Self*. Berkeley, Los Angeles and London: California University Press.

Grimm, J. and Grimm, W. (1980) *Kinder – und Hausmärchen. Band 2*. Stuttgart: Reclam.

Grimm, J. and Grimm, W. (1982) *Selected Tales*. Harmondsworth: Penguin Books.

Grimm, H. and Hinrichs, G. (eds) (1963) *Briefwechsel zwischen Jacob und Wilhelm Grimm aus der Jugendzeit*. Weimar: Hermann Boehlaus Nachfolger.

Hennis, W. (1988) *Max Weber: Essays in Reconstruction*. Tribe, K. (trans.) London: Allen and Unwin.

Hinkle, G. (1986) 'The Americanization of Max Weber', *Current Perspectives in Social Theory* 7: 87–104.

Kent, S. (1983) 'Weber, Goethe, and the Nietzschean Allusion: Capturing the Source of the "Iron Cage" Metaphor', *Sociological Analysis*, 44: 297–320.

LaCapra, D. (1983) *Rethinking Intellectual History: Texts, Contexts and Language*. Ithaca New York: Cornell University Press.

Leonard, E. (1900) *The Early History of English Poor Relief*. Cambridge: Cambridge University Press.

Lepenies, W. (1988) *Between Literature and Science: The Rise of Sociology*. Cambridge: Cambridge University Press.

Levy, H. (1912) *Die Grundlagen des oekonomischen Liberalismus in der Geschichte der englischen Volkwirtschaft.* Jena.

McGann, J. (1983) *A Critique of Modern Textual Criticism.* Chicago and London: Chicago University Press.

McGann, J. (1985) *The Beauty of Inflections: Literary Investigations in Historical Method and Theory.* Oxford: Oxford University Press.

Mann, T. (1924/1952) *Der Zauberberg. Roman.* Berlin: S. Fischer Verlag.

Mauret-Saunders. (1910) *Enzyklopaedische englisch–deutsches und deutsch–englisch Wörterbuch.* Berlin-Schoeneberg: Langenscheidt.

Michaelis – Jena, R. (1970) *The Brothers Grimm.* London: Routledge and Kegan Paul.

Mommsen, W. (1984) *Max Weber and German Politics 1890–1920*, second edition. Chicago and London: Chicago University Press.

Mommsen, W. (1989) *The Political and Social Theory of Max Weber.* Cambridge: Polity Press.

Murvar, V. (1964) 'Some Reflections on Max Weber's Typology of Herrschaft', *Sociological Quarterly*, 5: 374–84.

Newton, K.M. (1990) *Interpreting the Text: A Critical Introduction to the Theory and Practice of Literary Interpretation.* London: Harvester Wheatsheaf.

Nietzsche, F. (1957) *Thus Spake Zarathustra.* London: J.M. Dent.

Palmer, R. (1969) *Hermeneutics: Interpretation Theory in Schleiermacher, Dilthey, Heidegger and Gadamer.* Evanston, Illinois: NorthWestern University Press.

Paul, H. (1966) *Deutsches Wörterbuch.* Tübingen: Max Niemeyer.

Poggi, G. (1983) *Calvinism and the Capitalist Spirit: Max Weber's 'Protestant Ethic'.* London; Macmillan.

Prawer, S.S. (1976) *Karl Marx and World Literature.* Oxford: Oxford University Press.

Scaff, L. (1989) *Fleeing the Iron Cage: Culture, Politics, and Modernity in the Thought of Max Weber.* Berkeley, Los Angeles and London: University of California Press.

Schluchter, W. (1981) 'Einführung in die Max Weber-Gesamtausgabe', in *Prospekt der Max Weber Gesamtausgabe.* Tübingen: J.C.B. Mohr (Paul Siebeck).

Seidman, Stephen (1983) *Liberalism and the Origins of European Social Theory.* Oxford: Blackwell.

Skinner, Q. (1988) *Meaning and Context: Quentin Skinner and His Critics.* Tully, J. (ed.). Cambridge: Polity Press.

Tanselle, G.T. (1990) *Textual Criticism and Scholarly Editing.* Charlottesville and London: University Press of Virginia.

Tenbruck, F.H. (1989) 'The Problem of Thematic Unity in the Works of Max Weber', in Tribe, K. (ed.) *Reading Weber.* London: Routledge.

Thiselton, A.C.T. (1992) *New Horizons in Hermeneutics.* London: HarperCollins.

Turner, B.S. (1992) *Max Weber: From History to Modernity.* London: Routledge.

Unwin, G. (1904) *Industrial Organization in the Sixteenth and Seventeenth Centuries.* Oxford: Clarendon Press.

Warnke, G. (1987) *Gadamer: Hermeneutics, Tradition and Reason.* Cambridge: Polity Press.

Weber, Marianne (1975) *Max Weber: A Biography.* Zohn, H. (trans.). New York and London: John Wiley.

Weber, M. (1904) 'Die protestantische Ethik und der "Geist" des Kapitalismus, I. Das Problem', *Archiv für Sozialwissenschaft und Sozialpolitik*, 20, 1: 1–54.

Weber, M. (1905) 'Die protestantische Ethik und der "Geist" des Kapitalismus. II. Die Berufsidee des asketischen Protestantismus', *Archiv für Sozialwissenschaft und Sozialpolitik* 21, 1: 1–110.

Weber, M. (1909) 'Zur Psychophysik der industriellen Arbeit II', *Archiv für Sozialwissenschaft und Sozialpolitik*, 28, 1: 219–77.

Weber, M. (1920) *Gesammelte Aufsätze zur Religionssoziologie I.* Tübingen; J.C.B. Mohr (Paul Siebeck).
Weber, M. (1930/1990) *The Protestant Ethic and the Spirit of Capitalism.* Parsons, T. (trans.), twenty-first impression. London: Unwin Hyman.
Weber, M. (1948) *From Max Weber: Essays in Sociology.* Gerth, H and Wright Mills, C. (eds). London: Routledge and Kegan Paul.
Weber, M. (1949) *The Methodology of the Social Sciences.* Shils, E. and Finch, H. (trans. and ed.). Glencoe, Illinois: The Free Press.
Wells, C.J. (1985) *German: A Linguistic History to 1945.* Oxford: Oxford University Press.
Zeller, H. (1975a) 'Struktur und Genese in der Editorik. Zur germanistischen und anglistischen Editionsforschung', *Zeitschrift für Literaturwissenschaft und Linguistik*, 5: 105–26.
Zeller, H. (1975b) 'A New Approach to the Critical Constitution of Literary Texts', *Studies in Bibliography*, 28: 231–64.

Chapter 2

Max Weber and contemporary sociology of organizations

Stewart R. Clegg

Max Weber's relevance for the sociology of organizations today is not as self-evident as it might once have seemed. Major contemporary schools, such as population ecology, or contingency theory, appear to have little or no relationship to his thought or the body of work that he bequeathed. The legacy may be interpreted as an injunction to conduct organization analysis as a branch of cultural studies. Historically, few have seen it this way.

In the 1950s a series of landmark case studies by researchers as influential as Etzioni, Blau and Gouldner disconfirmed much of what he said about bureaucracy as an ideal type. In the 1960s the Aston researchers pronounced the irrelevance of Weber's typological construct for the understanding of organizations. Yet, they built on one aspect of his legacy in doing so, the notion that organization design was a variation on bureaucratic structure. The benign neglect continued. In the 1970s the rediscovery of 'alternative' forms of organization could have led to a revival of interest in Weber's work but did not. Nor did the widespread rediscovery of 'culture' within more conventional habitats recharge Weberian approaches.

The development of so-called 'critical' or 'radical' approaches in the later 1970s and earlier 1980s in part reintroduced Weber to the discourse. Yet, it did so in a way that left his legacy under-explored and somewhat stereotyped as a foil to Marx and Marxian concerns (Clegg and Dunkerley 1980). By the early 1980s the revival of an 'institutional' theory in the United States, particularly in the work of DiMaggio and Powell (1983), led to Weber's cultural theory of organizations being somewhat better understood, if little explored.

If organizations adopt representations for reasons of culturally valued beliefs, then these organizations become a key conduit in the structuring of modernity. Yet this linkage between modernity and organizations, so central to Weber's work, remains strangely underdeveloped. When Weber's work gained wider diffusion in English (in the United States) after the Second World War it was not only in translation but also through a subsequent series of independent empirical studies that qualified aspects of Weber's thesis. In Weber, it appeared as if the appropriate organizational form for modernity was one that was rational, where 'rational' had a precise definition. Some post-war landmarks in the analysis of organizations suggested Weber's thesis to be overdrawn. This overdrawn representation, one that seeks to equate rationality and efficiency in determinate and limited ways, has continued to prefigure the ground of much contemporary organization analysis. So the classical scope of this thesis narrowed down somewhat into an argument that sought to prescribe the limited organizational forms that modernity might adopt. The focus in organization analysis on Weber as principally a theorist of 'bureaucracy' has led to a relative neglect of other aspects of his work. These other aspects still have a methodological role to play in contemporary organization analysis, even while the illuminative powers of the modernist representation of bureaucracy fade into dusk in our increasingly post-modern organizational times (Clegg 1990).

MODERNITY AND ORGANIZATION

Sociology, conceived as a discipline that sought to understand the contours of modernity as they appeared in the nineteenth century, appeared coterminous with its object of analysis. Invariably, modernity, understood as the history and future trajectory of a single process of modernization, admitted of no common understanding. From diverse nineteenth-century representations modernism took intellectual shape for organizational analysis.

Marx and Durkheim represent two significant reactions to modernization from within intellectually contrasting but sophisticated modernist positions. For Marx (1976) modernization meant the advance and eventual overcoming of capitalism as a dominant world-wide mode of production. In Marx's (1965) youthful writings, at least, this entailed overcoming the division of labour that earlier writers such as Smith (1961) saw as the very essence of capitalist rationality. Implicitly, the future fully modernist society would be characterized by simple organization structures, multi-skilled individuals, an absence of hierarchy and high degrees of job rotation.

Durkheim (1964) saw an increasing division of labour in societies. One consequence of this was a potentially morally hazardous increase in the differentiation of available social identities. Differentiation, although organizationally generated, was contingent upon the relationship constructed between two key variables. These were the degree of marketization of social life and its political incorporation within authoritative, hierarchical forms. Thus, both hierarchy and complexity would characterize organizational modernity for Durkheim, as market society. Compared to Marx, Durkheim's (1964, 1957) view of modernization, although it stressed a process that was still economically embedded, conceptualized it as far less economically contained. Durkheim focused on what he saw as the consequences for social disorganization of the extreme development of the division of labour (see Clegg and Dunkerley 1980: ch. 1).

Irrespective of their particular vision, what the major nineteenth-century social theorists shared was a similar 'universalistic' conception of modernization leading to modernity. The similarity of their views resided in their depiction of the imagined future. It would be one in which there would be a 'gradual obliteration of cultural and social differences in favour of an increasingly broad participation of everyone in the same general model of modernity' (Touraine 1988: 443). The model, defined differently in each case, though always through similar processes of 'applying the general principles of reason to the conduct of human affairs' (ibid.), became the leitmotiv of modernism.

For most theorists the importance of 'organization' depended on it being purposeful, goal-oriented action encapsulated within routine, recurrent repro-duction of social action, social relations and social structures. Typically these 'complex organizations' remain an implicit mechanism of social change in general sociology. This would be as true of Marx's concern with the revolu-tionary impetus of changing productive forces and production relations as of Durkheim's moral concern with the increasing differentiation of labour and identity in the modern world. The specifically organizational aspects tend to be neglected.

Organization as a process and organizations as an object of analysis are almost implicit themes in the writings of the 'founding fathers' of sociology such as Comte, St Simon, Durkheim and Marx (argued in detail elsewhere: Clegg and Dunkerley 1980). Although witnesses to the birth of modernity, their work was not widely used to construct foundations for the systematic study of organizations as one cornerstone of modernity. Such distinction was to be granted to Max Weber's scattered observations on the nature of bureaucracy, on economic life more generally, and on the role of the 'Protestant ethic' in introducing the 'spirit of capitalism', work that became adopted as a foundation of the rigorous study of organizations (Weber 1948, 1976, 1978).

MAX WEBER AND THE ANALYSIS OF ORGANIZATIONS

Weber evidently had not intended to found a specialist field of organization studies: his comparative concerns were much wider than organizations *per se*. They ranged over a dazzling array of sources, questions and issues. The under-standing of the major world cultures and their relation to secular, rational modernity expressed in the major world religions was a crucial theme. It was one that organization scholars were not to focus on. In the 1950s several scholars followed the traces of pioneers such as Philip Selznick (1943, 1948) and Robert Merton (1940) to begin the systematic sociological study of organizations. The focus was on organizations as formal, complex constructions of human ingenuity. In search of a sociological heritage for their enterprise they turned to the recently translated works of Weber (1947, 1948). Peter Blau (1955), Alvin Gouldner (1954) and Amitai Etzioni (1961) were the principal researchers. The organiz-ational themes in Weber's work became the focus in a move that saw the broader context of Weber's thought decline in clarity and relevance in favour of explicitly organizational concerns.

There were other foundational sources. The interpretation of Weber had to be fitted to these. For instance, there were the more pragmatic 'formal administration' developed by consultants, engineers and successful m.. Chester Barnard (1938) in the United States (see Perrow 1986) or Henri I. (1949) in Europe (see Clegg and Dunkerley 1980) were cases in point. In additio. there was the body of work indelibly associated with Elton Mayo's (1933, 1975) critique of 'industrial civilization'. Originally crafted as a critique constructed against the individualistic image initially developed for American industry by Frederick Winslow Taylor (1911) subsequently it became elaborated throughout the Western world (Maier 1970; Clegg and Dunkerley 1980; Braverman 1974; Littler 1982; Dunford 1988). This critique spawned a body of work that became known as 'Human Relations Theory', work that stressed the importance of informal social organization within formal organization.

These, and other sources, were of considerable theoretical and practical importance. Yet none of them shared the same academic status or distinction, the same honour, as did the much more intellectually demanding work of Max Weber. It was in part the sheer magisterial quality, the depth of scholarship and the breadth of vision in Weber's work that first attracted scholars. Weber's inheritance became the legitimate capital with which to differentiate one's intellectual work from the more mundane concerns of a Fayol or the ideological visions of a Mayo.

In the analysis of organizations a process of selective attention occurred with respect to Weber's work as a whole. His broad-ranging concerns became increasingly interpreted far more narrowly by later organization theory. Weber became a precursor, a legitimate forebear, for organization theory. It is hardly surprising: intellectual seed, once sown, may reap many a strange fruit.

Once constituted as a legitimate forebear Weber could be seen to have

> analysed three general types of organizations stemming from the bases of wielding authority, and drew attention to the fact that in modern society the bureaucratic type has become dominant because, he considered, of its greater technical efficiency. In doing so he formed the starting point of a series of sociological studies designed to examine the nature and functioning of bureaucracy, particularly to draw attention to the dysfunctions of this structural form left out of the original analysis.
>
> (Pugh 1971: 13).

It is not so much that this account is wrong. There is no shortage of similar interpretation in the literature. Such interpretation is clearly selective in its focus, as Albrow (1970: 63) argues. Weber's evident insights became pressed into service in a discipline that had neither framed nor generated them. The process was not inexplicable. It involved, (to use a term that Weber [1976] derived from nineteenth-century chemistry, via Goethe) an 'elective affinity'. Elective affinity meant that aspects of the two distinct discursive strands of Weber's sociology and the systematic study of organizations were sympathetic to each other. Arguments in one resonated with arguments in another. Weber's sociological vision, in

etation, and the more 'efficiency' oriented concerns
ganization theory interpenetrated each other.
nity derived from his 'cultural pessimism'. From this
ation of the world' would, he anticipated, produce for
'iron cage of bondage'. Organizations would become
le feature of whatever pathway modernity was to tread,
citly to a 'socialist' or a 'capitalist' drum. This prognosis
into aspects of contemporary organization theory as it
it contributed to the efficiency of organizational design. It
seemed ... ot so much organizations (in the plural) that constituted
modernity, but that a particular form of organization would increasingly and
inexorably become definitive.

'Modernity' could be conceived of as the 'capacity to respond to a changing
environment and to manage complex systems' (Touraine 1988: 452). Modernity
and 'organization' became set on a fateful convergence, by which a specific
conception of the latter became the essence of the former. It was not to be a purely
formal concept of 'organization' for achieving purposeful, recurrent and routine
action, but a substantive concept that was to carry explicit values and meaning in
its definition. The capacity of modernity became identified with a specific form
of organization. In this way the nineteenth-century adaptation of the Enlightenment project of imposing general laws of reason, implicitly became adopted –
albeit in a changed form.

It is worth recalling just what the Enlightenment project entailed, in particular
for those deemed too ignorant to know that they ought to submit to what is
inevitable. It might be said that such people were those who could be regarded as
anthropologically estranged from the normative universe of the nineteenth
century. Above all this was a universe defined in terms of conceptions of reason
held by Europeans, by males, by the governing classes. Excluded from this
definition, in general, were non-Europeans, however civilized they might appear
to be; native peoples in the world's wilderness areas; the industrial working
classes at home, also most women *in toto*. Literally, it meant the destruction of
any claims to a form of life on terms other than those that were ascendant. At one
extreme this frequently entailed something close to genocide (of the 'savages' of
the Americas, Africa, Asia, Oceania and Australasia). Closely related to the
destruction of these peoples was the attempted remaking of other 'exotic'
cultures in a subordinate mould. Not only the annihilation of tribal peoples but
also cultural genocide, the loss of their languages and their land were at issue.
The armoury of moral reform could just as easily be targeted at the savages
abroad, as colonial subjects, as it could be at those indigenous aliens who took the
form of the working classes at home. The same missionaries could be despatched
to the East End of London with as much fervour as accompanied their adventures
in East Africa. Alternatively, forms of life could be subject to a process of
'ghettoization' within victorious civil society, such as occurred with the location
of women in the bourgeois home.

Such destruction was not an explicit part of Weber's project. Weber's acute sociological vision was more closely focused than the preceding characterization of the implications of the Enlightenment project, even if it shared a similar focus. The focus was not on gross annihilation but on the rationalization out of existence of less 'rational' forms of life. Incidentally, as Zygmunt Bauman (1990: 420–2) has argued with his customary insight, this focus was intrinsic to his very method, not something incidental to it. It is another way in which Weber stands as a quintessentially modernist theorist. The social world of modernity narrowed down the possible modes of existence in an elimination of difference best seen through the metaphor of 'the iron cage of bureaucracy'.

THE IRON CAGE OF BUREAUCRACY

In Weber's view the coming of modernity saw the 'discipline' of bureaucracy encroaching on almost every sphere of life. The cause of this encroachment was the irresistible spread of organizations in the twentieth century. What made this advance inexorable was their 'purely technical superiority over any other forms of organization' (Weber 1948: 214). In many respects Weber regarded bureaucracy with a highly sceptical eye. While it was technically superior to other forms of administration it was still a human product. Yet, in his view its humanity fatefully compromised its technical functioning. The efficient bureaucracy was a human creation increasingly out of control. A human creation, once unleashed, could turn and devour the humanity that had produced it, as the following passage, taken from a speech Weber made late in his life, clearly suggests:

> Already now, rational calculation is manifested at every stage. By it, the performance of each individual worker is mathematically measured, each man becomes a little cog in the machine and aware of this, his one preoccupation is whether he can become a bigger cog . . . it is horrible to think that the world could one day be filled with these little cogs, little men clinging to little jobs, and striving towards bigger ones . . . this passion for bureaucracy is enough to drive one to despair.
>
> (Weber, in Mayer 1956: 127)

In Weber's view bureaucracy is to be regarded almost as if it were a scientific creation that has turned and devoured its human creators. Rational calculation has become a monstrous machine. All significations of humanity, those 'relationships that are important to us due to their connections with our values' (Weber 1949: 76), get devoured and denatured by this triumph of human ingenuity. What remain are 'cogs', as its chronicler despaired.

A common romantic myth of the nineteenth century had it that scientific ingenuity and creativity would unwittingly invite its own self-destruction. The products of imagination turning on their producer were a popular theme for an age equally impressed and anxious about the scope of scientific achievement. We know the myth best today in the form that Mary Shelley (1969) recorded in

Frankenstein (1818). Dr Frankenstein, a scientist obsessed with the creation of a technically perfect form of human being, creates an all too fallible creature. It is one that resembles humanity, but imperfectly so. Finally the creature turns in revenge and tragedy upon its creator and destroys him. An underlying theme of the story is clear. Nothing, it seems, can save us from the forces that rationality has unleashed.

Weber is in some respects replaying aspects of this myth, but with an important difference. No final act of revenge will be exacted by the technical form upon its human makers. Instead, humanity will become ever more captive in the thrall and bondage of technical perfection. As Haferkamp (1987: 31) reminds us, for Weber bureaucracy was 'necessary', 'unavoidable', 'unstoppable', 'inescapable', 'universal', and simply 'unbreakable' (Weber 1920: 3ff.; 203ff; 1958: 318ff). It is these adjectives that serve to display Weber's 'cultural pessimism', in the simply irresistible but utterly unattractive face of the 'fate of our times'.

In the name of reason the nineteenth century attempted to impose a philosophy of progress upon the world, remaking it in one image. The late twentieth-century version of this tragedy differs markedly from Weber's metaphorical entrapment and enveloping myth. It also differs from the viciousness of the civilizing process that imposed this reason upon recalcitrant subjects. Yet, as we shall see, within organization theory today there are some highly influential currents that would analytically annihilate the possibilities of variety in contemporary forms of organizational life. The elimination proposed will again take place in the name of efficiency and effectiveness (Donaldson 1985). It might just as well nail the flag of 'cultural pessimism' to its mast – at least, if it did, it would display the true colours of its genesis.

Grumley (1988) suggests that the work of Max Weber represents what is probably *the* most impressive intellectual attempt to come to terms with the sudden transition from pre-modernity to modernity. Launched under particular conditions, those of Germany's national formation in and through the experiences of modernization, unification, industrialization and secularization, Weber's theory sought to understand its context. In Weber's work it is the theme of *rationalization* that threads these disparate experiences into several interlocking, contingent processes whose outcome is modernity as defined: the capacity to respond to changing environments and to manage the complexity that this entails.

At the core of this modernist capacity was a unifying rationalistic principle. This principle could be seen in the rationalization of various institutional arenas such as the market, technology, law, the state. It could be seen in various general processes. The increasing depersonalization of social relations, particularly in work, the increasing importance of specialization for modern life, and the concomitant intellectualization of realms of knowledge, especially culture, scientific and religious life, were the key features. The major mechanism of its transmission was the increasing differentiation of spheres of existence and of phenomenon within them. The growing pervasiveness of rational calculation in all spheres of life wrought these transformations as modernity. It was this pervasiveness that created that phenomenon identified by Weber as the 'de-enchantment' or 'disenchantment' of the world. What he meant by these terms was a process by which enchantment became stripped away from everyday life and belief, through a progressive loss of faith in the unseen but enchanted movers of the human drama provided by folk beliefs and by superstitions as well as by organized religions. These were not the only sources of enchantment nor was it merely a historical phenomena. In Weber's view contemporary parties organized from a putative universalizing 'historical subject', such as the proletariat, were captive to a more modern form of enchantment.

Disenchantment meant an end to ultimate values and to sacred meanings. It entailed exposure to a world in which meaningfulness was never 'given' but had to be struggled for, had to be secured, even against the resistance of others. Only the rare charismatic leader, whose personal grace, sense of calling, duty and devotion to some ultimate ideal was unshakeable, could in the future impose this meaning on life. Even this would not 'smash' the 'iron cage', but merely make it meaningful for an efficient bureaucracy and a subordinated mass. Adrift from the meaningful frame of superhuman powers, more lowly beings could only hope to live their lives bereft of meaning. Trapped within the iron cage of their increasingly rationalized, bureaucratized existence, wrenched from their traditional forms of life by the irresistible pull of modernity, organizational bondage stretched out as the inexorable vision of the future. In this way modernity was coeval with disenchantment: it was the latter that grounded the capacities for rational action of the former. Rational action consisted precisely in the capacity to respond to the new uncertainties of a world without meaning. The modern world was, by definition, an age of uncertainty. This applied equally whether the political system was totalitarian or democratic, the economy socialist or capitalist. Therefore, the siren of rationality, in Weber's interpretation, would be the likely clarion call whatever the socio-economic and political system.

Uncertainty both defined and limited freedom. It defined freedom through posing the existential and environmental conditions under which rational action was possible. It limited freedom by imposing an ethic of calculation, as a totally objective rationality, upon this freedom to act. From now on, one could only ever hope to master uncertainty through the experience of modernity. Modernity entailed a loss of freedom as one submitted to the constraints of rationality. It also entailed a loss of faith: as one became free of the old dogmas one became condemned without any authoritative basis for one's life other than rationality itself. Such rationality, when working properly, would allow no other citadels of ultimate value to be crafted in modernity's mentality. The achievement of this rationality involved a profound emptying and opening up of the human condition as it battled to confront the nihilism of modernity. The process of rationalization unyoked new possibilities from dogma for cultural construction in all spheres of knowledge. Yet no one of these could reunify the cultural spheres liberated, because of the necessity of rationality, a constant witness against any new architects of domination.

In Weber's view rationality had only a few sources. It might derive from those individuals forced to confront the world and choose how to impose value and meaning upon it. The world did not already confront such people as if it were resolutely unyieldingly, already absolutely and unbreakably cast in a mould. There were precious few such people in Weber's vision, other than the charismatics and leaders, the 'Caesarists'. Most people, one will recall, were 'trapped' within the 'iron cage'. On the other hand it is precisely this 'iron cage' that is the instrumental, disciplined repository of rationality. The unfreedom of the many within the organizational apparatuses of modernity was the necessary foundation of the rationality and freedom for action of the few, a freedom and rationality gained through the instrumentality of bureaucracy.

The 'iron cage' is not only a prison but also a principle. As a principle it 'makes us free' to be modern. It makes us free because it is only through the purposefulness and goal directedness of organization that the uncertainties of disenchanted modernity could be coped with. Uncertainties were no longer explicable in terms of the enchanted but unseen, the knowing but unknown, the controlling but uncontrollable fates of divines, demons and devils. Such past bulwarks of individual beliefs held against the uncertainties of an enchanted age were in certain decline, thought Weber. In Weber's view it would be only false prophets who would insist otherwise. Rational calculation would limit uncertainty to a world that was, in principle, manageable.

The freedom of modernity, experienced in the loss of entrapment within received meaning, is not something that is merely one-dimensional, something wholly positive. It is also something simultaneously experienced negatively – as a loss of freedom to organizational and rational constraint. For the future, irrespective of the political values that modernity infused, Weber argued that 'the fate of our times' was such that the reproduction of this modernity was absolutely dependent upon the existence of vast public and private sector bureaucracies. The very existence of these would act as a further deepening of the rationalistic principle. Although large economic organizations would demand greater specialization within bureaucracy, this would not create greater individuality. Rational discipline would permeate all authoritative relations of modernity. The rise of the professional expert would greatly restrict the scope for individualism in any guise. 'Specialists without spirit', as the new breed of organization expert, yoked to bureaucratic cogs, epitomized modernity's future organizational trajectory for Weber. Its tracks were clear. Organizational servants would be required to subordinate personality to impersonal, objective rules and functions. Work was a sentence of bondage for prisoners in a vast mechanism and chain of command. To work was to be organized rationally, to obey prescriptions laid down from above and to meet the functional requirements of a system determined by objective, calculable rules for optimal performance, precisely as Grumley (1988: 30) describes it.

THE VARIABLE TENDENCIES OF BUREAUCRACY

Bureaucracy, for Weber, was a mode of organization. The concept of organization was such that it subsumed such differing substantive entities as the state, the political party, the church or sect, and the firm. The defining characteristic of an organization was the presence of a leader and an administrative staff. These persons, ordered into specific types of social relationship, depending upon the type of rule to which action was oriented in the organization in question. Weber termed these rules 'the order of the organization', which he based upon his well-known typology of different types of authority.

In an organization, whatever bases of order it might have, the administrative staff has a dual relationship to this order. On the one hand the behaviour of the administrative staff is regulated by rules; on the other hand it is the task of the ruling body to see that other members also follow the rules of the organization. These rules comprise an order governing the organization to which members are subject, by virtue of their orientation towards it:

> The validity of an order means more than the existence of a uniformity of social action determined by custom or self interest. The content of a social relationship will be called an order if the conduct is, approximately or on the average, oriented towards determinable maxims. Only then will an order be called valid if the orientation to all these maxims occurs among other reasons although because it is in some appreciable way regarded by the actor as in some way obligatory or exemplary for him.
>
> (Weber 1968: 31)

Weber suggests that actors orient their actions to a similarly defined order because collectively recognized rules guide their individual enactments. An order is not merely a form of codification of conventional and legal rules, but the existence of a dominant set of social rules more generally. Different types of rule exist in different orders to which one orients one's behaviour. They will afford differential probability that different types of command, under differing conditions of rule, will be obeyed. Such command will be authorized and made legitimate by reference to the rule, submission to which we would normally call authority. Different forms of belief in the legitimacy of authority associate with different authority structures and therefore with different organizational forms.

The most important of these for contemporary analysis would be where people obey orders because they believe that the person giving the order is acting according to the duties stipulated in a code of legal rules and regulations. Five related beliefs support such a claim. Following Albrow (1970: 43) we can summarize these in an abbreviated form as follows:

1 that a legal code can be established that can claim obedience from members of the organization;
2 that the law is a system of abstract rules; these rules apply to particular cases,

and administration looks after the interests of the organization within the
limits of the law;

3 that the person exercising authority also obeys this impersonal order;

4 that only as a member does a member obey the law;

5 that obedience is due not to the person who holds authority but to the impersonal order that has granted the person this authority.

Bureaucracy was not a distinctively modern phenomenon, yet Weber (1948: 204)
argued that it existed 'in ever purer forms in the modern European states and,
increasingly, all public corporations since the time of princely absolution'. Before
this what had characterized the absolutist state were forms of patrimonial bureaucracy premised on patrimonal authority or domination. Weber thought that
modern bureaucratic organization formulated on rational legal precepts could
sweep other forms of organization before it:

> The decisive reason for the advancement of bureaucratic organization has
> always been its purely technical superiority over any other form of organiz-
> ation. The fully developed bureaucratic mechanism compares with other
> organizations exactly, as does the machine with the non-mechanical modes of
> production.
>
> (Weber 1948: 214)

The emergence of this modern bureaucratic form of organization rationality is not
accidental. It is a necessary feature of modernity. 'The peculiarity of modern
culture, and specifically of its technical and economic basis, demands this very
"calculability" of results':

> Today it is primarily the capitalist market economy that demands the official
> business of the administration be discharged precisely, unambiguously, con-
> tinuously, and with as much speed as possible. Normally, the very large
> modern capitalist enterprises are themselves unequalled modes of strict bur-
> eaucratic organization. Business management throughout rests on increasing
> precision, steadiness and above all, the sp*eed of operations* . . . . Bureaucratiz-
> ation offers above all the optimum possibility for carrying though the principle
> of specializing administrative functions according to purely objective con-
> siderations. Individual performances are allocated to functionaries who have
> specialized training and who by practice learn more and more. The 'objective'
> discharge of business primarily means a discharge of business according to
> calculable rules and without regard for persons.
>
> (Weber 1948: 215)

It is in *General Economic History* (1923) that Weber enumerates what he takes
to be the peculiarity of modern culture. Its organizing principle is the existence
of a capitalist market economy. Central to this are several factors. These include
the existence of a 'formally free' labour force; the appropriation and concentration of the physical means of production as disposable private property; the

representation of share rights in organizations and property ownership and the 'rationalization' of various institutional areas such as the market, technology and the law. In particular, rationalization of the market depends upon the existence of an economic surplus and its exchange in monetary terms. Markets are the historical product not of reason but of might: 'money prices are the product of conflicts of interest and compromise' (Weber 1948: 211).

The outcome of this process of rationalization, Weber suggests, is the production of a new type of person shaped by the dictates of modern bureaucracy. Such a person, whether in business, government or education, is one with a restricted, delimited type of personality. Characteristically, this is the specialist, the technical expert who increasingly, Weber feels, will come to replace the ideal of the cultivated person of past civilizations.

Weber argues that rationalization is a process that affects almost all aspects of social life, and he distinguishes two notions of rationality. First, means–end relationships, referred to as formal rationality. Formal rationality involves the attainment of definitely given and practical ends through increasingly precise calculation of means adequate to the achievement of those ends. The focus of this means–end rationality is very much on the means. Ends, being 'given', require no explanation. The end, for instance, may be a religious or mystical end, or it may be the genocide of a people in concentration camps. Whatever ends may be served they could still be gained through rational calculable means.

Weber offers a second conception of the term rationality, which he terms 'substantive rationality'. This is the kind of rationalization that a systematic thinker does on the image of the world: the theoretical mastery of reality by increasingly precise and abstract concepts. It was this aspect that Weber sometimes called the de-enchantment or disenchantment of the world. It is the process by which all forms of magical, mystical, traditional explanation are stripped away from the world. The world lain bare is open and amenable to the calculation of technical reason. Calculable means connect to given ends. As Weber put it:

> It is not sufficient to consider only the purely formal fact that calculations are being made on grounds of expediency by the methods which are amongst those available technically the most nearly adequate. In addition it is necessary to take account of the fact that economic activity is oriented to ultimate ends of some kind: whether they be ethical, political, utilitarian, hedonistic, the attainment of social distinction, of social equality, or of anything else. Substantive rationality cannot be measured in terms of formal calculation alone, but also involves a relation to the absolute values or to the content of the particular ends to which it is oriented.
>
> (Weber 1947: 185).

The 'absolute values' that Weber focuses on were ones that initially sanctified capitalist activity. These turned out to be the religious values of Calvinism, especially the stress on 'this-worldly' asceticism (Weber 1976). Yet, ultimate values would be in inexorable decline with the coming of modernity, in large part because the 'calculability' of formal rationality progressively erodes values from the world. Such belief systems would no longer be necessary to sustain the technical rationality of contemporary life:

> Since ascetism undertook to remodel the world and to work out its ideals in the world, material goods have gained an increasing and finally an inexorable power over the lives of men as at no previous period in history. Today the spirit of religious ascetism – whether finally, who knows? – has escaped from the cage. But victorious capitalism, since it rests on mechanical foundations, needs its support no longer. The rosy blush of its laughing heir, the Enlighten-ment, seems also to be irretrievably fading, and the idea of duty in one's calling prowls about in our lives like the ghost of dead religious beliefs.
>
> (Weber 1976: 181–2)

Clearly Weber was not a naive or unqualified proponent of bureaucratic ration-ality. Yet he did not believe that despair would be sufficient to see bureaucracy overcome. This was because of his view of bureaucracy as an instrument or tool of unrivalled technical superiority, at least for as long as it retained legitimacy. At the base of any bureaucracy are its members' beliefs in the legitimacy of its existence, its protocols, its personnel and its policies. Given these beliefs, and serving to reproduce them, there will exist a specific form of administration and organization that is bureaucracy. It would be defined most precisely in terms of several tendencies.

1   Task discontinuity is achieved by functional specialization. Tasks are specific, distinct and done by different formal categories of personnel who specialize in these tasks and not in others. These official tasks would be organized on a continuous regulated basis to ensure the smooth flow of work between the discontinuous elements in its organization: thus, there is a tendency towards *specialization*.
2   The functional separation of tasks means that the personnel charged with their despatch must have a level of authority and sanction available to them that is commensurate with their duties. There is a tendency towards the *authorization* of organizational action.
3   Because tasks get functionally separated, and because the personnel charged with each function have precisely delegated powers, there has to be some relation of hierarchy between these: thus, there is a tendency towards *hierarchization*.
4   The delegation of powers, expressed in terms of precise contracts of employ-ment that specify duties, rights, obligations and responsibilities leads to a *contractualization* of organizational relationships.
5   Because officials are appointed by a contract, one that specifies what the qualities demanded for the job are, there is a tendency towards the specifi-cation of organizational qualities in terms of qualifications measured in terms of formal credentials: thus, there is a tendency towards *credentialization* in organizations.

6 One requires differentially stratified credentials to enter different positions in the hierarchy of offices; thus, there is a career structure and promotion is possible either by seniority or by merit of service by individuals with similar credentials, depending on the judgement of superiors made according to the rules. Without the appropriate credentials one cannot be promoted to the next rung in the hierarchy: thus, there is a tendency towards *careerization* (striving to be bigger cogs in the machine) within organizations.

7 Different positions in the hierarchy get differential pay and other rewards, such as pensions, superannuation rights, travel allowances and so on. Thus there is a tendency towards a process of status differentiation in organizations. We may term this a process of *stratification* in organizations.

8 The hierarchy, expressed in specific rights of control by superordinates, as well as specific powers to resist improper attempts at control on the part of subordinates, tends towards a specific *configuration* of authority within the structure.

9 Functional separation, task-discontinuity and hierarchical relations require that the actual work of the organization and its superintendence should be formally rule-bound. This can be either technical or legal, but rules should be followed without regard for persons; that is, without fear of offence. The rules serve to justify and produce legitimate action: so, there is a tendency towards *formalization* of rules in organizations.

10 The formality of rules requires that administration must be based on files of written documents. Thus, the office, where files are filed and consulted by those whom the files give such rights, is the hub of the organization. A consequence of this is that organizational action assumes a standardized form – a tendency towards *standardization*.

11 The relationships in the organization are not just hierarchical. The centrality of the office develops communication, coordination and control routed through the hub: consequently, there is a tendency towards *centralization*.

12 Legitimate action within bureaucracy requires a sharp boundary between what is bureaucratic action and what is particularistic action by personnel. Thus, it is a requisite that the resources of the bureaucracy must be maintained as something separate from those that belong to and can be used by the members of the bureaucracy in their private capacity: thus there is a tendency towards the *legitimization* of organizational action.

13 Power belongs to the office and is not a function of the office holder. Office holders are bearers of powers that they cannot appropriate personally: thus, there is a tendency towards *officialization* of organizational action.

14 Because powers get exercised in terms of the office instead of the person there is a tendency towards *impersonalization* of organizational action.

15 This impersonalization occurs according to disciplinary systems of knowledge. These are both organizationally developed and adopted from external professional bodies of knowledge: thus, there is a tendency towards a *disciplinization* of organizational action.

Each of the fifteen tendencies of bureaucracy can be represented as a variable; that is, there may be more or less of a given process in any specific organization (for empirical instances of this in organization analysis see the work of writers such as Hall 1962, 1963; Hall *et al.* 1967; Pugh and Hickson 1976, and Hage 1965; Hage and Aiken 1970). Universities may tend to place a greater degree of emphasis upon the process of credentialization of personnel compared to another organization less concerned with the categorization of knowledge *per se*. Weber (1978) used the notion of an 'ideal type' to capture this sense of a variable quality. The ideal type 'froze' the qualities of bureaucracy in an idealized representation, one that provisionally alerts us to the kinds of empirical phenomenon that we would expect to find if the organization in question had bureaucratic tendencies. 'Such types consciously and expressly accentuate value-relevant aspects of reality in an artificial model that serves as an interpretative and explanatory scheme' (Clegg and Dunkerley 1980: 38). Rendering the central typical elements as processual variables provides one with a clearer idea of what Weber thought was important than does a precise reiteration of the type itself. Taken together, these processes represent his view of how the world will be turned into a complex of iron cages.

Weber's views have been deservedly influential, but require considerable revision in several respects. Empirical researchers began to study organizations using the Weberian ideal type of bureaucracy as their guide. When they did they quickly found that in the real world of modernity, rather than in Weber's theorization of it, bureaucratic tendencies did not always come together in a complete rational-legal package. One interpretation of Weber's model might have suggested that it was a guide for ideal practice. This proposes an obvious, if erroneous, interpretation of what an 'ideal type' is: that it is a model for perfect practice. Acceptance of Weber's pessimism concerning the necessary rationalization and bureaucratization of the modern world proved to be misplaced, even in terms of his system of concepts. As subsequent researchers showed (see the discussion in Clegg 1990) they do not form a systematic, coherent package. They are a set of tendencies that can be accentuated in many possible ways (much as one might expect of an ideal type). They are not as easily conceptualized as a correlate of modernity as might appear at first glance. So, much of Weber's tragic vision relating to the iron cage of bureaucracy proves to be misplaced.

Rationalized, bureaucratized organization is not the necessary 'fate' of our times, according to the findings of some classic studies in the sociology of organizations. It appears that plenty of scope remains for creativity and imagination. Still, these findings have not succeeded in dispelling that persistent pessimism noted in Weber's 'foundations' for organization theory. The latter, in an influential and sophisticated version, has irrevocably tied modernity to a particular concept of modernization, one carried by a particular substantive rationality of organizations, which Weber identified as the 'fate of our times'.

MODERN ORGANIZATIONS FOR MODERN TIMES: THE TRIUMPH OF THE SYSTEM

Touraine captures a central and pervasive aspect of the understanding of modernity: it is a complex system embedded in a dynamic environment. The image is one of some body or entity seeking to create order out of the chaos of complexity. The ideas developed in the realms of natural science, particularly in biology (von Bertalanffy 1968). As a social scientific metaphor for modernity nowhere has this image received a more elaborated development than in the application of 'general systems theory' to the field of organization analysis. General systems theory was introduced into organization analysis in the decade after the initial exploration of Weber's ideas. Its innovatory phase was the decade stretching from the mid-1950s to the mid-1960s, when writers like Boulding (1956), Katz and Kahn (1966), and above all, Thompson (1967), developed the notion that an organization was like an 'open system'.

Systems frameworks conceptualize the organization as having a definite boundary through which flow environmental inputs and outputs. It strives to maintain this boundary to ensure its own distinctive survival as an entity composed of several system components that exist together in a state of dynamic interdependency, processing throughputs and reflexively monitoring their environment through the re-entry of outputs as new inputs, a process known as feedback.

Systems ideas are now so much a part of the modernist consciousness that they barely require elaborate iteration (see Morgan 1986). Not only did they produce a major reconceptualization of organizations striving for orderliness in an otherwise chaotic world; they also successfully reinterpreted the past development of organization theory. Reading backward from an open systems perspective, much earlier conceptions could now be interpreted as an excessively internalist and closed system account of organization structure and processes.

The ideal type of bureaucracy, with its affinities with early managerial and mechanistic approaches to organizations in writers like Taylor (1911) and Barnard (1938), could now be regarded as an example of a flawed closed system approach to the analysis of organizations. Instead of conceptualizing the openness of the organization to the environment as a necessary corollary of its existence, these earlier theorizations had assumed the fixity of organization boundaries. What went on outside the organization became unimportant. What becomes important is the ability of those in positions of authority inside organizations to manipulate internal characteristics, such as employee morale, motivation and teamwork (Mayo 1975) to affect output variables like productivity.

The open systems framework allowed for a far more dynamic conceptualization of organizations. A closed system, whether it be conceived as an organization or a machine, does not monitor and respond to the environment. By contrast, it is the very essence of an open system to do this. Its openness consists precisely in the capacity to import resources and energies from the environment, to use them for the benefit of the internal system. Open systems are inherently adaptive. Like biological organisms their adaptive capacity is to be thought of in terms of the processes of differentiation and specialization by which organisms evolve in changing environments.

Two of the key processual variables from the Weberian model, specialization and differentiation, could now be thought of within the framework provided by evolutionary biology and ecology. Organizations were just like other organic entities. The root metaphor triumphed. A new organicism was born in which the preservation of organic equilibrium and the maintenance of boundaries were the central drives for organization systems. Because no organization can ever be a closed system, organic growth and survival requires boundary-spanning to secure resources. Partly in consequence of this, different elements of the organizations' internal system will be more or less functionally specialized on either internal or environmental processes and monitoring. The more environmentally oriented they are, one would anticipate, the more 'loosely coupled' they will be *vis-à-vis* other elements of the organization system (Weick 1979). Complex organizations have variable coupling of their sub-system elements.

The reconceptualization had one considerable advantage. It easily avoided a substantive problem that the typological approach to organizations had encountered. Where a specific substantive feature of organizations, such as rule-use or benef- iciaries, was the basis for categorization then the population of organization types was always potentially incomplete. New bases for typologization were always empirically possible or could theoretically suggest themselves. By contrast, systems theory operated at a level of abstraction and generality such that the substantive qualities of specific organizations were of less conceptual importance. All organizations could now be conceptualized as structures and patterns of behaviour that enjoyed relative stability, were slow to change and could cope successfully with the uncertainties posed by environments. Simon's (1957) and March and Simon's (1958) stress on organizations as the embodiment of pragmatic, bounded rationality became predominant. In this way common properties of organizations, irrespective of function, could be highlighted. Different functional types of organization that dealt with different types of environment might adopt similar patterns of behaviour to deal with them. A high degree of uncertainty in the environment, for instance, might lead to a reinforcement of credentialization and specialization as strategies for dealing with it. It only remained for the actual process of organization work to be de-substantivized. Thinking of it as the reduction of uncertainty, through Weick's (1979) stress on 'organizing' as the reduction of 'equivocality', is the classic case. Now any organization could be abstractly compared with any other. On the one hand its patterns of behaviour, built up out of the variable expression of Weber's tendencies to bureaucratization, were supplemented from time to time by processes produced by new insights. On the other hand, there were more or less uncertain environments. Connecting them were system flows of inputs, throughputs, outputs and feedback, conceptualized as the sources of change in the patterns of organizational behaviour.

A distinction made by Gouldner (1959) could be said to have overlain the historical construction of what was, by the 1960s, a burgeoning field of organization theory (Scott 1981). The distinction was between 'rational' and 'natural' conceptions of organizations as systems. The 'rational system model' is one that 'views the organization as a structure of manipulable parts' (Gouldner 1959: 405). The 'natural system model' regards the organization as a 'natural whole', in that, irrespective of 'the plans of their creators', organizations 'become ends in themselves and possess their distinctive needs that have to be satisfied. Once established, organizations tend to generate new ends that constrain the manner in which the nominal groups can be pursued' (Gouldner 1959: 405). The rational model is an instrumental view, one that regarded organizations as human tools capable of more or less appropriate design for different purposes. By contrast, the natural conception is altogether more organic: organizations are to be seen not so much as humanly shaped tools but as creatures with attributes and vitalism. As such, organizations conceived of as natural systems are likely to be regarded as primarily oriented towards a singular formal rationality, hierarchy, planning, impersonality, goals or efficiency, instead of a plurality of modes of substantive rationalities, alliances, strategies, persons, needs or futures.

In terms of systems representations, early writers on organizations were overwhelmingly 'closed' and 'rational' theorists, whether they were sociologists like Weber (1978), management consultants like Fayol (1949) or engineers like Taylor (1911). From the 1930s until about the late 1950s the focus of analysis shifted towards conceptions of the organization as an evolving natural organism. In this conception it had emergent properties, such as informal groups, that developed within the formally rational structure and that could be tapped into to increase the efficiency of the organization (Mayo 1975). The iron cage could now seemingly be made to reproduce its bondage from the only freedoms it contained: the freedom of informal group processes to flourish within it.

INSIDE THE IRON CAGE, ENMESHED BY UNAVOIDABLE CONTINGENCIES

The iron cage of bureaucracy could be built out of any of fifteen possible dimensions in terms of the earlier characterization of Weber's theoretical tendencies to bureaucratization. Fifteen proved to be too complex for the empirical research imagination: less proved best at Aston. In the early 1960s, using an open systems model, several researchers began to think systematically about Weber's variables and their relative weight in the structuring of organizations. Some went one stage further and commenced applying their systematic thought to the collection and analysis of empirical data describing organization structure. The most influential of these empirical studies of organization structures became known as the 'Aston studies' (Pugh and Hickson 1976). These studies derived their name from the place where the studies were conducted: the University of Aston, located next to the city centre of Birmingham in the West Midlands region of England.

The fifteen possible dimensions of organization structure located in Weber's variables were not all explored in the empirical study. Preliminary research by the Aston team suggested that organization structure was likely to be built out of just five of the dimensions: specialization, standardization, formalization, centralization and configuration, defined as follows:

Specialization: the degree of division into specialized roles;
Standardization: the degree of standard rules and procedures;
Formalization: the degree of written instructions and procedures;
Centralization: the degree of decision-making authority at the top;
Configuration: long versus short chains of command and role structures, and percentages of 'supportive' personnel.

(Pugh 1988: 128)

These variables were to be the key building blocks for a major landmark in organization analysis. Intensive study of the prior theoretical literature on organizations grounded the analysis. Another important catalyst for its production proved to be exploratory field work carried out in several organizations in the immediate West Midlands region. This remarkable research project is perhaps the most significant contribution from Europe to the mainstream of North American organization theory. (See Pugh and Hickson 1976; Pugh and Payne 1977 and Hickson and McMillan 1981.) In addition, Donaldson (1986), in a paper that subjects the Aston data bank to reanalysis, is a useful source for the great many comparative studies that have developed from the original research. The project as a whole has been subject to 'cogently comprehensive' critique by Starbuck (1981), as Pugh (1988) suggests. An alternative critique may be found in Clegg and Dunkerley (1980). While the Aston researchers had evident links with Weber they were with Weber conceived not as a cultural theorist. The translation begun in the 1940s by Parsons, continued by researchers since, was completed by the empiricism of Aston. In this way the Weberian bequest to European scholarship of a cultural studies of organizations became broken in the most influential example, the major North American market, that Europe offered. Instead, Weber was presented as a magnificent but now irrelevant ancestor of the structural analysis of bureaucracy.

Five structural variables were arrived at from Weber's fifteen tendencies. Empirically they derived from a wider pool of hypothetical structural properties of organizations. Data was collected from a representative random sample of 46 work organizations. The sample was stratified by size and product or purpose (Standard Industrial Classification) from the total population of West Midlands employing organizations. Five structural variables displayed certain consistent inter-correlations, or dimensions, replicated often, in many samples, derived from many countries (Donaldson 1986). These dimensions were as follows.

Structuring of activities: specialization, standardization and formalization are all highly related. Collectively, this package of correlationally consistent interrelationships became known as the structuring of activities, primarily related to the size of the organization, and secondarily to the degree of routinization of its technology. The larger the organization, defined in terms of the number of employees contracted to it in a stable employment relation, the more specialist, standardized and formalized it would be. In other words, larger organizations had more highly structured activities. These tendencies would be exacerbated particularly with a routinized, automated and integrated technology.

Concentration of authority: centralization negatively relates to specialization, summarized in a single structural dimension called 'concentration of authority', a measure that increases as the dependency of an organization upon other organizations increases.

Line control of workflow: this was a factor that comprised the percentage of superordinates and the degree of formalization and standardization of procedures concerning personnel decisions. Organizations with less routinized technologies tended to have a higher line control of the workflow.

The Aston studies found that size was the major determinant of these central features of organizational structure. This finding has gained considerable support from other research programmes (e.g. Blau and Schoenherr 1971). In particular, larger organizations have their activities more highly structured; that is, they have more specialization, more formalization and more standardization than smaller organizations, although there was no strong relationship between size and either the concentration of authority or the line control of workflow.

Drawing the Aston findings on the importance of size together with the related Woodward findings on the importance of technology in determining organization structure (1958, 1965), several conclusions present themselves. First, that technology has the most impact on organization structure the closer to its technical core one moves (Hickson *et al.* 1969). Secondly, that the smaller the organization, then the more influence its technology will have upon it (Pugh and Hickson 1976: 154; Child and Mansfield 1972). Of course, there are notorious difficulties in sorting out technology from industry effects in these comparisons, as Child and Mansfield observed. Often the same technology will be used in organizations in the same industry and not in others. What are the causal factors at work in such a situation?

Weber's cultural pessimism derived from the importance he attributed to values, values that he saw eroded inexorably by the rationalization of the world. Both the Aston researchers and Woodward identify the mechanisms that are enclosing the iron cage around us. For Woodward they are the types of technology developed, chosen and adopted. For the Aston researchers technology had a more delimited role to play compared to the mechanism of organization size. Size becomes *the* determinant of the iron cage in these accounts:

> In all countries, big organizations will be the most formalized and specialized in structure. This is because everywhere growth means reaping economies of

scale and expertise by dividing labour still further, and as the knowledge possessed by any one person of what is happening in the organization becomes a smaller part of the whole, so it requires more formalized documentation of action and intended action for control. Non-formalized custom is inadequate to control large numbers in organizations with a turnover of personnel.

(Hickson *et al*. 1979: 37)

Simply stated, if Indian organizations were found to be less formalized than American ones, bigger Indian units would still be more formalized than smaller Indian units.

(Ibid.: 59)

There is a logic of organization. It is an inescapable logic. As organizations grow in the number of employees that they have then they will become more bur-eaucratized. It is not possible for it to be otherwise. There is no alternative to the increase in bureaucratization wherever there is an increasing size of organization. If one were of a whimsical turn of mind one might want to name this the TINA tendency within organization theory: *There Is No Alternative*. Or at least there is very little.

The TINA tendency is an organizational specification of one argument about modernity: the modernization thesis associated with Kerr *et al*.'s (1973) prognosis that there is a 'logic of industrialization' (as has been remarked elsewhere in Clegg and Dunkerley 1980: 247–51). It is a straightforward argument. Industrialization is the driving force behind modernization. Industrialization takes place through the medium of large-scale organization. The corollary of this, to adapt Michels, is that 'whomsoever says large scale organization says bu-reaucracy'. TINA. The iron cage shuts, the lock bolts, the key turns. Some suggest that the lock is size and the key efficiency.

EFFICIENCY RULES, OK?

In what are probably the most frequently cited words that Weber ever wrote on the subject of organizations, it seems as if the inexorable spread of bureaucracy is due solely to its competitive advantage in terms of efficiency:

The fully developed bureaucratic mechanism compares with other organizations exactly as does the machine with the non-mechanical modes of production.

Precision, speed, unambiguity, unity, strict subordination, reduction of fric-tion and of material and personal costs – these are raised to the optimum point in the strictly bureaucratic administration, and especially in its monocratic form.

(Weber 1948: 214)

Some interpretations of this passage in Weber suggest that it offers a eulogy to bureaucracy (e.g. Blau and Scott 1963). Yet, as Albrow (1970: 63) points out, 'It would be quite misleading to equate Weber's concept of formal rationality with the idea of efficiency.' What Weber realized only too clearly was that 'technical formal rationality' was not necessarily the equivalent of 'efficiency'. Not only was 'efficiency' a 'foreign' term to Weber (see Albrow 1970: 64), but, even in those terms he made his, its achievement would have required more than sheer technique alone. It also required a normative, moral context of value that could only be given culturally, instead of instrumentally. It is not that the spread of bureaucracy is due solely to its instrumental efficiency, according to Weber. It would be more correct to point to the cultural conditions of 'rationalization' as the appropriate explanation. Such a 'cultural' explanation points to the *institutionalization* of value as the overarching factor in interpreting the rise of particular types of organization. The iron cage is a cultural construct instead of a rational constraint.

Had Weber wanted to make an argument linking 'efficiency' to 'bureaucracy' he would have found it easy to do so. He was, after all, thoroughly familiar with a tradition that drew such connections, that of Austrian marginalist economics (Therborn 1976: 290–5). Yet, had he followed this path it is unlikely that the linkage would have been a positive one. Had Weber embraced an argument that linked bureaucracy to the achievement of efficiency it would have been necessary to mount a counter-argument to the marginalist position. From the perspective of marginalism what was most striking about bureaucracy was its inefficiency, not its efficiency. Simply stated, this position regarded voluntary and reciprocally oriented transactions between individuals to be the maximally efficient form of exchange. Bureaucracy, instead of facilitating the market in these, interposes the heavy hand of centralized authority that overrides freely contracting individuals.

From a marginalist economic perspective, order does not have to be organized: it is something that can emerge spontaneously, if it is not subject to interference. As Friedrich von Hayek (1976: 21) argues, 'the commands as well as the rules which govern an organization serve particular results aimed at by those who are in command of the organization', as opposed to that 'spontaneous order' that the market can provide. Organizations, whether public or private bureaucracies (but particularly those of organized labour), distort the spontaneous order of the market (Hayek 1976: 134). Against the necessity of organization which Weber argues for, Hayek would favour decentralization and de-authorization of action to aid the spontaneous formation of coalitions entered by freely contracting subjects, untrammelled by the hands-on authority of any organizations.

For Hayek the market is a source of spontaneous order. It is the market that resolves the Hobbesian mystery. Social order is possible because of the myriad free and independent decisions to buy and sell on the market that the price mechanism allows. No system of central planning could obtain the same effects, he argues. Thus, organizations, as such systems, must be a second-best alternative to markets (and their very existence, of course, destroys 'fair' markets). The emergent basis of market order, premised upon the free decisions of many disconnected individuals, often based upon the most tacit and implicit of knowledge, brings people into a relationship with each other simply through decisions to buy and sell, decisions effected through the 'price mechanism'. Planning could not hope to replicate the implicit, tacit and differentiated bases of this order. It could only ever be a stage on *The Road to Serfdom* (Hayek 1944).

Where planning fails and markets are absent Hayek believes that a vicious cycle will set in. Otherwise, ever grander and more ambitious plans will seek to compensate for the failures of earlier ones. Such a fetish of planning will be doomed to failure. Planning fails because of the impossibility of any omnipotence which can centralize and synthesize all the data necessary for decision-making. Besides, such omnipotence is unnecessary. According to Hayek the market can do whatever a plan can do so much more effortlessly and economically. The order that it produces does not need to be contrived. This uncontrived order is not purely a result of the serendipitious 'hidden hand' of the market: it is also a moral order. Hayek (1960: 62) writes that the freedom that is the market 'has never worked without deeply ingrained moral beliefs . . . coercion can be reduced to a minimum only where individuals can be expected as a rule to conform voluntarily to certain principles' (cited by Hindess 1987: 130).

Interestingly, Hayek, the advocate of freedom through the market, does not oppose the existence of enterprise organization *per se*. Hayek recognizes the existence of organizations as goal-oriented systems, at least where they are profit-oriented corporations. Whatever other goals an organization has ought to be rigorously subordinated to 'the profitable use of the capital entrusted to the management by the stockholders' to secure 'the single aim' of obtaining 'the largest return in terms of long-run profits'. Without this dedication 'the case for private enterprise breaks down' (Hayek 1967: 300, 312). Hayek makes an exception to the rhetoric extolling the pleasures of unbridled liberalism and the purity of the market as the most sacred of institutions. Large organizations are allowable where every aspect of their functioning subordinates itself to the market principle of profit raised to an overarching goal.

Hindess (1987: 127) notes that the central idea buttressing the market in Hayek's thought is that of 'liberty'. It is because planning reduces liberty that it is to be avoided. Yet, he does not regard the organizational basis of enterprise calculation as a reduction of liberty. In this respect, as Hindess (1987: 129) observes, he is a far less astute and realist commentator than was Weber (1978): 'The fact that employees are not legally prevented from resigning and seeking alternative employment does not mean that they are not subject to coercion by their employers. The extension of freedom of contract in a society may well go hand in hand with the development of highly authoritarian relationships in the sphere of employment.' Exactly so. A certain blindness about this issue is a peculiar affliction of 'market' premised approaches to organization analysis in their delimitation of a sphere of efficiency other than the market. There is no doubt that Weber's analysis of 'efficiency' as a cultural concept, instead of as one that is economic, is a more appropriate premise for analysis. In contemporary theory it is only the 'institutionalist' school that retains the sense of the centrality of culture to organization analysis. Unfortunately, they do so in a way that leads frequently to a somewhat one-dimensional functional determinism.

Weber's approaches to bureaucracy and to organizations as structures of value have provided the central core of his legacy for the sociology of organizations and organization theory more generally. In the wider context of his work there were at least two other routes open for exploration in considerably more detail. One would have been the large-scale comparative historical sociology which Weber pioneered. The other would have been the sociology of organized economic action. Neither endeavour has been noticeably attractive for the subsequent exponents of organization analysis. To the extent that there has been any interest in either of these two alternate routes from Weber, then it is the latter that has commanded attention.

ECONOMIC EMBEDDEDNESS, INSTITUTIONAL FRAMEWORKS AND MODES OF RATIONALITY

Organization analysis could have started, but on the whole has not, from Weber's conceptualization of the sociological categories of economic action, the title of the second chapter of *Economy and Society* that deals with the vexed relationship between formal and substantive rationality. A good deal of the force of Weber's analysis derives from his exploration of the differentially distributed powers of control and disposal of productive resources that underpin the characteristic form of a modern market economy, which is 'a complete network of exchange contracts in deliberate planned acquisitions of powers of control and disposal' (Weber 1978: 67). Not only does this characterization put paid to economic-liberal representations of the market as a sphere of freedom and equality in a contractual universe, such as those of Williamson (1963), which at best present only one side of the social process involved, but it also sets the stage for the conflict between different modes of economic rationality as well as demonstrating the importance of trust, often implicit and embedded in economic action.

Organizations exist because, in all probability, 'certain persons will act in such a way as to carry out the order governing the organization' (Weber 1978: 49). In other words one premise of organization is the expectation that one can trust in the obedience of others. The order recognizable as that of an effectively functioning organization gets constructed out of this trust and obedience. In Weber's terms this order refers to the constitution of the organizational 'structure of dominance'. Structures of dominance are cultural in context and always substantive sources of rationality. Specific substantive sources may be indistinguishable from formal rationality under conditions where a specific substantive rationality is treated as if it were the essence of reason. This identity would occur if the formal categories of a purely accounting notion of efficiency were to be the dominant element shaping organization designers and elite judgements, for example. In such a situation a specific cultural value – efficiency, defined in terms of the categories of a particular form of knowledge – would be raised to the status of an 'ultimate value', culturally prized for its own sake, as an end in itself, as something in which we trust.

For Weber, economic action is *formally* rational to the extent that it rests on the best technically possible practice of quantitative calculation or accounting. Yet no such precise notion of *substantive* rationality is possible as this is a generic concept designating goal-oriented action where the goals are variable. Economic action is substantively rational to the extent that its motivation and assessment proceed according to an ultimate goal of some sort. Such a substantive orientation, Weber notes from the start, may lead the actor to see formal, quantitative calculation as unimportant, or even inimical to the achievement of ultimate ends. The probability that this will be so lessens the more that the world approximates to a formally rationalized ideal of capitalist accounting in which ultimate ends hardly figure (Weber 1978: 165). Ironically, of course, this denial of ultimate ends in the face of technical rationality elevates technical reason itself to the value of an ultimate end. It becomes 'iconic'. It is no longer in obedience to God that we place our trust but in obedience to the rational techniques that He once sanctified.

The immediate lure of formal rationality in a money economy occurs because money itself is the most rational formal means of orienting activity. It can be used as more than a medium of exchange. It apparently offers a universal measure of quantification and calculation for all elements of capital, including heterodox physical capital and present and future monetary claims, obligations and expectations. Working from real or fictional transactions both between enterprises and within them, accountancy offers the formal possibility of global assessments of gross and net capital worth. It can do so at selected moments both now and in the future. The formal possibility of calculating profit and loss becomes available.

Weber's discussion of accounting practice suggests something of a relapse into marginalist economics' quasi-objectivist problematic, a suggestion that is confirmed instead of scotched by his repeated proviso that the formal rationality of monetary calculation rests on 'real' prices, that is, prices obtained on an unfettered market. The ideal rationality of economic enterprise *per se* conflates to the economic system *in toto*. Weber was not unaware of having done this. He observes that there is an unavoidable element of irrationality in all economic systems. It is evident because a 'structure of dominance' always conditions their operations in ways substantively alien to purely technical rationality (Weber 1978: 942).

At this highest level of formal rationality Weber (1978: 108) begins to note the systematic entry of elements of substantive irrationality. There is an irony here. It is from a purely technical interest that the possibility of diverse modes of rationality becomes constituted. He isolates three circumstances in particular where the ramifications of monetary calculability induce this 'irrationality'. The first of these is the relevance of autonomous and antagonistic enterprises, which produce according to no other criterion than arbitrarily distributed demand. The second concerns the environmental conditions upon which capital accounting depends. The latter presupposes absolute property rights over capital goods, a purely commercial (as opposed to technical) orientation of management, and favours speculative behaviour based on these unfettered rights. Capital accounting thus approaches technical optimality under ideal economic-liberal conditions. The specification of these is simple. Unqualified proprietorial prerogatives and market freedom, including control over appointment of managers, is necessary. Also, labour would be freely available on an unfettered labour market where complete freedom of contract prevailed. Mechanically rational technology; a formally rational administration and legal system, and a complete divorce of enterprise from household organization would also be evident. Weber singles out the exclusion of workers from control over capital ownership as well as from its returns, with their subordination to entrepreneurs, as a specific form of substantive irrationality (Weber 1978: 129, 161–2, 138; also Clegg et al. 1986: 60–1).

The third circumstance in which Weber sees formal rationality compromised is where the economic organization becomes prey to the calculations of outside interests: it becomes, in effect, a potential locus of contradictory calculations instead of being a single discrete calculating subject (Cutler et al. 1979a; 1979b). 'Expropriation of workers from the means of production' and the concentration of control in proprietorial interests are entry points for external influences of two kinds. First, credit and financial institutions; secondly, predators who acquire the issued share capital for speculative purposes. Either way, the outside interests pursue their business interest, 'Often foreign to those of the organization as such' and 'not primarily oriented to the long-term profitability of the enterprise' (Weber 1978: 139; also see the discussion in Clegg et al. 1986: 61–2). This problem becomes acute when these interests 'consider their control over the plant and capital goods of the enterprise . . . not as a permanent investment, but as a means of making a purely short-run speculative profit' (Weber 1978: 140). Familiarity with the gamesmanship, argot and institutions surrounding corporate takeovers (Hirsch 1986) only serves to underscore the contemporary salience of these aspects of Weber's account of the substantive bases of mistrust, despite their relative neglect in the literature dealing with organizations.

The earlier part of this chapter traced how the concern with formal rationality and efficiency that pre-dated Weber's translations, in Barnard (1938) for instance, effectively structured the context within which Weber's work was assimilated into the sociology of organizations. Lost in this process were the broader comparative concerns with the religious roots and societal consequences of 'rationalization'. Also, the central focus on substantive sources of rationality and their existential tension with formal rationality became displaced. A narrower focus on 'bureaucracy' prevailed, one in which an instrumental concern with 'efficiency' overshadowed the historical, institutional, political and economic sociology of the market which Weber (1978) had pioneered. By 1968, when the first translation of the whole text of *Economy and Society* appeared, the sociology of organizations, already constituted as 'normal science' (Kuhn 1962 and see Donaldson 1985), found little resonance with Weber's broader concerns.

CURRENT CONTINUITIES WITH THE WEBERIAN PROJECT FOR THE ANALYSIS OF ORGANIZATIONS

Weber's problematic did not go entirely unheeded. It is to be found in aspects of an institutionalist perspective, in the emphasis on institutional iconicization, as one might term it. Moreover, it is necessarily central for proponents of the power perspective, if they are to match Weber's sense of *realpolitik*. In France, for instance, Lucien Karpik (1972a, 1972b, 1977, 1978) developed a critique of what he took to be the thrust of Marx and Weber's writings on organizations. In so doing he resuscitated themes in Weber's work which organizational sociology had neglected. The organizational theory of the firm (Baumol 1967; Marris 1964; Cyert and March 1963; Williamson 1963), coupled with the concern with the organization as an arena that individuals attempt to dominate, in concert with others, as a locus of calculation and decision, became the central focus. These attempts at capture proceed through coalitions engaged in competitive bargaining for organizational resources and positions, to enforce their ends on the organization. Within this arena organizationally dominant coalitions appropriate the organization, from time to time, through various forms of strategic calculation. They consolidate 'structures of dominance'. In crypto-Foucauldian anticipation of later themes in the study of power/knowledge, these coalitions can be analysed through the study of various forms of strategic practice, modes of rationality sometimes termed 'logics of action' (see Karpik 1972a; Clegg and Dunkerley 1980: 502). The organization, conceptualized as a multiplicity of centres of power (also see Clegg 1989), has no necessary empirical structure apart from that which, locally, power and knowledge fabricate. Within the organizational arena agents with varying strategies struggle to constitute the capacities of the organization in policy terms that represent their conceptions of their interests. In so doing, they will bargain with whatever resources can be constituted as strategic. Such resources may be located either within or without the organizational arena. It is not just that there are resources waiting to be used. Instead resources get constituted through struggles represented discursively as diverse ways of being 'rational' in Weber's sense of substantive rationality. Hence 'modes of rationality'.

Structures of dominance articulate around more or less abstract cultural values and achieve their expression through organizationally situated actions and vocabularies of motive (Mills 1940). These are the normal ways of accounting for action (where 'accounting' is not being used in the technical sense of the discourse of accountancy). It is through such 'accounting' that one may refer to the socially available and publicly accountable complexes of reasons with which one might seek to justify organizational actions. Such 'rationalities' when considered collectively may be seen as 'modes' of rationality. No assumption of 'unity' or 'coherence' should be read into this designation. It is conceivable that organizations, and the agents located in and around them, may construct diverse and simultaneous rationalities that cohere neither across space nor through time.

Modes of rationality, built out of locally available conceptions, embed economic action. These may be derived either from local custom or practice, shaped either by culture or by the institutional framing of available vocabularies of motive. These cultures of local knowledge and local practice are the object of an institutional focus. These may be composed out of a complex pot-pourri of ingredients. One may be dealing with aspects of a traditional local culture, an occupational or organizational culture, or the clashes between them. One may be dealing with the way in which frames of meaning are subject to regulation by legislation, the norms of professional practice, or rationalized bureaucracy. Even contracts, seemingly the most rational and transcendent of forms, when studied empirically in local practice, require large elements of trust that may not be forthcoming for all sorts of good economic reasons that have nothing to do with the 'trustworthiness' of the parties but everything to do with substantively rational action (Clegg 1975).

Elements of trust are frequently at the centre of economic action. (The papers collected in the volume edited by Gambetta (1988) are a valuable resource for understanding the nature of trust, as is the classic text in organization analysis, Alan Fox's *Beyond Contract, 1974.*) Trust, with a limited range of other devices such as the structuring of members' (and clients', customers' etc.) conceptions of their self-interests in ways that are compatible with organizationally approved actions, serves to produce 'rationalities' conducive to organizational understanding: that is, stable patterns of action extending beyond immediate co-presence and through space and time.

The rationalities that can be called upon tend, in the first instance, to derive from whatever seems to work best in a particular environment. They are culturally available in a particular place and time. Here, elements of the population ecology argument are useful. Innovation may occur for all sorts of contingent reasons and when it does some forms will tend to survive and reproduce with a greater frequency than will others. Thus, organizations may well persist in displaying the characteristics that attended their formation, as Stinchcombe (1965) suggests. The structure of organizations 'sediments' as different concerns and issues become laid down in it. Sedimentation will occur particularly as organizations have to take on functions to deal with aspects of their institutional environment externally mandated by authoritative regulation by government, for instance, which seeks to see that organizations comply with some statutory objectives, for example as equal opportunity employers or ecologically acceptable manufacturers or disposers of waste. Frequently, the criteria of regulation develop in the context of professional practice, as DiMaggio and Powell (1983) have suggested. What survives organizationally may not be most 'efficient' but survives because at some time in the past of the organization it became instilled with value in that specific institutional context. It is this that is the essential insight of the institutional school. Things, forms and practices may be valued for and in themselves, irrespective of their contribution to the efficiency of the organization. Historically one might think of the place the Latin mass once had in the Roman Catholic church, or the role that the confessional still plays. Such practices do not necessarily make priests more efficient, but have value as legitimate icons. They are constitutive parts of a ceremonial fabric with an explicable past cultural context.

At the centre of analysis will be organizational agencies. Such agencies may be individuals or they may be collective agencies of some sort that have developed mechanisms for both the calculation and the representation of interests. They can make these calculations through the various discursive forms available to them. In particular, one thinks of the articulation of the various scientific, technical and other knowledges that constitute the primary occupational identities and resources of organizational agencies. Other sources of discursive availability will be drawn from whatever regulative (i.e. political, legal, economic, accounting etc.) and local frameworks of meaning present themselves, as well as from the many competing sources of value representation that surround any agency.

Local frameworks of meaning may be embedded in an infinite variety of contexts. 'Local' refers to specific sites of organizations, sites that empirically offer a plenitude of possible meanings and memberships with which to organize or to resist. In Hong Kong, for instance, it would be an imprudent Chinese organization that did not consult the *feng-shui* specialist in designing its buildings, moving into new offices, choosing a chief executive's office or determining the layout of the furniture, the location of doors and windows. As a visitor at the University of Hong Kong I was once witness to such a ceremony conducted when a department moved into new offices in a new building. The ritual consists of sprinkling water around the corners of the room and at the threshold, placing lighted candles in strategic positions, burning 'paper money' (not real currency but ceremonial money for *feng-shui* purposes), offering roast duck and oranges that subsequently one eats, and conducting a formula of words and actions appropriate to the ceremony. *Feng-shui* rituals may look like the height of irrationalist geomancy to those trained in rationalities such as microeconomic calculation. Still, in the Hong Kong local context they enter the modes of rationality in use in important ways.

It should be clear from the *feng-shui* example that in considering local context one is thinking of the discourse of various substantive rationalities that can be regarded as 'ultimate values' of some kind: discourses pertaining to represent the interest of efficiency, of equality, of the market, of the ecology, of a specific ethnicity or place, of *feng-shui*, of other forms of disciplinary knowledge-practice, such as forms of microeconomic or accounting calculations. It is precisely a part of my argument that no privilege attaches to forms of the latter in any *a priori* way. Whatever privilege is constituted can only be achieved through the stabilization of 'circuits of power' (Clegg 1989). Almost any abstractions might prevail. Practices in and around organizations will be constructed on the contested terrain of these various knowledges. It is not clear that the outcome of these struggles will always be decided in terms of the technically rational, as the limited success of 'green' values should serve to demonstrate. Whichever values obtain stable articulation as necessary nodal points through which organizational discourse must pass become what Weber referred to as 'principles of dominance' (see Clegg 1989 for a discussion of 'necessary nodal points'). The triumph of efficiency as such a value lacks necessity attached to it. As Weber was well aware, efficiency is ultimately a technical term, derived from the discourse of accounting conventions. These will vary widely with national frameworks. As is anthropologically self-evident, these principles of domination necessarily derive from the complex fabric of the surrounding material culture of members' knowledges and the practices that these knowledges can be claimed to license, to authorize, to enable or to approve. Where these practices can be represented as the principal conduits serving ultimate values, such as efficiency, they will be that much more secure against the strategic play of alternative discursive forms.

Discursive forms of knowledge and the practices that are coterminous with them, are not random, happenstance nor merely contingent. Actions are produced and reproduced according to rules constructed, reconstructed, transformed and innovated through mundane and institutional practice. An evidently material structure such as a building is an application (and sometimes an extension or innovation) of design, engineering, and other construction rules. An organization form is only marginally a less material structure composed through available rules. Taken together, where these achieve dominance in and as an organization form then they may be seen to be displaying a 'mode of rationality'.

CONCLUSION

Theoretical arguments since the translation of Weber's work have tended to be more deterministic in their analyses than the sketch presented here. The most obvious examples of this were to be contingency theories of what became known as a 'culture-free' variety (Hickson *et al.* 1974).

From the non-deterministic and highly contingent perspective developed here, power-players within and around the organizational arena will seek to use whatever resources are available to them in constructing local organizational practice, shaped to whatever mode of rationality, against the last of whatever stabilized circuits of power define as organizational imperatives. Organizations are thus arenas within which some things will tend to 'hang together' and power-players may adopt them while other forms of combination may be far less likely to occur as a coherent package, perhaps because they are less coherent, or perhaps because the alliance that could make them so lacks a position in the field of power able to constitute the necessity of its choices. Power, knowledge and organization are culturally irremediable. The theory of organizations must always also be an institutional and cultural theory. On this interpretation, it must also focus on the role of power and knowledge in organization. Any organization will always stand as a precise specification of distinct ensembles of these practices, fabricated in action and in structure. None of this is too far away from a plausible interpretation of Weber's concerns.

Max Weber has a continuing relevance for the sociology of organizations not so much because of what he wrote about organizations – the famous 'ideal type' of bureaucracy – but more for how he recommended analysis of the cultural constitution of any phenomena. Necessarily, one must reject some problematic aspects of the legacy of the theory; in particular, the vexed role of the legislative relationship between analysis and lay knowledges that, in common with other theorists of modernity, Weber was to prescribe (Bauman 1990). Consistent with the general approach that I would propose (Clegg 1989, 1990) this chapter resolves the issue by making these knowledges and the strategies of power that secure, reproduce and transform them the object of inquiry. Power/knowledge is thus at the core of a cultural science which, on this reading, is the nature of organizational analysis.

In general, this depiction of where Weber's analysis might direct us was not the legacy that organization theorists found in Weber. The iron cage held them captive, in many ways. Gouldner's earlier work on organizations,despite the fact that it is often interpreted as yet a further refutation of the ideal type of bureaucracy rather than as a practical exemplification of a mode of analysis with some affinities to the interpretation sketched here, is the exception. There is little point in resuscitating the modernist ideal type of bureaucracy today. We live in plural, partly postmodern, times and roadmaps to the essential bureaucratic soul of modernity are of little use as aids to navigation. The future focus may well be less on the inescapable sources of bondage and more on the imagination of difference that can release energies held captive. Bureaucracy, and its variants, as a specific ideal type, one whose influence has been so baneful for organization theory in its preoccupations with modernity, no more captures the necessary fate of our times than it did in the past. The past is always uncertain and the future remains unexplored outside the possibilities of dreams, fantasies and the projects of our imagination. Organization studies can play a role in charting the future by breaking free of the grip that the iron cage has held for so long on our imaginations and realities.

Breaking out of the iron cage, finding freedom in new constraints, discovering dark sides on the road to bright futures-what the organizational implications of this will be and how it might be achieved – this must be another story, one that remains barely scripted, even if touched upon elsewhere (Clegg 1990). Max Weber is dead: let us bury the reverberations of his pessimistic insights with him, leave the corpse interred and rewrite the epitaph and obituary. There is a continuing relevance in the thought of Max Weber for the sociology of organizations today. It is not what might be thought. The central focus is the inescapability of substantive values – even in their formal denial. These are at the core of organizations.

REFERENCES

Albrow, M. (1970) *Bureaucracy*. London: Pall Mall.

Aldrich, H.E. (1972) 'Technology and Organizational Structure: A Re-examination of the Findings of the Aston Group', *Administrative Science Quarterly*, 17: 26–42.

Barnard, C. (1938) *The Functions of the Executive*. Cambridge, Mass.: Harvard University Press.

Bauman, Z. (1990) 'Philosophical affinities of postmodern sociology', *Sociological Review*, 38(3): 411–44.

Baumol, N. (1967) *Business Behaviour, Value and Growth*. New York: Macmillan.

Blau, P. (1955) *The Dynamics of Bureaucracy*. Chicago: Chicago University Press.

Blau, P.M. and Schoenherr, R. (1971) *The Structuring of Organizations*. New York: Free Press.

Blau, P. and Scott, W.R. (1963) *Formal Organizations: A Comparative Approach*.

Boulding, K. (1956) 'General Systems Theory: The Skeleton of Science', *Management Science*, 2: 197–208.

Braverman, H. (1974) *Labor and Monopoly Capital: The Degradation of Work in the Twentieth Century*. New York: Monthly Review Press.

Child, J. and Mansfield, R. (1972) 'Technology, Size and Organization Structure', *Sociology*, 6: 368–93.

Clegg, S.R. (1975) *Power, Rule and Domination: A Critical and Empirical Understanding of Power in Sociological Theory and Organizational Life*. London: Routledge and Kegan Paul.

Clegg, S.R. (1989) *Frameworks of Power*. London: Sage.

Clegg, S.R. (1990) *Modern Organizations: Organization Studies in the Postmodern World* London: Sage.

Clegg, S.R. and Dunkerley, D. (1980) *Organization, Class and Control*. London: Routledge and Kegan Paul.

Clegg, S.R., Boreham, P. and Dow, G. (1986) *Class, Politics and the Economy*. London: Routledge and Kegan Paul.

Cutler, A., Hindess, B., Hirst, P.Q. and Hussain, A. (1979a) *Marx's Capital and Capitalism Today (Volume 1)*. London: Routledge and Kegan Paul.

Cutler, A., Hindess, B., Hirst, P.Q. and Hussain, A. (1979b) *Marx's Capital and Capitalism Today (Volume 2)*, London: Routledge and Kegan Paul.

Cyert, R. and March, J. (1963) *A Behavioral Theory of the Firm*. Englewood Cliffs, NJ: Prentice-Hall.

DiMaggio, P. and Powell, W. (1983) 'The Iron Cage Revisited: Institutional Isomorphism and Collective Rationality in Organizational Fields', *American Sociological Review*, 48(2): 147–60.

Donaldson, L. (1985) *In Defence of Organization Theory: A Response to the Critics*. Cambridge: Cambridge University Press.

Donaldson, L. (1986) 'Size and Bureaucracy in East and West: A Preliminary Meta Analysis', pp. 67–91 in S. R. Clegg, D. Dunphy and S. G. Redding (eds), *The Enterprise and Management in East Asia*. Hong Kong: University of Hong Kong Centre of Asian Studies.

Dunford, R. (1988) 'Scientific Management in Australia': A Discussion Paper', *Industry and Labour*, 1(3): 505–15.

Durkheim, E. (1957) *Professional Ethics and Civic Morals*. London: Routledge.

Durkheim, E. (1964) *The Division of Labour in Society*. New York: Free Press.

Etzioni, A. (1961) *The Comparative Analysis of Complex Organizations*. New York: Free Press.

Fayol, H. (1949) *General and Industrial Management*. London: Pitman.

Fox, A. (1974) *Beyond Contract: Work, Power and Trust Relations*. London: Faber and Faber.
Gambetta, D. (ed.) (1988) *Trust: Making and Breaking Cooperative Relations*. Oxford: Blackwell.
Gouldner, A.W. (1954) *Patterns of Industrial Bureaucracy*. New York: Free Press.
Gouldner, A.W. (1959) 'Organizational Analysis', pp. 400–28 in R.K. Merton, L. Broom and C. Cottrell (eds), *Sociology Today*. New York: Basic Books.
Grumley, J. (1988) 'Weber's Fragmentation of Totality', *Thesis Eleven*, 21: 20–39.
Haferkamp, H. (1987) 'Beyond the Iron Cage of Modernity? Achievement, Negotiation and Changes in the Power Structure', *Theory, Culture and Society*, 4(1): 31–54.
Hage, J. (1965) 'An Axiomatic Theory of Organizations', *Administrative Science Quarterly*, 10: 289–320.
Hage, J. and Aiken, M. (1970) *Social Change in Complex Organizations*. New York: Random House.
Hall, R. H. (1962) 'Intraorganizational Structure Variation: Application of the Bureaucratic Model', *Administrative Science Quarterly*, 7: 295–308.
Hall, R.H. (1963) 'The Concept of Bureaucracy: an Empirical Assessment', *American Journal of Sociology*, 69: 32–40.
Hall, R.H., Haas, J.E. and Johnson, N.J. (1967) 'Organization Size, Complexity and Formalization', *American Sociological Review*, 32: 903–12.
Hayek, F.A. (1944) *The Road to Serfdom*. London: Routledge and Kegan Paul.
Hayek, F. A. (1960) *The Constitution of Liberty*. London: Routledge and Kegan Paul.
Hayek, F.A. (1967) *Studies in Philosophy, Politics and Economics*. London: Routledge and Kegan Paul.
Hayek, F. von (1976) *Individualism and Economic Order*. London: Routledge.
Hickson, D.J. and McMillan, C. (eds) (1981) *Organization and Nation: The Aston Programme IV*. Aldershot: Gower.
Hickson, D.J., Hinings, C.R., McMillan, C.J. and Schwitter, J.P. (1974) 'The Culture-free Context of Organizational Structure: A Trinational Comparison', *Sociology*, 8: 59–80.
Hickson, D.J., Pugh, D.S. and Pheysey, D.C. (1969) 'Operations Technology and Organization Structure: An Empirical Reappraisal', *Administrative Science Quarterly*, 14: 378–97.
Hickson, D.J., McMillan, C.J., Azumi, K. and Horvath, D. (1979) 'Grounds for Comparative Organization Theory: Quicksands or Hard Core?', pp. 25–41 in C. J. Lammers and D. J. Hickson (eds) *Organizations Alike and Unlike: International and Inter-Institutional Studies in the Sociology of Organizations*. London: Routledge and Kegan Paul.
Hindess, B. (1987) *Freedom, Equality and the Market: Arguments on Social Policy*. London: Tavistock.
Hirsch, P.M. (1986) 'From Ambushes to Golden Parachutes: Corporate Takeovers as an Instance of Cultural Framing and Institutional Integration', *American Journal of Sociology*, 91(4): 800–37.
Karpik, L. (1972a) 'Sociologie, économie, politique et buts des organizations de production', *Revue Française de Sociologie*, 13: 299–324.
Karpik, L. (1972b) 'Les Politiques et les logiques d'action de la grande enterprise industrielle', *Sociologie du Travail*, 1: 82–105.
Karpik, L. (1977) 'Technological Capitalism' pp. 41–71 in S.R. Clegg and D. Dunkerley (eds) *Critical Issues in Organizations*. London: Routledge and Kegan Paul.
Karpik, L. (1978) 'Organizations, Institutions and History' pp. 15–68 in L. Karpik (ed.) *Organization and Environment: Theory, Issues and Reality*. Beverly Hills, CA: Sage.
Katz, D. and Kahn, R.L. (1966) *The Social Psychology of Organizations*. New York: John Wiley.

Kerr, C., Dunlop, J.T., Harbison, F. and Myers, C.A. (1973) *Industrialism and Industrial Man*. Harmondsworth: Penguin.

Kuhn, T.S. (1962) *The Structure of Scientific Revolutions*. Chicago: University of Chicago Press.

Littler, C.R. (1982) *The Development of the Labour Process in Capitalist Societies*. *London*: Heinemann Educational Books.

Maier, C.S. (1970) 'Between Taylorism and Technocracy: European Ideologies and the Vision of Industrial Productivity in the 1920s', *Journal of Contemporary History*, 5: 27–61.

March, J.G. and Simon, H.A. (1958) *Organizations*. New York: John Wiley.

Marris, R. (1964) *The Economic Theory of 'Managerial' Capitalism*. Chicago: Free Press of Glencoe.

Marx, K. (1965) *Economic and Philosophical Manuscripts*. London: Lawrence and Wishart.

Marx, K. (1976) *Capital* (Volume 1). Harmondsworth: Penguin.

Mayer, P. (1956) *Max Weber and German Politics*. London: Faber and Faber.

Mayo, E. (1933) *The Human Problems of an Industrial Civilization*. New York: Macmillan.

Mayo, E. (1975) *The Social Problems of an Industrial Civilization*. London: Routledge and Kegan Paul.

Merton, R.K. (1940) 'Bureaucratic Structure and Personality', *Social Forces*, 18: 560–68.

Mills, C.W. (1940) 'Situated Actions and Vocabularies of Motive', *American Sociological Review*, 5: 904–13.

Morgan, G. (1986) *Images of Organizations*. London: Sage.

Perrow, C. (1986) *Complex Organizations: A Critical Essay*, third edition. New York: Random House.

Pugh, D.S. (ed.) (1971) *Organization Theory: Selected Readings*. Harmondsworth. Penguin.

Pugh, D.S. (1988) 'The Aston Research Programme', pp. 123–35 in A. Bryman (ed.) *Doing Research in Organizations*. London: Routledge and Kegan Paul.

Pugh, D.S. and Hickson, D.J. (1976) *Organizational Structure in its Context: the Aston Programme 1*. London: Saxon House.

Pugh, D.S. and Payne, R.L. (eds) (1977) *Organizational Behaviour in its Context: The Aston Programme 111,* Aldershot: Gower.

Scott, W.R. (1981) *Organizations: Rational, Natural and Open Systems*. Englewood Cliffs, NJ: Prentice-Hall International.

Selznick, P. (1943) 'An Approach to a Theory of Bureaucracy', *American Sociological Review*, 8: 47–54.

Selznick, P. (1948) 'Foundations for a Theory of Organizations', *American Sociological Review*, 13: 23–35.

Shelley, M.W. (1969) *Frankenstein: Or, The Modern Prometheus* [1818]. London: Oxford University Press.

Simon, H.A. (1957) *Administrative Behaviour*, second edition. New York: Macmillan.

Smith, A. (1961) *An Enquiry into the Nature and Causes of the Wealth of Nations*. Indianapolis: Bobbs-Merrill

Starbuck, W.H. (1981) 'A Trip to View the Elephants and Rattlesnakes in the Garden of Aston', pp. 167–97 in A. H. Van de Van and W. F. Joyce (eds) *Perspectives on Organizational Design and Behaviour*. New York: John Wiley.

Stinchcombe, A. (1965) 'Social Structure and Organizations', pp. 142–93 in J.G. March (ed.) *Handbook of Organizations*, Chicago: Rand McNally.

Taylor, F.W. (1911) *Principles of Scientific Management*. New York: Harper and Row.

Therborn, G. (1976) *Science, Class and Society*. London: New Left Books.

Thompson, J.D. (1967) *Organizations in Action*. New York: McGraw-Hill.

Touraine, A. (1988) 'Modernity and Cultural Specificities', *International Social Science Journal*, 118: 443–57.

Von Bertalanffy, L. (1968) *General Systems Theory: Foundations, Development, Applications*. New York: Brazillier.

Weber, M. (1920) *Gesammelte Aufsätze zur Religionsssoziologie*. Tübingen: J. C. B. Mohr (Paul Siebeck).

Weber, M. (1923) *General Economic History*, translated by F. H. Knight. London: Allen and Unwin.

Weber, M. (1947) *The Theory of Social and Economic Organization*, translated by T. Parsons and A. M. Henderson, with an introduction by T. Parsons. New York: Free Press.

Weber, M. (1948) *From Max Weber: Essays in Sociology*, translated, edited and with an introduction by H. H. Gerth and C. W. Mills. London: Routledge and Kegan Paul.

Weber, M. (1949) *The Methodology of the Social Sciences*, translated and edited by E.A. Shills and H.A. Finch. New York: Free Press.

Weber, M. (1958) *Gesammelte Politische Schriften*. Tübingen: J. C. B. Mohr (Paul Siebeck).

Weber, M. (1968) *Economy and Society: An Outline of Interpretive Sociology* (3 vols), edited and with an introduction by G. Roth and C. Wittich. New York: Bedminster Press.

Weber, M. (1976) *The Protestant Ethic and the Spirit of Capitalism*, translated by T. Parsons and with a new introduction by A. Giddens. London: Allen and Unwin.

Weber, M. (1978) *Economy and Society: An Outline of Interpretive Sociology* (2 vols), edited by G. Roth and C. Wittich. Berkeley: University of California Press.

Weick, K.E. (1979) *The Social Psychology of Organizing*, Second edition. Reading, Mass.: Addison-Wesley.

Williamson, O.E. (1963) 'A Model of Rational Managerial Behavior' pp. 237–52 in R. M. Cyert and J. G. March (eds) *A Behavioral Theory of the Firm*. Englewood Cliffs, NJ: Prentice Hall.

Wilson, H.T. (1983) 'Technocracy and Late Capitalist Society: Reflections on the Problem of Rationality and Social Organization', pp. 152–238 in S. R. Clegg, G. Dow and P. Boreham (eds) *The State, Class and the Recession*. London: Croom Helm.

Woodward, J. (1958) *Management and Technology*. London: HMSO.

Woodward, J. (1965) *Industrial Organization: Theory and Practice*. London: Oxford University Press.

Woodward, J. (1970) *Industrial Organization: Behaviour and Control*. London: Oxford University Press.

Chapter 3

Work and authority: some Weberian perspectives

John Eldridge

It is perhaps Weber's greatest achievement that he succeeded in assessing the character of modern bureaucratic institutions both in the instrumental-rational perspective of their specific capabilities and in the substantive-rational perspective of the seemingly irreversible impact of bureaucratisation as a rationalising force as well as a threat to open societies like our own and indeed to the future of mankind as a whole.

(Mommsen 1989: 120)

This chapter endorses Wolfgang Mommsen's contention and will attempt to tease out and reflect upon some of its implications. My starting point is with the evergreen *Protestant Ethic and the Spirit of Capitalism* (1930). There we have Weber's justly famous discussion of the springs of action that contributed to the formation of the modern economic order. What were the motivations that generated and energized the spirit of capitalism among entrepreneurs? What were the social sources of obedience to authority that underpinned workers' compliance with their employers' orders? This opens up the general issue of the break with traditionalism, which is a crucial benchmark in Weber's exposition. I recognize the force of this rupture. At the same time I want to reconsider the concept of traditional action, in relation to both workers and employers. This leads me to suggest that traditional action should not be treated as a residual category in contrast to Weber's typology of rational action. Weber's ideal types were only ever intended for heuristic purposes, so the notion of traditional action as unreflective, habituated behaviour is not something which, in its pure form, we should expect to find in concrete situations. My inference is that the label 'traditional behaviour' can actually turn out, on inspection, to cover forms of substantive rationality. This does not, as it were, 'refute' Weber, but it does nuance some of the argument. And it does challenge what might be termed a vulgar Weberianism, which would equate traditional with irrational behaviour. Moreover, once we have an image of society as one in which there are competing rationalities entailing with different values and interests (including traditional orientations) then we can appreciate why Weber's ideal type of capitalism, in terms of its formal rationality, was not realized in practice. Nor did he claim it was or expect it to be.

This is clearly indicated in *Economy and Society* (1978). There Weber writes of formal rationality, applied to economic action as a way of referring to quantitative calculations or accounting. In its own terms this was clear enough, 'at least in the sense that expression in money terms yields the highest degree of formal calculability'. He then adds, characteristically, that 'naturally, this is true only relatively, so long as other things are equal' (1978: 85). This, we soon discover, is not a casual qualification. It is a way of introducing us to the ambiguities and complexities of substantive rationality. The term itself, he suggests,

> conveys only one element common to all 'substantive' analyses: namely, that they do not restrict themselves to note the purely formal and (relatively) unambiguous fact that action is based on 'goal-oriented' rational calculation with the technically most adequate available methods, but apply certain criteria of ultimate ends, whether they be ethical, political, utilitarian, hedonistic (*ständisch*), egalitarian, or whatever, and measure the results of economic action, however formally 'rational' in the sense of correct calculation they may be, against these scales of value rationality – or *substantive* goal rationality. There is an infinite number of possible value scales for this type of rationality, of which the socialist and communist standard constitute only one group.
>
> The latter, although by no means unambiguous in themselves, always involve elements of social justice and equality; others are criteria of status distinctions, or of the capacity for power, especially of the war capacity, of a political unit; all these and many others are of potential 'substantive' significance. These points of view are, however, significant only as *basis* from which to judge the *outcome* of economic action. In addition and quite independently, it is possible to judge from an ethical, ascetic, or esthetic point of view the spirit of economic activity. All of these approaches may consider the 'purely formal' rational of calculation in monetary terms as of quite secondary importance or even as fundamentally inimical to their respective ultimate ends, even before anything has been said about the consequences of the specifically modern calculating attitude.

(1978: 85–6)

It is scarcely an exaggeration to say that *Economy and Society* consists in unpacking the significance of that position and pursuing the implications. This extends to and connects with Weber's treatment of modern bureaucracy, hence the quotation from Mommsen with which this chapter began. But again, the importance of the distinction between formal and substantive rationality is crucial. In formal terms bureaucracy is a form of social organization, which through its administrative efficiency makes for a high degree of calculability within its sphere of activity. Questions about who controls the bureaucracy, who the bureaucrats themselves are, and who is controlled by these forms of administration with what consequences, are never far away from Weber's mind. These point clearly to the varieties of substantive rationality. The interrelationship of modern capitalism and legal-rational bureaucracies is clearly recognized and stated by Weber. Paradoxically, we may think, these rational instruments, by definition collective organizations, can be seen as essential elements in the ideological and practical pursuit of competitive individualism But what about socialist societies? It would, argued Weber, be a question,

> whether in a socialistic system it would be possible to provide conditions for carrying out as stringent a bureaucratic organization as has been possible in a capitalistic order. For socialism would, in fact, require a still higher degree of formal bureaucratization than capitalism. If this should prove not to be possible, it would demonstrate the existence of another of those fundamental elements of irrationality – a conflict between formal and substantive rationality of the sort which sociology so often encounters.

> (1978: 225)

What kind of bureaucracy did it turn out to be? Weber only lived to see the very early years of the Bolshevik regime in the Soviet Union. Seventy years on the bureaucracy of the planned economy in Eastern Europe and the Soviet Union had, in a different paradox, come to be defined with reference to red tape, stagnation and corruption. In the case of the KGB, especially under Stalin, the bureaucracy of surveillance also became an instrument of terror.

This chapter explores these paradoxes of unintended consequences in relation to both capitalism and socialism. Both can lay claims to being rational economic orders, yet both give evidence of substantive irrationality. Weber put markers down to indicate his own value position. There were features of modern capitalism that disturbed him, as indicated in *The Protestant Ethic* and elsewhere. But he was sceptical of the socialist alternative. I agree with Mommsen, however, when he argues that 'neither on the political nor on the theoretical level did he consider the dialogue with socialism to be definitely closed. He felt that the final word on this issue had not yet been spoken' (Mommsen 1989, 73). There are many who now feel the final word has indeed been spoken. But my reference to Nove's *Economics of Feasible Socialism* (1983) in what follows makes clear my dissent from that view. The substantive irrationalities of modern industrial societies constitute perhaps, a prefiguring of what Beck terms *Risk Society* (1992). The question I raise at the end of the chapter is: are there any resources of hope that can take us beyond Weber's value position and his accompanying pessimism?

WORK AND THE CAPITALIST SPIRIT

Weber's *Protestant Ethic and the Spirit of Capitalism* was a seminal treatment of the role of religious ideology in the economic sphere. From the first publication as articles in the *Archiv für Socialwissenschaft und Socialpolitik* in 1904, 1905 and 1906, the study has been a provocation and stimulus to academic debate, much of it very fierce, to which Weber himself responded vigorously. In the foreword to the 1930 Parsons translation, R. H. Tawney saw it as a study that was valuable not only for historians and economists but for all who were concerned to explore the deeper issues of modern society: 'In emphasizing . . . the connection between religious radicalism and economic progress, Weber called attention to an interesting phenomenon, at which previous writers had hinted, but which none had yet examined with the same wealth of learning and philosophical insight' (Weber 1930: 6). Nevertheless, as he was to salute the 'masterly ingenuity' of the work, Tawney also noted with some understatement, we may feel: 'His conclusions are illuminating; but they are susceptible, it may perhaps be held, of more than one interpretation' (ibid.: 10). Weber offers us a view of the way in which entrepreneurship could be legitimized and its practice motivated, together with comment on the social sources of obedience among the emerging workforces of industrial capitalism. Much of it hinges on the distinction between traditional economic behaviour and capitalism. The breakdown of traditionalism, almost by definition, was not an easy matter:

> A man does not 'by nature' wish to earn more and more money, but simply live as he is accustomed to live and to earn as much money as is necessary for that purpose. Where ever modern capitalism has begun its work of increasing the productivity of human labour by increasing its intensity, it has encountered the immensely stubborn resistance of this leading trait of pre-capitalist labour. And today it encounters it the more, the more backward (from a capitalistic point of view) the labouring forces are with which it has to deal.
>
> (Ibid.: 6)

He goes on to give an example of traditional workers, in this case German women, who, with a significant exception that illustrated his point, were unwilling to respond to new methods of work even though they would have earned more:

> Increases of piece rates are of no avail against the stone wall of habit. In general it is otherwise, and that is a point of no little importance from our viewpoint, only with girls having a specifically religious, especially a pietistic background. One often hears, and statistical investigation confirms it, that by far the best chances of economic education are found among this group. The ability of mental concentration, as well as the absolutely essential feeling of obligation to one's job, are here most often combined with a strict economy which calculates the possibility of high earnings, and a cool self-control and frugality which enormously increase performance. This provides the most favourable foundation for the conception of labour as an end in itself, as a calling which is necessary to capitalism: the chance of overcoming traditionalism are greatest on account of the religious upbringing.
>
> (Ibid.: 62–3)

Necessary it may have been but it was also strongly contested by the workforce. Weber cites examples of Methodist workmen who were persecuted and their tools destroyed because of their willingness to work. Indeed, a parallel split occurred among employers. There was the traditional spirit and there was the capitalist spirit. Weber gives a pen picture of the traditional form of economic activity in the Continental textile industry, under the putting-out system:

> The number of business hours was very moderate, perhaps five to six a day, sometimes considerably less; in the rush season, where there was one, more. Earnings were moderate; enough to lead a respectable life and in good times to put away a little. On the whole, relations among competitors were relatively good, with a large degree of agreement on the fundamentals of business. A long daily visit to the tavern, and with often plenty to drink, and a congenial circle of friends, made life comfortable and leisurely.
>
> (Ibid.: 66–7)

Interestingly, Weber distinguishes between the form and spirit of capitalist activity. These textile businesses were capitalist in form, with rational book-keeping and the use of capital in the turnover of the business, but:

> It was a traditionalistic business, if one considers the spirit which animated the entrepreneur; the traditional manner of life, the traditional rate of profit, the traditional amount of work, the traditional manner of regulating the relation-ships with labour, and an essentially traditional circle of customers and the manner of attracting new ones. All these dominated the conduct of the busi-ness, were at the basis, one may say, of the ethos of this group of business men.
>
> (Ibid.: 67)

Yet it was the dynamism of the capitalist spirit that was to win out. Even before the factory system it was there, represented in those individuals who system-atically pursued the principle of low prices and high turnover, who introduced stricter methods of supervision over those they employed, adapted more knowl-edgeably to the needs of their customers, reinvested profits into their business rigorously. This activity brought the sharp edge of the competitive struggle into the traditional arena and did not leave the traditionalist untouched. Indeed, and not surprisingly, these innovators could be on the receiving end of hatred and moral indignation. The point for Weber was not that such people were amoral but that it was the motivating ethic of what, for them, constituted 'good business' which sustained them and enabled them to withstand and overcome the attacks of the traditionalists. Convinced of the rightness of what they were doing, their very methods made them more successful than the traditionalists. They were the harbingers of the triumph of bourgeois capitalism.

We may recall that, in Weber's ideal types of social action, traditional action is defined as a habit-bound response. It is distinguished from two types of rational action: action rationally oriented towards an absolute value and action rationally oriented to a system of discrete individual ends, in which the ends, the means and the secondary results are all rationally weighed and taken into account (Weber 1978). Yet we ought to question whether traditional action can be so easily contrasted, because it is, after all, entirely possible to give good reasons for habitual action, if asked, other than 'we've always done it'. Even Weber referred to the traditional business routine, perhaps ironically, as an 'idyllic state'. There are values which inform and guide habits. These might have to do, for example, with valued rhythms of work connected with the seasons, established patterns of relationships which are valued and contribute to a person's sense of identity. The significance of some of this is well exemplified in the work of E.P. Thompson (1968, 1991). If we pick up Weber's cue on Methodism, for example, we can see that in *The Making of the English Working Class* (1968) Thompson contrasts the ethos of Methodism with the older, half-pagan popular culture with its fairs, sports, drink and picaresque hedonism. Tradition, therefore, was not a matter of cultural hegemony, such that the lower orders deferred unquestioningly to those in authority; traditional behaviour also contained the seeds of disrespect for authority and the capacity for protest and rebellion. In *Customs in Common* (1991), Thompson argues that, in eighteenth-century England there can be found the paradox of a rebellious traditional culture:

> The conservative culture of the plebs as often as not resists, in the name of custom, those economic rationalisations and innovations (such as enclosure, work discipline, unregulated 'free market' in grain) which rulers, dealers or employers seek to impose. Innovation is more evident at the top of society than below, but since this innovation is not some normless and neutral technological/sociological process ('modernisation', 'rationalisation') but the innovation of the capitalist process, it is most often experienced by the plebs in the form of exploitation, or the expropriation of customary use-rights, or the violent disruption of valued patterns of work and leisure. Hence the plebeian culture is rebellious, but rebellious in defence of custom.
>
> (Thompson 1991: 9)

As Thompson sees it, this plebeian culture is in one sense the people's own, with its fairs, taverns, rough music and defences against the gentry and clergy. But when a legitimation of protest was offered, against the encroachments of capitalism, interests could be defended and justified by reference to specific legal codes, which underpinned certain aspects of traditional behaviour. Thompson refers, for example, to the Book of Orders, established and developed between 1580 and 1630, which in essence gave power to local magistrates and juries to inspect stocks in barns and granaries and, in times of market scarcity, to order quantities to be sent to market. It was the failure of the authorities to enforce this legislation in times of scarcity that led the food rioters to take the law into their own hands. This is extensively illustrated in Thompson's essay, 'The Moral Economy of the Crowd' (in Thompson 1991: 185–258). There is, behind these riots, a sense that the common good has been violated. The Rev. Charles Fitzgerald, in a sermon before the sessions at Bodmin, denounced the hoarders of corn in no uncertain terms:

these Man-haters, opposite to the common good, as if the world were made only for them, would appropriate the earth, and the fruits thereof, wholly to themselves . . . As quails grow fat with Hemlocke, which is poison to other creatures, so these grow full by Death.

(cited in Thompson 1991: 253–4)

Whether it was a reference back to the Book of Orders in the case of food rioters, or to the Tudor labour code in the case of artisans, who saw their rights and livelihoods affected by economic and technological change, the specific tradition out of which the nineteenth-century English working class was hewn was neither wholly independent nor wholly subordinated and passively moulded by the dominant classes and their ideologies. The conflicts were real and significant, although sometimes their meanings need to be decoded in order to disclose the rules that governed particular protests. If we do this, then, in Thompson's view, 'we can read much eighteenth century social history as a succession of confrontations between an innovative market economy and the customary moral economy of the plebs' (1991: 12).

The robustness, spontaneity, mutual loyalty, and neighbourliness, picaresqueness and quasi-insurrectionary practices of eighteenth-century plebeians were, then, part of the inheritance, with all the forms and complexities of experience they embodied, of the workforce of the nineteenth century. In such a way was the working class 'made'; we can see, from this perspective, that a phenomenon such as Luddism can be recognized as a link between the old ways of life with their own rationale and, even if idealized, sense of the common good, and the new forces of production which were sweeping all before them. But we cannot put such resistance into a residual category of 'tradition' without coming to terms with the real conflicts of values and interests that were at stake.

Now we can certainly see some affinity here with Weber's often quoted comments on asceticism descending like a frost on the life of Merrie old England, affecting in different ways both the labouring classes and their employers. Traditional joys and worldly merriment were marginalized, if not crushed, by sobriety and utility in the economic order, with decisive consequences. As Weber put it: 'That powerful tendency toward uniformity of life which today aids the capitalistic interest in the standardisation of production, had its ideal foundations in the repudiation of all idolatry of the flesh' (Weber 1974: 169).

Thompson's point is that it was not victory without a struggle, nor was it total. But it does explain why his hostility to Methodism was so strong, given the effects imputed to it. The real nature, extent and significance of the influence of Methodism, which Weber and Thompson both highlight in the English case, remains a matter for debate. But whatever our verdict on that, the underlying point I wish to emphasize is that we cannot treat the category of tradition as irrational or non-traditional by definition. This is to recognize that value-laden activities and practices within what may be termed tradition or traditional society have their own substantive rationality. This is not to assume, of course, that all such action was logically consistent, or always demonstrably in, what is an inherently contentious concept, 'the best interests' of the relevant individuals and groups. Still, as Weber himself was to write in the footnotes accompanying *The Protestant Ethic* (surely the longest subtext in the history of sociology):

> A thing is never irrational in itself, but only from a particular rational point of view. For the unbeliever every religious way of life is irrational, for the hedonist every ascetic standard, no matter whether measured with respect to its particular basic values, that opposing asceticism is a rationalisation. If this essay makes any contribution at all, may it be to bring out the complexity of the only superficial simple concept of the rational.
>
> (Weber 1974: 194)

In commenting on this very text, Roger Brubaker, in his illuminating study of Weber, *The Limits of Rationality* (1984), points out that this pinpoints two axioms of Weber's thought. The first is the view that rationality does not inhere in things, but is ascribed to them; the second is that rationality is a relational concept – what is rational is only so from a particular point of view, never in and of itself. This is why the logic of Weber's own argument points, in my view, to the conclusion that once we unpack the concept of traditional action to show its particular meanings and import in particular cultures, it can be seen as another form of rationality rather than a contrast to it; so, for example, it is clear that some forms of sabotage, machine destruction and restrictive practices can be related to traditional forms of action. Hobsbawm and Rudé's study, *Captain Swing* (1969) draws attention to the markedly ambivalent attitudes of farmers, and even magistrates, to the destruction of threshing machines by farm labourers. In his essay on the machine breakers, Hobsbawm cites examples of machine breakers in various parts of England who were not brought to justice, even though the masters knew well enough who had broken their frames. In Rossendale, he noted, merchants and woollen manufacturers passed resolutions against power looms before their employees smashed them. He went on to argue:

> The small shopkeeper or local master did not want an economy of limitless expansion, accumulation and technical revolution, the savage pursuit of which doomed the weak to bankruptcy and wage earning status. His idea was the secular dream of all 'little men', which found periodic expression in Leveller, Jeffersonian or Jacobin radicalism and small scale society of modest property owners and comfortably-off wage earners without great distinction of wealth or power; though doubtless in its quiet way getting wealthier and more comfortable all the time. It was an unrealisable ideal, never more so than in the most rapidly evolving of societies.
>
> (Hobsbawm 1964: 13)

The rapid changes to which Hobsbawn alludes are what Weber had described as the movement of victorious capitalism – the infamous iron cage: 'since asceticism undertook to remodel the world and to work out its ideals in the world,

material goods have gained an increasing and finally a̶ [...]
the lives of men as at no previous period in history' (Web̶ [...]

This indeed is what he forcefully describes as the tremen̶ [...]
modern economic order, and his clear dislike of what modern̶ [...]
to, despite all his well known hesitations about value judgemen̶ [...]
sciences, is plainly registered at the end of *The Protestant Ethic*. Fr̶ [...]
commitment to a spirituality whose goal was profit making to God's̶ [...]
asceticism of the market place to the secular replacement of the puri̶ [...] ork
ethic by the utilitarian work ethic, where moral values are judged against their
utility in promoting economic success – Weber observes the growth of an
instrumental rationality in the service of profit. The consequences of this for
people who live in such a society seemed, for Weber, to be very bleak. The
original moral impetus has gone. The optimism of the Enlightenment, linking
reason, progress, liberty, and even happiness, was also disappearing. The cosmos
Weber delineates is the consumer society grounded in the mechanical foundations of the economic order. Bourgeois he may be, happy he is not. Bearing this
in mind, I think Mommsen is right to point out that Weber was not a champion of
the capitalist system. In fact, he suggests, almost the opposite is true:

> With eyes open, Weber analysed the working of the capitalist system as well
> as its social consequences, both in the short and the long term, and he was not
> inclined to make it appear better than it actually was. He perceived clearly that
> capitalism creates social trends which are detrimental to a humane social
> order. But he could not discover any easy way out of this.
>
> (Mommsen 1974: 70)

While he saw this development as a site for many conflicts at the level of
substantive rationality and therefore subject to varying outcomes in terms of
power relations, there was a generally pessimistic motif to his thought in this
respect. His own ultimate value position, as he sought to come to terms with the
competitive dimensions of this capitalist future, was to give priority to the nation
state in its struggle for power. This was quite evident early in his work. When he
produced a report on agricultural workers he put it precisely within the context of
the national question. Käsler, in his commentary, makes it clear that Weber
wanted the absolute exclusion of Russo-Polish workers from the east of Germany
and the development of internal colonization in that area though the state's
encouragement of peasant smallholding. Weber wrote: 'Here I am regarding "the
question of rural workers" quite exclusively from the viewpoint of *staatraison*
(reasons of state): for me it is not a question of agricultural workers, thus *not* the
question "are they having a good or a bad time, how can they be helped."' (in
Käsler 1988: 60). The reason of state Weber had in mind was the peaceful
defence of Germany's eastern border.

REAUCRACY, CAPITALISM AND SOCIALISM

But the break with traditionalism is also considered from another, albeit related, thematic perspective in Weber's work: the growth of rational-legal bureaucracies in the modern world. Whereas Marx had emphasized the separation of the worker from the ownership of the means of production, Weber extended this by noting that the soldier was separated from ownership of the means of warfare, the scholar from ownership of the means of scholarship, the scientist from ownership of research facilities. And the official, in a bureaucratic organization, is separated from the ownership of the means of administration.

In the industrial sphere, Weber saw bureaucratic organizations and machine technology as conjoining to shape factory discipline. This was true for capitalist but also for socialist societies. In his essay on socialism, commenting on the Germany of 1918, he wrote:

> What characterises our current situation is this, that private economy bound up with private bureaucratisation and hence with the separation of the worker's tools of his trade, dominates the sphere of *industrial* production which has never before in history borne these two characteristics together on such a scale; and this process coincides with the establishment of mechanical production within the factory, thus with a local accumulation of labour on the same premises, enslavement to the machine shop or pit. It is the discipline which lends to the contemporary mode of separation of worker from materials its particular stamp.
>
> (Eldridge 1971: 200–1)

But bureaucracy, whether in capitalist or socialist societies, was not going to disappear. For this reason Weber was sceptical concerning the more utopian views imputed to the consequences of socialism. Indeed, he assumed that in a socialist state the bureaucratic apparatus would assume greater significance. As against the formula of the dictatorship of the proletariat in the conventional communist view of the transition from capitalist to socialist society, Weber, more perceptively, wrote of the dictatorship of the official. That dictatorship could, of course be subject to political dictatorship, as the Stalin years in the Soviet Union were to demonstrate graphically. So, too, did the post-Stalin period, albeit more benignly. Under Tsarist rule, as Bendix, in his pioneering study *Work and Authority in Industry* (1956) pointed out, the relations between managers and workers had been subject to outside authoritative control. The Bolshevik revolution under Lenin maintained that position, but with a different authority. Industrialization, for Lenin, required the combination of capitalist techniques, including Taylorist principles of organization, with Soviet government and administration. Thus the factory boss could be an autocrat within his own enterprise and controlling his own bureaucracy, but he was subject to the party boss controlling the political bureaucracy, and ultimately to one person, the leader of the Party, who represents 'the experience of the masses'. This gives a context for Lenin's contention:

> We must learn to combine the 'meeting' democracy of the toiling masses – turbulent, surging, overflowing its banks like a spring flood – with *iron* discipline while at work, with *unquestioning obedience* to the will of a single person, the Soviet leader, while at work.
>
> (Bendix 1956: 250)

With the collapse of the Soviet Union, the record of these years became more available; the 'official', bureaucratic secrets are brought to light, revealing something of the terror, tragedy and tyranny. Alongside this dictatorship in the name of democracy, there was another contradiction. For when all has been said about bureaucracy as an efficient form of administration (and recognizing the comparative sense in which Weber wrote about this) the examples of its practice in socialist societies has come to stand for inefficiency and failure to deliver. Is this, then, as triumphalist capitalist voices would have us think, simply a matter of coming to terms with the failure of socialism?

This was the question that provoked and informed Alec Nove's study, *The Economics of Feasible Socialism* (1983). Writing of the Soviet Union, he described the shortages, the production bottlenecks, the failure to fulfil plans and the waste of resources. He then comments:

> No one who reads the Soviet press can doubt the high priority which the leadership gives to correcting these and other defects. However, since they still reject the 'market model' the reforms they are announcing cannot possibly cure the disease: the tighter central control, the imposition of centrally determined 'norms' (normed value added, normed material utilisation etc.) stricter allocation of a longer list of materials and machines, exhortation to achieve a higher quality of planning and production, more severe penalties for non-fulfilment of planned delivery contracts and so on. While no-one would deny that some aspects of the system could be made to function more efficiently, the basic problems are either untouched or actually exacerbated by 'reforms' such as these. The chronic crisis of the centralised system may be reaching its acute stage with consequences as yet unforeseeable.
>
> (Nove 1983: 113)

How right he was! Yet, it is worth remembering that, for him, the question was whether a feasible socialism could emerge that would avoid the over-concentration of power, the over-centralization of management and diseconomies of scale: 'Inflexibility, inefficiency, human alienation and the unrepresentative nature of authority are part of the same unattractive package . . . But it should be possible for socialism to present a much more humane and acceptable and human face.' (ibid.: 113).

Nove writes as an advocate of democratic socialism, accountable through and to its elected representatives and to its consumers, but also grounded in the development of a participative industrial democracy. For him, it is not a question of planning or markets but rather what kind of planning in a competitive world with scarce resources. This is an invitation to reconsider the question of political choice. Bureaucracy cannot be spirited away from complex industrial societies but we can still consider the differing politics and options that are available without being impaled on the false dilemma of market or plan.

> 'Socialism' is thought of as an alternative to a society still based largely on private ownership and private profit. Generations of reformers and revolutionaries envisaged a world in which there would be no great inequalities of income and wealth, where common ownership would prevail, where political (and economic) power would be more evenly distributed, where ordinary people would have greater control over their own lives and over the conditions of their work, in which deliberate planning for the common good of society would replace (at least in part) the elemental forms of the market place.
>
> (Nove 1983: 7–8)

In other words, for Nove the critique of Soviet-style socialism was a critique of a society in crisis, but one which is offered from a perspective that does not embrace capitalist values.

Throughout the 1980s the crisis in authority relations in the Soviet Union intensified, and the legitimacy of the state was called into question. Thus, in July 1989, strikes took place in the Siberian and Ukranian mines that were widely regarded as the most serious manifestation of labour unrest in the Soviet Union since the 1920s. Over 100,000 miners were involved. What was particularly significant was that the strikes were not only about pay and working conditions. They were also about demands for workers' control over state enterprises, industrial democracy and the insistence that more of the fruits of industry should be ploughed back into the coal-producing regions. In that respect it represented an anti-Moscow, pro-decentralization view.

More strikes were to follow. Attempts from the centre to institute political and economic reform (*glasnost* and *perestroika*) served to make the protest more visible and challenge the basic legitimacy of the Soviet Union and the efficiency of economic restructuring, with the unravelling consequences that the world was later to witness. In the 1920s, the solution to challenges from below in the name of workers' control and workplace democracy had been to institutionalize a massive bureaucratic structure and centralize control from above. In the 1980s, the Gorbachev reforms stressed the importance of modernization and increased productivity. Yet the method of achieving these ends was much contested, not least by the bureaucratic party functionaries. And the difficulties were further interlaced, not only with regional issues – how much and what kind of economic decentralization – but with longstanding, if repressed, questions of nationalism.

The dictatorship of the official is not easily overthrown. In December 1987, a young man wrote a letter to the journal *Selskaya Molodezh* (Rural Youth eds). He was a peasant who had moved from the country to the town:

> It seems to me that some do not understand the situation that has arisen in agriculture . . . Millions of people have abandoned their villages and have gone to the town, where they live in hostels . . . wallowing in sorrow and in drink. Those who remain in the villages are in a still worse state. The land is no longer theirs. They are not peasants any more, they are just *batraki* (landless labourers). Where is it known for a *batrak* to work well on someone else's land and wish to have children? What for? So they too should be *batraks*? What is the consequence of the fact that today the land is controlled not by those who work on it but by officials – bureaucrats? Our agriculture is three to five times behind America's. I consider that the granting of land (to the peasants) is the most vital and immediate task. It would be as significant as were in their time the abolition of serfdom and the agrarian revolution. One must save the peasants from final degradation and rural officialdom from nervous and mental breakdown or else they will fall victim to the most clumsy, chaotic and senseless agricultural policy.

> (Nove 1989: 206–7)

Even so, the fate of the socialist societies of the Soviet Union and Eastern Europe do present a challenge to bureaucratic theory. These countries became a by-word for the proverbial red-tape version of bureaucracy, yet in the political sphere there were repressive and coercive state organizations, not least the highly bureaucratized KGB. Yet for all the power of the bureaucratic machine, the fear it could generate and the sanctions it could deploy, despite its reservoirs of knowledge, it could not in the end prevail, once the legitimacy of the state was itself called into question. These administrative frameworks, notwithstanding the resources they placed in the hands of their political controllers, could not, in perpetuity, keep the lid on ethnic, national, regional and industrial conflicts, all of which had a political dimension to them.

But let us call to mind again what, Weber had to say about bureaucracy. It was the capitalist market economy which required official business to be conducted with precision, speed and unambiguity. Normally, the very large capitalist enterprises were unequalled models of strict bureaucratic organization. Bureaucracy, in this respect, could be viewed as a social technology that deals with problems of control, planning, monitoring and coordination. The emergence of such forms of bureaucratic organization would, Weber saw, have enormous consequences for social structure and the exercise of power:

> Once fully established bureaucracy is among the structures which are hard to destroy. Bureaucracy is *the* means of transforming social action into rationally organized action. Therefore, as an instrument of rationally organized authority relations, bureaucracy was and is a power instrument of the first order for those who control the bureaucratic apparatus. Under otherwise equal conditions,

rationally organized and directed action is superior to every kind of collective behaviour and also social action opposing it. Where administrations have been completely bureaucratized, the resulting system of domination is practically indestructible.

(Weber 1978: 987)

Viewed in this way, bureaucracy can be seen as an instrument for containing crisis and managing conflict by those who control them – the official managers of society. It is as though, just at the time when class struggle might have intensified in capitalist societies, *vis-à-vis* a Marxist analysis, or collapsed through unregulated competition, as in Durkheim's discussion of acute anomie, the bureaucratic form of administration can be used by its controllers for maintaining social and organizational stability and, by the same token, blunting the capacity for resistance, both practically and ideologically. Practically because of their control of knowledge and resources and the ability to apply sanctions embedded in legal regulations; ideologically because they embody the power to define social reality and to set agendas within which discussion takes place. In such ways are we confronted with the 'common sense' of bureaucratic logic.

At the same time, the rationality of the bureaucratic enterprise or administration does not eradicate conflict. It remains present at the level of substantive rationality, even within a bureaucracy for example, between production and marketing, personnel and line management, between different levels of hierarchy, in an industrial enterprise. This touches on the multi-faceted issue of pluralism. It is one thing to define organizations in terms of their formal characteristics, or 'missions', but another to view them as sets of relationships that may be differently articulated and experienced by their participants. Tom Burns has written:

In practice working organisations seem to be makeshift assemblies of relationships and activities which operate in accordance with several quite different sets of principles and assumptions and different rationales. They are, to use Lévi-Strauss' useful word, *bricolages*, composed out of second-hand bits and pieces of second of rather general notions and traditions of how to go about things, each having its own semblance of legitimacy.

(Burns 1981: 3)

Even so, while recognizing the element of contingency and the many and sometimes discrepant faces of organizational life, we can still observe the inequalities, ties, skill, knowledge, power and resources within them and the ways that these can crucially affect outcomes that come to be defined as decisions. There is still hierarchy, even if it is fragmented and subject to challenge. Furthermore, rationality within the enterprise, with all its micro-conflicts, is not sealed off. This was precisely understood by Weber who had, after all, studied the German Stock Exchange:

The fact that such 'outside' interests can affect the mode of control over managerial positions, even and especially when the highest degree of formal rationality is attained constitutes a further element of substantive irrationality specific to the modern economic order . . . The influence exercised by special-ist interests outside the producing organisations themselves on the market situation, especially that for capital goods, is *one* of the sources of the phen-omenon known as the 'crisis' of the modern market economy.

(Weber 1978: 140)

Comments like these remind us of the Chinese box character of rationality in Weber's work, but also of the fundamental instability of capitalist societies, such that issues of control and the continuous need for ideological labour to sustain social orders and organizations are the very hallmark of modern times. Weber, for his part, was not a supporter or advocate of an unfettered capitalist market economy; rather he looked to legal checks on unbridled competition through state intervention and recognized the role of trade unions in defending their members against pure market forces. At the same time he sensed that the planned econo-mies of socialism would lead to a formal rationalization of bureaucracy that would end in stagnation. In both cases, for different reasons, the autonomous personality and the scope for personal freedom would, in his view, be diminished.

In a way, from a socialist standpoint Nove makes substantive qualifications. Given the existence of relative scarcity, he recognizes the inevitability of social conflict. This is not just a matter of the private ownership of the means of production. Nevertheless, he believes that although the distinction between governors and governed, rulers and ruled, managers and managed, cannot be eliminated it is possible in substantive terms to devise barriers to the abuse of power and to aim for the maximum possible democratic participation in social and political life. This, for him, entails intervention by the state to prevent the market mechanism from creating intolerable social inequalities. This would include an appropriate taxation policy, intervening to restrain monopoly power, excluding sectors such as education and health from being judged and admini-stered in terms of market criteria, and setting ground-rules for the operation of the competitive market. Nove abandons any claims to a utopian socialism, but his values can certainly be linked to the socialist tradition. And he is robust enough to maintain that 'compared with the inflation, exchange rate fluctuations, zig-zags in interest rates, unemployment, of what passes today for capitalism, decision makers might well have better means for being right more often' (Nove 1983: 230).

TOWARDS A POLITICS OF HOPE

To hope for the future for societies with destructive capacities to kill one another and irreversibly pollute the planet, does not depend on a master narrative – history is on no-one's side – or a utopian fantasy. We can see readily enough the formidable accomplishment of advanced technology and bureaucratic control in the conduct of war. The Gulf war was presented to us as a high-tech triumph and, horrific though it was in its consequences, it was an example of sophisticated, coordinated organizational activity. Yet that does not, or need not, lead to the absence of critique. As long as questions of value are not inevitably reduced to questions of interest, space for critique will remain. Not only so, but we can see, on the basis of the historical record, that powerful, seemingly impenetrable bureaucracies can be challenged. They can be reshaped and redirected by social movements, even if in a world of competing substantive rationalities, which generates its own irrationalities, they are not successful in achieving all their goals. This, as I see it, underlines the work of Alain Touraine and brings us back to questions of ultimate values, which Weber himself did not shirk. Consider Touraine's discussion of the term 'crisis':

> A crisis is being declared on all sides by the defenders of capitalist economy, themselves uneasy as they see the sources of capitalist industrialisation – the propensity to sound long-term investment in productive activities and the stability of the currency – threatened by a consumer society and in a more spectacular manner by those who oppose unsatisfied real demands to over-satisfied artificially stimulated demands. The latter ask, how can one not be sensitive to a crisis in societies that respond to needs only when such responses increase profit.

(Touraine 1981: 317)

From his perspective, the term 'crisis' itself is one which is seen from the point of view of ruling forces – the official managers of society. To speak, on the other hand, of transformation would be to reckon with the birth of new social movements which can shape new forms of power and identify new possibilities in social relations and cultural practices. This could well involve what for Weber was a core value position: the ultimate value of the nation state. By the same token, it could lead to a reappropriation of the concept of crisis: 'We must speak of crisis when we see some population abandoned to hunger and death, while others speak only of relaxation, identity and pleasure' (Touraine 1981: 340).

Yet, in an odd way, this does bring, us back to *The Protestant Ethic*:

> No one knows who lives in this cage in the future, or whether at the end of this tremendous development entirely new prophets will arise, there will be a great re-birth of old ideas and ideals, or, if neither, mechanised petrification, embellished with a sort of convulsive self-importance. For of the last stage of this cultural development it might well be truly said: 'Specialists without spirit, sensualists without heart; this nullity imagines that it has attained a level of civilisation never before achieved.

(Weber 1974: 182)

We know too well the power of bureaucracies in advanced societies. We know their capacity for surveillance and control. We know that they can be put to the service of powers, which through their 'rational' practices can destroy the very planet we live on. But we also know that, for all their apparent indestructibility, bureaucracies and their controllers are not immune to resistance and to transformation, even as we acknowledge the recuperative powers they can display in the wake of the challenge of a social movement. But it is now within our imaginative scope to think about the human condition in global – and interconnected – terms, rather than the narrower Weberian terms of national self-interest. This in itself can lead us to think about new forms of authority relations, the purpose of productive activities, the role of international social organizations in regulating this one earth which, for all its abundance and recuperative powers, does not have unlimited resources. In other words, questions of values and questions of politics cannot be indefinitely repressed by even the most powerful bureaucratic machine, or the most virulent market forces. In this sense, and with hope, we can endorse Weber's view that to the cultural sciences is entrusted the gift of eternal youth.

REFERENCES

Beck, U. (1992) *Risk Society* London: Sage.
Bendix, R. (1956) *Work and Authority in Industry*. Chichester: John Wiley.
Brubaker, R. (1984) *The Limits of Rationality. An Essay on the Social and Moral Thoughts of Max Weber*. London: Allen and Unwin.
Burns, T. (1981) 'Rediscovering-organisation.' London: Social Science Research Council report, mimeo.
Eldridge, J.E.T. (ed.) (1971) *Max Weber: the Interpretation of Social Reality*. London: Michael Joseph.
Hobsbawm, E. (1964) *Labouring Men: Studies in the History of Labour*. London: Weidenfeld and Nicolson.
Hobsbawm E. and Rudé, G. (1969) *Captain Swing*. London: Lawrence and Wishart.
Käsler, D. (1988) *Max Weber. An Introduction to his Life and Work*. Cambridge: Polity Press.
Mommsen, W. (1974) *The Age of Bureaucracy*. Oxford: Blackwell.
Mommsen, W. (1989) *The Political and Social Theory of Max Weber*. Cambridge: Polity Press.
Nove, A. (1983) *The Economics of Feasible Socialism*. London: Hutchinson.
Nove, A. (1989) *Glasnost in Action. Cultural Renaissance in Russia*. London: Unwin Hyman.
Thompson, E.P. (1968) *The Making of the English Working Class*, Harmondsworth: Penguin
Thompson, E.P. (1991) *Customs in Common*, London: Merlin.
Touraine, A. (1981) 'The New Social Conflicts: Crisis or Transformation?' in C. Lemert, *French Sociology*. New York: Columbia University Press.
Weber, M. (1971) 'Socialism', in J. Eldridge, (ed.) *Max Weber: the Interpretation of Social Reality*. Nelson.
Weber, M. (1930) *The Protestant Ethic and the Spirit of Capitalism*. London: Allen and Unwin.
Weber, M. (1978) *Economy and Society*. Berkeley: University of California Press.

Chapter 4

Accounting for organizational feeling*

Martin Albrow

The 1980s saw a new and fuller appreciation of the amplitude of Max Weber's work. This volume demonstrates how it is leading to a complete revision of the dominant view that Weber's work on organizations was about their rationality and little else. Michael Reed (1985: 17–18) pointed out that this was a lazy reading, fitting Weber into a particular kind of functionalist interpretation which highlighted problems of technical control. Energetic readers can find many other possible points of entry into a new Weberian sociology of organizations. We could begin with his theory of the social relationship, as does Gangolf Peters (1988), or with values and authority, as does John Eldridge in this volume, or, also here, with culture, as Stewart Clegg suggests. My own choice in a recent paper (Albrow 1992) was to apply a view on action theory elaborated in an earlier book (Albrow 1990) where the complex interplay of motives and structures of meaning was seen as the animating impulse for Weber's interpretative sociology.

That paper argued that Weber's interest in irrationality, and in particular affectivity, had been submerged by twentieth-century rationalistic models of organization. But it conceded too that Weber had given the rationalists some good excuses for a one-sided interpretation of his work since his writing on bureaucracy was not the best example of his general approach. It reproduced, in an unacknowledged manner, the peculiarities of German bureaucracy, and played down the place of emotions, to which his interpretative method elsewhere (as in his sociology of religion) gave greater weight. The 'other Weber' was, then, set against the received version and consequently against the tradition of rationalistic technocratic theories of organization for which that received version had so long served as the classic text.

In brief, the case was made for elaborating the place of the emotions within the framework of organizational analysis, not as byproducts, interferences or even repressed potentialities and resources, but as integral and essential modalities of organizational performance. Stated at its strongest it was asserted that, just as organizations act, so they equally have feelings. This chapter is a sequel, backing the earlier claims by elaborating the consequences for organizational analysis if one takes affectivity seriously.

This cannot be a routine exercise, if only because the obstacles which rationalistic models have erected to such analysis are formidable. They extend even to the equation of analysis with rationality itself, which leads to emotions being seen as alien objects passing across the analyst's gaze. That rationalism is evident at the deepest level in the form of analysis which has most directly been concerned with emotion: psychoanalysis. By concentrating on repressed feeling and emphasizing the cognition of unconscious processes, psychoanalysis effectively devalues the emotional content of everyday experience and subordinates it to a discursive rationality shared between analyst and patient. In the context of organizations this outlook presumes a shared rationality of organization and analyst, which locates organizational failure in the individual manager's neurosis (for an example see Kets de Vries *et al.* 1985). Older approaches to organization, which do address emotional aspects of human behaviour, such as the socio-technical systems theory of the Tavistock school (e.g. Trist *et al.* 1963) or the self-actualizing theory of McGregor (1966) share this rationalistic bias of psychoanalysis in treating as both normal and ideal a state in which individual feelings are gathered up in, and absorbed by, rational organizational performance. Radical critiques of this position simply offer a transvaluation of the same ontology, individual feeling viewed as constrained and trapped, as opposed to being enabled or realized, in organizational structure, e.g. as in Morgan's (1986) image of the organization as psychic prison. The contrasting position offered here is quite different. Purpose, cognition and emotion are seen as intertwined modalities of action *both for individuals and for organizations*. The opposition 'individual feeling': 'organizational rationality' as a guiding principle for organizational analysis is replaced by 'personal action': 'organizational action'.

This approach is broadly Weberian in several respects: organizations will be treated as realities, but existing only in and through people's behaviour; they will be seen as facticities, but constructed out of motives and systems of meaning; they will be seen as systems of action, enduring and cohering only in so far as people sustain them. These conditions make organizations contingent in a double sense, namely they depend on people doing things, and also upon their ability to demonstrate that things have been done. The empirical study of organization has, therefore, a constitutive relationship to organization. The possibility of demonstrating the facts of organizations is a requirement for their functioning. Getting the facts wrong about them means they won't work as expected. If we leave out the facts of people's emotions in our accounts of organizational behaviour, the accounts will be distorted to the detriment of both organizations and people (Albrow 1980).

My account of Weber gives pride of place to the empirical thrust of his work, to the establishment of facts as constitutive of social reality, and hence to the strictly subordinate position of the ideal type. His was an anti-foundationalist faith in empirical science, which trusted intellectual constructions only as far as they helped to illuminate the facts (Albrow 1991). From that point of view the constructs of organization theory over the years have been one-sided distortions of reality, as inappropriately reified as Weber's own ideal type of bureaucracy.

The history of twentieth-century theorizing about organizations is very largely one of accounts born of interests and ideology, leaving large areas of organizational reality out of the frame (Albrow 1980). Actors' own accounts have kept closer to reality, and empirical sociology of organization has an honourable place in keeping a firm relation to those accounts. It can recognize the complex interweaving of reason and feeling that makes up the course of daily work. It registers the daily behaviour which constitutes organization, recording the feelings which are as much integral to it as timetables and work schedules.

This chapter then presupposes the validity of an empirical sociology where organizations are constituted by people and their feelings are as much elementary facts of the situation as their plans, knowledge and resources. To be sure we could draw on some old-established areas of organizational analysis where emotion has been acknowledged e.g. in accounts of morale, work satisfaction or leadership (where charisma has recently become an important focus of discussion: Pauchant 1991), but these were primarily adjuncts to rationalistic models, betraying their origins in large-scale industrial manufacturing to which human feeling is explicitly made subordinate and regarded as alien by advocates and opponents alike.

The decline of the old industrial sector does make the task of taking emotions as a serious side of organizational analysis much easier for two reasons. The first is that the ever growing weighting of the advanced economies towards the service sector has led to increasing departures from the classic hierarchical pyramidal shape of organization. Innovative potential is sought in different forms of social relations. As Burns and Stalker (1961: 234) pointed out, emphasis on organizational change may reduce subordination but at the same time it increases incorporation, placing greater demands on the whole personality, including emotions.

The other reason for the new prominence of the emotions in organizations is that the service sector intrinsically orients itself to a market of expressed non-material needs. Treating the customer as a person means focusing on interaction and may result, as Hochschild has vividly portrayed (1983: 10), in such practices as training employees to smile, paying them for emotional labour. In this respect the attempt is made to rationalize feelings much as any other kind of human capacity has been in Taylorized manufacturing. But emotions have been brought back into the frame of reference and the alienation which results from lack of authenticity means that they force themselves upon the attention of analysts in a more pressing way than was the case with Fordist manufacturing or Prussian bureaucracy. They were never absent in the factory or the government office, but they could be left unthematized. Now even the authentic display of emotion in work can be posed as an imaginable possibility.

Recovering emotion will mean a return to older verities where the language of action weaves purposes, moods, plans and sentiment into complex descriptions of situations which take account of the cirumstances of time and place. Rationalism has distorted the language of social description in general and the place of emotion in particular. Contemporary organizational structure must make it impossible any longer simply to elaborate the language of rationality while consigning emotion to an unanalysed motivational reservoir. Any account of organizational affectivity is in effect bound to adopt the full range of appraisal terms for human action which are available in the wider society and employed in everyday life. Language with a far more direct moral and political content must dispel the pretence of a uniquely privileged rational way of describing organizational action.

However, the gain in intelligibility achieved by approaching more closely to everyday language will for many analysts be more than outweighed by the loss of systematic rigour and the sense that the lines of organizational structure are blurred or even fractured. This is a necessary loss, for the relations between emotions are more empirical than they are rational, and it is in fact the case that organizational structure is becoming less categorical and more ambiguous. It is a changed social reality which gives rise to notions of postmodern organization and makes postmodernist analysis relevant (Cooper and Burrell 1988, Burrell 1988, Cooper 1989, Parker 1992) but that reality will only be grasped with a revitalized empirical sociology which seeks to describe and account for this new open texture of organization.

One obvious way to test this approach to organizational affectivity is through the case study. Examples already exist in Hochschild (1983) and Fine (1988). Another is to confront the concepts of rationalistic organizational analysis with dissonant empirical material and to rework them by dislocating them from their pre-established frame. This is the method which I choose to adopt here.

The chapter proceeds by taking four classic areas of organizational analysis – goals; work performance; communication; and authority – and reworks each by recovering the emotional aspect. The choice of those four spheres is of course dictated by the rational model. But we cannot expunge rationality from organizations; it is intrinsic to them. There is every reason for saying that it has developed as organizations have developed and will continue to do so. (For an interpretation of what it means to assert that the rationalization process has continued to develop ever since Weber's day see Albrow 1987.) The new recovery of emotionality may indeed prove only to be the next phase of the rationalization process. But it will not leave things as they were. The outcome of reworking the classic themes is the final section of the chapter, 'Emotions and Organizational Structure', which finds more extensive grounds for reasserting the conclusion of the previous paper (Albrow, 1992), namely that emotions have to be seen as a property of organizations. They are integral to them and the accomplishment of their tasks. Organizations, viewed as webs of action and interaction, are emotional entities as much as they are rational units.

ORGANIZATIONAL GOALS

Statements about organizational objectives are notoriously slippery as focal

points for organizational analysis, yet traditionally have had a privileged place
(Katz and Kahn 1966: 15; Albrow 1968). Rational models of ends/means behaviour appear to require behaviourally defined, unambiguous targets to permit
mutual orientation to a common goal by a multiplicity of actors and the possibility of subsequent performance measurement. But that in itself does not assimilate
the notion of objectives to rationality. In respect of individual behaviour
economists have long allowed for the non-rationality of goals in their use of the
Latin tag 'de gustibus non disputandum' ('there is no accounting for tastes') and
Weber too shared the presumption of classical economists and liberals that there
was no rational way of judging between individual purposes. It was linked to the
unbridgeable gulf between facts and valuations, something about which Robbins,
professor of economics at the London School of Economics said, 'I confess I am
quite unable to understand how it can be conceived to be possible to call this part
of Max Weber's methodology in question' (1935: 148). For economists it was
only in the means by which individuals pursued their goals or in the consistency
of preferences between them that degrees of rationality could be distinguished.
But Weber also addressed a new sociological theme which was to be applied to
organizational purpose: the idea that purposes could be rationalized even if their
origins were irrational.

Non-rationality in organizational objective setting has received little attention,
probably for two main reasons. The first is that the commonality of organizational
purpose, breaking as it does with the liberal individualism that underpinned so
much of classical economics, could be considered in some way to reduce the
non-rationality of individual behaviour. The second is that organizational objectives, notwithstanding that their origins may be deemed irretrievably irrational,
may, much more than individual goals, be publicly 'rationalized', that is made
rational and open to inspection through specification, formalization, operational-
ization, measurement.

Taking the commonality of purpose first, we are bound to recognize that for
many analysts it is the acceptance of the common objective which creates an
organization and on which its rationality hinges. There is a paradox here since the
purest common-goal organization, if by that is meant one where all members take
that goal equally to be their personal objective, specifies much more the religious
organization than the capitalistic enterprise which depends on more limited
inputs and allegiances. The current frequent use of the idea of a 'mission statement' with its religious overtones is indication enough that the language of
common goals is some way from economic rationality, and that something more
than self-interest is needed to motivate members.

The roots of many of the themes of modern organizational thinking are to be
found in Christianity (alienation, responsibility, vocation, hierarchy, recently
given a new boost with subsidiarity) which should be sufficient to alert us at least
to the possibility of an emotional dimension to all aspects of organization theory.
In this context we simply have to recognize that religious goals are in themselves
non-rational, and this regularly applies to common-goal organizations of all

kinds. The favourite recourse to shared goals and values as a remedy for worker alienation should be seen as a secular restatement of religious salvation needs rather than a contribution to organizational rationality. The sharing of objectives as such is dependent on so many aspects of trust, commitment and mutual understanding that a verdant field of sentiment opens up before us. As I pointed out in the previous paper (Albrow 1992: 315) the emotionality of cooperative work organization was regarded in the earlier periods as its essential feature.

If it is not commonality which rescues organizational purpose from emotions is it rationalization, the second possibility mentioned above? The radical separation of organizational purpose from individuals' objectives as effected by the public choice theorists makes a virtue of the alienation effect. It assumes that each person is indeed only interested in organizational participation for his or her own benefit. The organizational objective is then elevated into an entirely instrumental position for each member of the organization rather than a terminal value. Provided it is unambiguous, precise and measurable it appears as a rational focus. But this is a recent intellectual development which has kicked away the ladder of meaning upon which organizational purpose has climbed to this elevated position. For whence this purpose? And if no one believes in its intrinsic worth, how does it survive?

It is another version of the Hobbesian problem of order. If we turn to Hobbes we can gain an intimation of how rationality finds a foothold in the individual setting of objectives. It was in addressing the problem of how selection was made between competing desires within the individual that Hobbes arrived at a formula for distinguishing between will and desire. He concluded that the will was simply 'the last appetite in deliberation' (1651: 40). A reflective process then, deliberation, contributes to the direction of human behaviour even if its selection among the appetites remains mysterious. We can already detect in this formulation the tendency to treat thought as adding the quality of rationality to goals.

This notion was developed by Ferdinand Tönnies (who had worked on Hobbes) within his seminal account of *Gemeinschaft* and *Gesellschaft* (1887) by shifting discussion of the will from the individual to the social group. It was the degree of explicitness and calculation which distinguished the social organization of *Gesellschaft* from that of the *Gemeinschaft*. It was the will of deliberation as opposed to the basic will of the natural community. Tönnies ushered in the age when rationalization became a watchword for the modernization both of industry and personal behaviour. The rationalization of objectives in industry and organizations generally became a movement in the early part of the twentieth century at the same time as the idea of rationalization of individual behaviour became a key term within psychoanalysis. In each case reflection transforms the objective, but in the case of organizations the result was much more likely to be incorporated into manuals, rule books and codes of practice. It was an easy step for Weber to generalize the process to all aspects of social life.

Organizational objectives, then, have had a privileged place in the rationalization process and individuals orientating to an organization have had a special interest in assisting the process. Quite apart from employers and employees, third parties who treat organizations as within their own field of action benefit from organizational fixity of purpose. As I have stressed before, in Weber's view it was this formal calculability and reliability that made bureaucracy indispensable, rather than its technical efficiency, about which he was far more ambivalent (Albrow 1970: 61–6). Objectives are rationalizable, even if in their origin and in themselves they are non-rational. It is a question of increasing the sphere of rationality in the interests of reducing uncertainty, the principle which Luhmann (1985) has made constitutive of the development of law.

But just how far can this reduction of uncertainty go? Every analysis of publicly defined objectives for organizations suggests that they ultimately run into fundamental, rationally unresolvable antinomies, as Weber stressed. Even if we take the simple case of the single overriding goal of the profit-maximizing organization we have to recognize that non-rationality has an irreducible hold. Let us imagine it hiring and firing at will, manufacturing a single product with the most advanced technology but requiring only the most modest skills on the part of the operatives, where labour is plentifully available and demand for the product buoyant. In this free-enterprise utopia there is no need to inspire the workers with common purpose, or anything other than a piece rate payment. Nor would there be any need for management consultants.

So it would have to be a sociologist who would put this question. Do we have here the purest possible case of rational objectives, conceding of course that in its origin the pursuit of profit is not in itself rational? Do we have clear-cut specified objectives which do not require or allow emotion to intrude? An affirmative answer would presumably require a demonstration that there were no dilemmas arising which required non-rational solutions. That is not easy. Take profit maximizing. Is it this year or next year? What time preference is involved? If it is twenty years, what determination and endurance does this require on the part of the decision makers? If it is this year how much impatience and recklessness does this imply? Determination and impatience are already terms of behaviour appraisal, with moral overtones and suggestions of character analysis. We may more readily see impatience as emotive, tallying with the explosive image of emotion. But emotion controlled is emotion employed and determination is as much part of the vocabulary of Western emotionality as is excitement.

Any account of the rise of self-discipline necessarily involves reference to the control of anger and fear, or any other emotion which calls for satisfaction. That is the basis of the psychoanalytic tradition, Freud's account of civilization and its discontents, but also equally of Weber's Protestant Ethic thesis and Elias' civilizing process. Each relies on the conversion of a disruptive primal energy into a controlled supply of motivation to behave in a socially acceptable manner. But Weber was also profoundly aware of the psychic economy of discipline: 'Enthusiasm and unreserved devotion may, of course, have a place in discipline; every modern conduct of war weighs, frequently above everything else, precisely the morale factor in troop effectiveness' (Weber 1968, 2: 1150).

In point of fact it is only by allowing the objectives of an organization to be entirely conventionally defined in terms of standard expectations of profits that the emotional qualities of decision making cease to be vital determining elements. It is not only time preference which has to be resolved arbitrarily. Equally there are questions of expansion and contraction, alternative routes to profit maximization where preferences cannot be resolved without resort to other criteria located ultimately within emotional structures (personalities, boardroom meetings, situational practices and pressures).

Under these circumstances it can scarcely be surprising that the personal qualities of the entrepreneur often become central features in estimates of the direction and future prospects of any organization which remotely approaches our ideal type. The counterpart of the mission statement is the vision, the imagined future state beckoning our hero towards higher things, sometimes even the dream, out of which arises the conviction pursued with iron resolution. Endowed with such characteristics it is small wonder that the entrepreneur will not rest with a strictly impersonal relationship with the wage labourers. Converts, followers, disciples provide more reassurance and replenish the store of confidence more effectively than the payment of wages to casual workers.

All of this disregards the changing environment, suppliers, competitors and customers, with whom relations will vary, in accord with markets but also with the climate of the times. Here the language of appraisal can convey excitement, energy, threat and attack. Hostile bids, dawn raids, frenzied dealing are the clichés of market relations which ruin lives and leave personal visions in fragments.

In such a context the emotions of self and competitors become signs and clues to each of the others' state of mind, of confidence in the future, willingness to take risks, ability to enter into commitments. Objectives themselves become subordinated to a frame of relationships and a status order which generate the guiding principles of entrepreneurial behaviour. The enterprise culture conquers the culture of the enterprise.

Where the sole entrepreneur is replaced by the board of directors and professional management, the objectives of the organization are both detached from personal control and at the same time the necessary focus for interpersonal rivalry, contradictory interpretation, ritual incantation. As a result the personal qualities of the business leaders are called to account in target setting at least as much as they are with the sole entrepreneur. The vision has to be negotiated and communicated as well as generated, while traces of past visions interfere with clarity of purpose.

Objectives, then, far from being fixed points for enduring reference, are constantly revised and renewed in the hands of professional leaders. The task may well be conceived as one of corporate transformation. The 'can-do' team player provides strategic planning and direction in a new model mix for an emerging global market. Purposiveness, rather than a specific purpose, is the animating spirit of the modern organization, and leaders are not the ones who adhere to a pre-given charter but rather those who take over the task of purpose setting. The organization becomes autopoietic, or self-maintaining, an open-ended resource for the discovery of new objectives rather than a means to achieving old ones. Where purposiveness itself is the product, it is scarcely surprising that those who can claim to create it acquire rewards beyond the dreams of older entrepreneurs.

The appraisal language for the new leadership emphasizes imagination and inspiration, endurance and flexibility, sensitivity and self-motivation, above all vision and creativity. All of these qualities may be seen as necessary accompaniments to the search for the means of organizational survival in a turbulent environment. As such, they are intimately bound up with a more profound organizational rationality. But that is not to deny their emotionality. The relations of rationality and emotionality in the organizational setting parallel their relations in individuals. The modern business leader is required to have the attributes of scientist, artist and politician. We should recall here that Weber's portraits (1947) of the vocations of scientist and politician highlighted emotional requirements. In each case creativity arises from both cognitive abilities and emotional resources. The excitement of discovery is common to each, simultaneously reward for past effort and spur to new achievement.

We have come full circle to the opening theme of this section. For the emotional climate in which these qualities of leadership for the renewal of purpose are going to be promoted is not one of sovereign individuals, or lone entrepreneurs. We will see when we address authority that the cooperative group is again valued as the setting in which the sparks of imagination can fly. The main difference from the early nineteenth century is that the extra impetus gained from the group is no longer feared for its subversiveness.

TASK PERFORMANCE

Goal setting is itself a variety of work and the descriptions employed above for goal-setting behaviour are simply special cases of work performance vocabulary. No description of work in real time which avoids reference to the state of feelings of the worker can provide an account which will satisfy a third party. Manual labour may be performed alertly, enthusiastically, vigorously, resentfully, steadily, carelessly, heedlessly, effortlessly, painfully, lackadaisically. Mental labour may be performed imaginatively, with concentration, with dour determination, haphazardly, painstakingly, with excitement, passionately.

Actually the lists are interchangeable although the incidence of some descriptions will be greater for the one sphere than the other. But manual labour can be imaginative, as anyone who has seen a good gardener at work will know, and no academic needs reminding that mental labour can be painful.

The demands on descriptive action vocabulary are enormously enhanced as soon as the social dimension of work is taken into the account. The scientist at work with others can be generous, defensive, disturbing, stimulating, self-satisfied;

the bricklayer perfectionist, demanding, arrogant, imperious. Here we are drawn easily into the spheres of authority and communication, about which more later. For the moment let us stay with the object environment, remembering always that those objects may sometimes be human beings whether on the operating table, on a passenger flight or on a payroll, all impersonal elements in someone's work schedule, all personally affected by the performance of that work without ever encountering the worker.

The atmosphere of the working situation of those who work collectively on impersonal tasks can easily affect the product or output. The alienation and resentment of the British car-worker in the 1960s was hardly unconnected with the reputation of British cars for poor workmanship. In the provision of services where there is a division of labour between production and delivery, there has to be particular stress upon the responses of those who move between the emotional setting of producers and those who deliver services. The air stewardess, to whose work Hochschild (1983) has given such close consideration, has to cope with the fallout of the air crew's feelings, protect the customer from them, and absorb the emotional demands of the passengers.

In the restaurant trade, the atmosphere in the kitchen can easily be conveyed to the customer in two ways: directly in the quality of the food, and indirectly through the serving staff who have to move between the two settings, in much the same way as the air stewardess. Gary Fine has provided an account based on ethnographic study of the work environment of a kitchen in which he argues that expressive behaviour is integral to the work situation. It is not merely, in his terms, 'letting off steam (in a psychological, hydraulic model)'. He says it contributes to the actual work, so that the boundaries of work and play are erased. He quotes a comment from one cook, 'I just love the activity . . . I concentrate totally, so I don't know how I feel . . . it's like another sense takes over' (Fine 1988: 125).

Such an account is wholly within the frame of analysis which this chapter is proposing. It is illuminating at many levels, structurally and ecologically. The kitchen as an emotional work cauldron, potentially requiring total absorption, has to be physically separated from the area in which food is consumed if the work is to be done to standard. At the same time the serving staff will be subjected to a dual pressure from cooks and customers. Conversely where the work of food preparation is conducted in the presence of its consumption, in a British home, or a fast food restaurant, conflict between the contradictory moods associated with each is an ever-present danger. The temperamental cook is a popular stereotype. But it is the work and its milieu which carries the emotional charge.

Work definitions which seek to minimize the emotional aspects of performance are either inadequate and misleading, or more usually in effect making tacit acknowledgement of their existence. The military and bureaucratic sectors have the reputation of requiring soulless automata. Each in its way is seeking to construct a factitious objectivity to force and administer, something which will convert the labile into the fixed immovable object. In each case the effort required to turn people into robots involves a harnessing of energy and determination, sometimes of deliberately frightening intensity. The parade ground sergeant bellows terror into the new recruit. Fear can prompt freezing to the spot as much as it can flight. Rigid, inflexible, cold behaviour is just as emotional as warm and loving responses. But for some sectors it is easier to call upon the rejection of emotions in the name of rationality than to acknowledge that the real requirement is the training of anger, disdain and contempt. The requirement as an aspect of role performance that a person should be prepared to use violence or even kill under some circumstances means inculcating a general preparedness for violence. There should therefore be nothing surprising about the regularity with which cases of police violence are reported and even less confidence that there is any simple remedy.

Without doubt the emotional requirements of work performance are now more widely acknowledged than ever in organizations, possibly because the military model has less and less influence on civilian life. The decline in what Andrzejewski called the military participation ratio (MPR) of the citizenry in the modern nation state (Andrzejewski 1954) means a decline in the general acceptability of military values of discipline. We can see this in contemporary job advertisements. No longer are descriptions confined to traditional leadership qualities as implied by military models. They extend into discretion, self-confidence, risk-taking, imagination, determination and a whole range of qualities which are required for working with other people, such as tact, empathy, assertiveness, cooperativeness. These involve a recognition that working in co-operation with other people draws upon and requires a set of responses which go far beyond cognitive aspects of job performance. (Paradoxically, advertisements for military careers now ape the civilian sector.)

Of course the decline in the MPR is matched by a rise in organizations linked with the defence industry, and in consequence a growth in secrecy and the acceptability of dissimulation, covertness and evasiveness. But it is a shift which allows for emotions to be invoked, even if their authenticity is in doubt. In fact, as we shall see, emotional ambiguity and the dissimulation of feeling are central issues of controversy in the discussion of organizational feeling.

COMMUNICATION

It was in the direct interpersonal communication of feeling that the nineteenth-century writers identified the special features of organized cooperation. The contagion of spirit enhanced the effectiveness of work and raised people to tasks which separately they could not manage. Twentieth-century management practices in effect did their best to bring such contagion under control and to limit communication to necessary instructions or data transfer. Production processes at the level of the small group were subordinated to the logic of large organizations and became defined very much as the informal sector, the human undergrowth patterned rules and procedures.

This concentration on the internal mechanisms of work group formation and process deflected attention from communication across groups, which is far more central to the working of the organization in which the work groups are located. This was seen as formal structure, inhabiting a rational sphere, and removed from sociological attention. But this meant that large sectors of organizational behaviour went unreported. Where lateral, or horizontal, relations were considered, it was often converted into issues of administrators versus professionals, and again seen as a matter of competing forms of knowledge rather than a matter of emotional expression.

The encounters, conversations and meetings of personnel in which business is transacted across departmental divisions constitute a large part of the work of organizations. These are complex occasions, involving much more than data exchange. Helen Schwartzman's recent study of meetings emphasizes how much they are a way of life in which one of the most salient aspects is the way they serve as an arena for the expression of emotion (1989: 134). The demeanour, expression and mood of each party are scrutinized for signs of the real factors which determine the working of other parts of the organization. Even the written memo has a vast range of stylistic cues which serve to convey feelings, and for this reason it often requires meticulous care both in preparation and in interpretation. Hostility, insecurity, approbation, dismay, agitation, esteem can all be conveyed in subtle variations of greeting, vocabulary and style. The memo is in McLuhan's terms a form of 'cool' communication because it invites so many interpretative activities on the part of the recipient (McLuhan 1964: 22–32).

The phenomenology of emotion in organizational communication has scarcely begun to be examined systematically. We have to rely on memoirs and biographies to get the full flavour. For good examples we can turn to Richard Crossman's *Diaries* and his reports of Cabinet meetings during Harold Wilson's first premiership (Crossman 1976): on 2 March 1967 Wilson accused his ministers of being out of touch with back-benchers. 'It was a long gloomy speech.' Callaghan 'weighed in'. Barbara Castle was 'staunch'. 'All the speeches were full of discontent' (ibid.: 259–60); on 4 May 1967 Wilson 'rebuked' the Home Affairs Committee. Crossman 'got more and more irritated'. Wilson's proposals were 'torn to shreds'. There was no one 'who had much sympathy with Barbara'. The 'Cabinet was absolutely solid against her' (ibid.: 342–3).

On 29 May 1967 Crossman wrote: 'Finally I must add that reading Cabinet minutes and comparing them with the accounts Roy and Barbara have given me of the meetings has made me realise once again how misleading the official record can be.' He reports how there had been a full discussion with weighty contributions from major Cabinet figures on aid for Israel. 'The discussion was passionate and extremely stirring yet when it had been boiled down and dehydrated by the Cabinet Secretariat very little of it remained' (ibid.: 356).

The disjunction which Crossman notes between the record and the events parallels the official–unofficial, rational–irrational, formal–informal dichotomies. Indeed what he describes is an episode in the regular construction of events, day

in, day out in any organization. It is a facet of the general process of organizational construction which is a key aspect of bureaucratic work and has been the
focus for a tradition of ethnomethodological research on organizations ever since
Bittner's seminal paper (1965). But it is the process of construction, rather than
the content, which preoccupies these studies. As one commentator writes, ethnomethodology 'yields subjectivist, idiographic descriptions of everyday situations'
(Hassard 1990): we can add that the accomplishment of those descriptions is well
described, but their content is regarded as subjective, and the forces which dictate
it are left in obscurity.

We can indeed acquire a lot of information about the use of written codes
describing what can be communicated in writing. We can at other times record
the shared understandings that are normally observed. One civil servant has told
me how an experienced official gave him advice when he first had to take Cabinet
committee minutes. It was 'Rewrite everything, omitting the adverbs; and then
rewrite everything again, omitting the adjectives.' Within the British civil service
'Cabinet Committee style' is as impersonal as a record can be, omitting reference
to speakers and views, concentrating on capturing decisions only. It is bound not
to satisfy Crossman's desire to record what actually happened. Other media will
be more inclusive in their scope, depending on the participants and purpose of the
work. But we are still some way from explaining why these forms of communication are shaped in the way they are to exclude some kinds of content.

Thus in one government department the normal written output is a typed Note
from one official to another, filed in the writer's files, on which however a
Comment may be handwritten by the recipient, and then passed on. The Comment
can express anything from pleasure to outrage. Written messages can be sent on
scraps of paper, sometimes stuck to a Note, and they too can convey emotion
information. The implicit rules on emotion reporting vary according to their
relation to organizational structure. The Note within a Department will be cool in
so far as its subject matter is confined to internal departmental matters, but strong
feelings may be expressed in the Note on external relations, with other organizations or other departments. Letters are only ever written to other organizations
or outside individuals, with one exception: the handwritten letter of thanks from
a minister to a top official, which is then circulated and is held to boost morale.
The cool nature of the Note will not be appreciated in relations between officials
adjacent to each other in the hierarchy, where a conversation might have sufficed.
The same elaborate conventions on emotional expression exist in relation to
meetings, with subtle gradations relative to rank and rank relations, numbers of
people involved, intra-or cross-departmental basis. Add to that discussion papers,
telephone conversations, and now computer communication, all of which are
governed by their own rules (information based on personal interview).

What is fully evident is that emotional expression is ubiquitous in organizational communication and its processing is a standard part of organizational
work. This is to reject one way of interpreting Crossman's account which would
be to argue, in ostensible debt to Max Weber, that the officials take the passion

out of the political process. But this is where we have to take a wider view of organizational structure. In Cabinet, ministers are part of the government machine. Their passions are replicated in any boardroom or managing committee. Nor do the officials inhabit a passionless sphere. They too can 'let off steam', urge their point of view passionately, in the right setting and through the appropriate medium. Only the official record becomes an anodyne, passion-free statement. Only if we confuse that with the reality of organizational process do we imagine that organizations are emotionless. The problem then arises: why are official records written in this way?

There is no easy answer to this question, to my mind, precisely because of the taken for granted nature of the practice. It is not something which the newcomer to an organization is supposed to question, and if they were to do so the answer would probably be something like: 'because you can't let feelings into it' or, 'because we just stick to the facts'. But these answers are themselves highly problematical and call for much more systematic inquiry. Emotions are in practice an acknowledged and essential part of organizational work. On the account here one area for research would be into the relationship between organizational structure and emotional disclosure. The 'official record' is an account which potentially can become public; emotional disclosure reveals information on the strength and weakness of the reporting unit, information which in a threatening environment may be used by others against you.

Another line of inquiry might be to look again at the notion of organizational objectives and outputs and see official records as part of that output, in so far as decisions are made and communicated through them, while emotions are part of the input, no more reportable than the skills or any other qualities of the members which contribute to their performance but are not being offered on for further consumption. Here again the question of unit interfaces arises, suggesting that it is in relations and not in bodies that we have to see the problematic of organizational emotion.

AUTHORITY

Affectivity has long found at least a foothold in organizational analysis by virtue of Weber's incorporation of charisma within his three types of authority. Moreover the relational perspective has had every chance to be explored, because Weber was emphatic that it was an imputed quality of the person (or office) rather than an objectively possessed characteristic which was the basis of the obedience a follower accorded to the instructions of the charismatic leader. The impressionability of the disciples rather than the capacity of the leader was the first requirement.

This analysis in part arose out of Weber's well known determination to avoid taking sides and his concern to keep to the recorded facts. He could report devotion, but the sociologist in a disenchanted world was unable to accept miracles. Moreover, again from Weber's well known disdain for popular democracy, masses could be credulous and leaders scoundrels. But this allowed in an element which fitted more within managerial ideology. There were ways in which leaders could awaken the devotion of followers, manipulation was possible, training in leadership was on the agenda. And it was clear that not just anyone would gain the charismatic accolade. Personalities could attract. The combination of tricks of the trade and personality characteristics has long made the selection and training of organizational leaders a suitable subject for psychological and psychoanalytical treatment. In each case emotions and their control have clearly been considered in depth. It was no accident that in the 1980s the explosion of interest in organizational culture should bring with it the widespread popular use of the term 'charisma'.

A double ellipsis is involved here. The managerial interpretation plays down the relational aspect of charisma and draws attention away from the members of the organization to the leader. But that in itself is possibly less important than the drastic curtailment of affectivity involved in Weber's own concept and typology of authority. For him authority (*legitime Herrschaft*), in full purity, rests on unquestioning obedience (Weber 1968, 1: 215). If on receipt of an instruction the official questions its basis, the authority is contaminated. Should the instruction be obeyed only because of fear of the consequences if it is not, then authority is secondary to power as the guarantor of obedience. In all cases of authority, whether rational, traditional or charismatic, it is the rightness, the unquestioning belief in the legitimacy of the instruction, which is the hallmark of the genuine article.

The result of this conceptual strategy is to displace organizational analysis onto questions of participants' beliefs, and since these are only one facet of motivational involvement, there is a severe restriction on the range of problems which can be pursued. It is this which explains Weber's own neglect of his category of affectual action in his account of bureaucracy. Feelings are suppressed (both empirically and for the purposes of analysis) by belief, and this applies even at the level of charisma: it is belief in the powers of the leader, not an emotional response to them, which is crucial (for a fuller elaboration of this point see Albrow 1972).

There is then no room for lengthy discussions of the legal basis of a decision, for consultation and conferences (elements of the collegialism which Weber considered doomed in the modern world), for securing the respect of one's staff through care and concern for them and routine competence at one's job. It is difficult to imagine Weber's bureaucrat requesting an opinion from a subordinate. As Carl Friedrich pointed out, his 'words vibrate with something of the Prussian enthusiasm for the military type of organization' (1952: 31). For there is no doubt that Weber's concepts were forged in a real setting and were indeed a rationalization of the practice of the time.

With authority, and more generally with the analysis of rules, sociology has long advanced beyond the Weberian position, and there is no need at this point to rehearse the pathbreaking work of Merton's students, Peter Blau (1955) and

Alvin Gouldner (1955) whose research can truly be said to be the foundation of the modern sociology of organization. If we add the further development of the ethnomethodological treatment of rules (and regard Weber's treatment of authority as a special instance of the rule 'always do what I am told by X') we can say that there is no justification whatsoever for regarding the reality of organizational behaviour as grounded in official definitions, legal or otherwise, however important these may be in some contexts. Again we have to say that Weber's treatment of bureaucracy, or indeed his sociology of law more generally, is not of a piece with the rest of his sociology (Albrow 1975a). But the argument I am setting out here is quite in accord with his critique of Stammler, whom Weber rejected precisely for giving law a foundational position (Albrow 1975b and 1976). Yet when it comes to legal-rational authority Weber removes all capacity for judgement from his bureaucratic dope.

Let us cut short the history of the interpretation of authority and suggest a new definition which may be more in tune with the spirit of the times in which the writer lives (Western democratic late twentieth century):

> We can call authority the regard an actor accords to a person or position when the decisions and associated actions issuing from that source are accepted by the actor as a regular and legitimate element in the actor's definition of the situation. The more actors accord this regard to a person or position the greater is the authority.

This avoids mention of orders or instructions. Although they may be involved they are not intrinsic to the idea of authority in our times which owes much more to the notion of professional judgement serving as the basis of a client's decisions than to the notion of military command. In fact Parsons (1947: 59) pointed to professional authority as a possible fourth type, an idea developed by Gouldner into his concept of representative bureaucracy (1955: 24, 187ff., 196ff.), and this definition adequately covers their objections to Weber's concept. Nor is there any suggestion that authority relations flow in one direction. Again paradoxically in Weber's account, while the subordinate was the source of authority, it depended on the duty to obey instructions coming from above. My definition allows for the regular situation of the subordinate's decisions prompting the superior to act, whilst the subordinate's authority and sphere of competence is recognized by the superior.

Undoubtedly the ramifications of this kind of definition are far more extensive than could be explored fully in this context. It opens up the question of how superiority and subordination are defined, and leaves unresolved just how far imperatives of one kind or another are involved in authority. But these are precisely the questions which have been opened up in the modern organization and which any contemporary conceptualization has to face.

Specifically, in this context such a definition of authority provides for the subsequent incorporation of the emotional subtleties of authority relations into the concept. Authority is constantly negotiated in situations where the emotional exchanges of the parties are a key element in the winning of that kind of regard which can prompt reciprocal responses. For instance authority can be won where competence is demonstrated, enthusiasm communicated, pleasure in the work displayed, there is readiness to accept criticism, confidence in outcomes is expressed, cooperation welcomed. Authority can be lost by an overbearing manner, displays of anger, unpredictable moods, disregard for others' feelings. But of course the more people who accord authority to someone the less likely it is that any particular defect or mistake on any one occasion is going to cause a serious diminution of authority, unless of course it should happen to be highly publicized and breach the codes for appropriate expression we discussed under the heading of communication.

A good instance of such code breaching has been provided by the former chief executive of the largest British jewellery firm, Ratners. Gerald Ratner made a much publicized announcement in a speech to the Institute of Directors in April 1991 that he was selling 'crap'. He intended it as a joke. Indeed he had used it as such in numerous private gatherings previously. According to press commentators' accounts, it was responsible for collapsing profits, nose-diving share prices and ultimately for Ratner's loss of his job in November 1992 (*Guardian*, Frank Kane report 26 November 1992; *Sunday Times*, Jeff Randall report 29 November 1992). Here again the situational appropriateness of a particular expression, not its intrinsic qualities, is the key determinant of its effects. In the privacy of the boardroom, Ratner presumably got his laughter and admiration for outrageousness. In the context of a prestigious public gathering the result was a loss of authority.

Situational logics provide the frame for emotional expression in organizations. They determine when and where it is appropriate for what kind of emotion to be expressed. This has long been recognized in accounts of ritual forms of tension release, the office party, or the works outing. But much of the impulse for this kind of account comes from an implicit psychoanalytical framework predicated on the repression of emotion in normal work routines. An approach drawing more on constructionist, interactionist and phenomenological sources can allow for the regular, even necessary expression of emotion in appropriate work situations.

In cases of pressure on a workforce to meet a deadline or production target it may be entirely appropriate for a manager to alternate between expressions of encouragement and exasperation. Where customers arrive in the showroom it would be perverse for the salesman to act with disdain and lack of interest. When a safety rule has been wilfully broken the culprit will expect an angry response, and not just from superiors, but from any colleague who could be threatened. The situated character of emotional display is a prerequisite for organizational functioning.

So necessary and expected is it that the question of the ownership of the emotions arises. Organizations depend on people behaving in ways which make sense in the frame of organizational meaning. They have to fit their actions to organizational structure, make sure that their own motives and interests are at least not contradictory to organizational requirements, at best make the organization's objectives their own. Nothing is done in organizations except by people, but a fair part of their actions belong to the organization. We do not find it incongruous if the manager says his target is to achieve an output of 3300 production units a month. That output is the collective product of the organization, his goal the organization's goal. Are his feelings of excitement when the target is beaten his alone, or his dismay when they fall short purely private and personal? If feelings are appropriate and required by the organization, just like goals and activities, can they not equally belong to the organization?

The bodily experience of the emotion does not belong purely personally to the individual any more than the visual inspection of a file in an office or the manual tightening of a nut in a workshop are outside the organization because they involve individual sense data. Moreover the visible display of emotional behaviour is so readily replicated for effect under the right circumstances that the question of whether the person 'really' feels that way often arises only as an academic question. Is the anger of the parade ground sergeant pulling up the slack raw recruit authentic or put on for effect? Does it matter? Could either of them tell the difference between the real and the simulated? Can we not have authentic performance? The dramaturgical perspective on human behaviour is often thought of as drawing an analogy between drama and life. The fact is that organizations require the acting out of roles not as a metaphor for real life but in order to instantiate the reality of organization. Employees are playing for real.

This approach which has much in common with the constructionism of Harré (1986) seeks to avoid the Goffman/Hochschild dilemma, where the former's stress on staged performance (1956) leaves the actor's core feelings vacant while the latter's stress on the falsity of emotional labour posits an alienated core. Nor does it assume or look to a normative harmony of organizational and personal feeling after the fashion of McGregor's Theory Y (1966). Rather it treats the expression of emotion in organizational situations as an authentic aspect of people's behaviour in organizations, part of the on-going process of constructing the organization. In principle it is neither more nor less alienated than what goes on in families or between friends.

EMOTIONS AND ORGANIZATIONAL STRUCTURE

The situated quality of emotions, the dramaturgical abilities of actors, and the differentiated structure of organizations constitute a theoretical frame for understanding a phenomenon which otherwise eludes organizational analysis, namely the often noticed fact of 'atmosphere', a feeling which appears to belong to the setting rather than the people, since each individual may be glad to get out of it, or alternatively – since 'atmospheres' may also be good – may be inspired on entering it.

An example of atmosphere may be taken from an insiders' account in the

British Treasury staff magazine *Chequerboard* which asked a former member of staff to describe how the 'feel' of his new Department of National Heritage (DNH) differed from that of the Treasury. In a brief space the author, Nicholas Holgate (1992) ranges confidently over many of the main aspects of the problematic of organizations. As a non-technical account it carries an authenticity which rationalistic models of organization fail to capture. It covers the variable of extra departmental contacts, greater with the public for the DNH, greater with other departments for the Treasury, differential satisfaction from 'owning' results, and the chance of a new Department developing a different culture. The author talks of the atmosphere of Treasury as 'a particularly studious school' and of the new Department having an 'uneven feel' with 'several mini-atmospheres that mix at the edges', which however provides 'a tremendous opportunity of establishing practices which suit the 1990s, not just adapting a common inheritance of procedure accrued over decades' (ibid.: 9).

This illustrates that total 'feel' for an organization which still eludes psychological research into 'climate' and which undoubtedly has fuelled the 1980s enthusiasm for the idea of corporate culture. In fact this insider's account with its emphasis on tradition coupled with the known relative stability of staffing in a British government department lends itself to a structural-cultural interpretation of organizational emotion. Anticipatory socialization linked with known personnel selection methods and then in-service training complete the ingredients for a theory of organizations which evokes the structure, culture and personality dimensions of an older mainstream functionalist sociological theory.

As Robert Merton pointed out to me in 1992, he was lecturing on emotions in organizations in Harvard in the 1930s. His concern there, as in his critique of Weber's bureaucrat (Merton 1940), was to ensure that the emotions were integrated into sociological descriptions of institutions. The thrust of this chapter and its predecessor (Albrow 1992) is to develop action and interpretative approaches in a broadly Weberian spirit, but equally to insist that this entails the full acknowledgement of the vital presence of emotions in organizations.

The theoretical frame is different from Merton's but just as Weber acknowledged the indispensable preliminary problem setting provided by functionalist questions ('It is necessary to know what a 'king', an 'official', an 'entrepreneur', a 'procurer' or a 'magician' does ... before it is possible to undertake the analysis itself', Weber 1968, 1: 18) so it is right to recognize a similar priority in relation to organizations. As the quotation from Weber makes clear, the major contribution the functionalist perspective made was to raise questions which demanded and got empirical investigation. The thrust of this chapter is to suggest that there is a further range of empirical issues raised by the interpretative approach.

By situating emotions in organizational contexts and seeing emotional responses as part of the repertoire of the organizational actor rather than as personality characteristics, provision is made both for disjunctions as well as for matches between organizational requirements and individual needs. Equally there is provision for variations over time and space in the incidence of emotionality within the organization. External contingencies and internal differentiation of task units will create very different emotional settings.

This theoretical locus for emotions provides the scope necessary for explaining otherwise neglected phenomena, like interdepartmental variations in atmosphere. Within British government departments, as opposed to between them, movement of personnel is rapid, and the staff of a division of a dozen people may have changed completely over a four year period. But the identity of the division may be associated with a 'feel' or an 'atmosphere' irrespective of the personnel occupying it.

It is not a question here of a personality type but of moods, and expressions appropriate to the situation. As so often is the case, the intuitive, everyday manner of speaking, that these departments have 'a feel to them', has a better hold on the reality of the situation than a rationalistic model which excludes emotions from organizational structure. The contention of this chapter and the previous paper is that 'organizations have feelings' is not a rhetorical flourish. It is a formulation required by the texture of work in contemporary organizations. Its necessity has been demonstrated by working through the emotional reality of four classic dimensions of organizational structure. In other words the case for a particular theoretical contention has been advanced through the accumulation of empirical illustration to show the inadequacy of rationalistic analysis.

This intellectual strategy is only one of many possible routes to re-establishing emotion in organization theory. But no single route alone will provide the necessary redirection, as evidence from earlier attempts shows. Merton's insights in his 'Bureaucratic Structure and Personality' (1940) were only in part exploited in the work of his pupils, Gouldner and Blau, probably because feelings were themselves tied too closely to the concept of personality. So Gouldner noted differences between miners' and surfacemen's personalities, expressed in dress or readiness to open aggression (1955: 136), but the theme was largely stillborn in the sociological literature on organizations as cognitive decision-making models came to exclude empirically based work.

The same continual pressure towards cognitive definitions of organizational problems probably accounts for another largely unfulfilled approach to emotion in the long-established tradition of writing on organizational climate. Although the concept arose out of the insight that there were relatively enduring qualities of the organizational environment and in early work attempts were made to specify dimensions of feeling in that climate (e.g Fiedler 1962, Tagiuri and Litwin 1968), over time the literature became heavily weighted towards studies of the methodological problems of measuring perception of that climate, and thence to seeing those perceptions as individual characteristics. A recent discussion (Patterson et al. 1992) concludes that it is necessary to specify clearly the unit of analysis on which individuals are asked to focus – job, team, organization etc. We can go further: it is necessary for the analyst to focus on the unit before interrogating individuals and to identify situated feelings before asking people about them. Nothing is more likely to convert emotional states into cognitive

maps than asking actors to complete formal grids. Good sociological observational studies are indispensable as ways of registering the emotional climate of
organization, matched only by participants' memoirs written in the heat of the
moment. Katz and Kahn (1966: 66) long ago pointed out that the organizational
climate and culture concepts could only be developed effectively on the basis of
participant observation, followed by depth interviewing, but their plea went
largely unheeded. In conclusion some work which fulfils this demand deserves to
be highlighted.

Hochschild (1983) has made the most important contribution to redressing this
cognitive bias by basing her account of emotion on observational study and by
seeking to develop a model drawing elements from Darwin, James, Freud,
Dewey, Gerth and Mills, and Goffman. Her own research led her to emphasize
the efforts individuals expend in the management of their emotions in the course
of paid employment and the controls which organizations exert on this process.
But her choice of organizational setting, the air flight attendant's work, results in
an emphasis on inauthenticity. She provides Goffman's otherwise hollow-souled
actor with personal feelings which are managed for money. Where emotional
display is less to the forefront as the actual product of work, we are less able to
set up a conflict between organizational requirements and individual feeling. The
excitement in a foreign exchange dealing room is no less authentic for being
situationally induced.

Hearn and Parkin's work on organization sexuality (1987) has, at first sight,
much in common with Hochschild's but, by emphasizing the ubiquity of feeling
in organizations, has more in common with the perspective of this chapter and
seeks to take issue with what they call the firm tradition of organization theory
and management as sexless disciplines. Flam (1990) takes as her starting point
the deconstruction of the rational model of the actor and carries her argument
through to constructing a model of the corporate body both as emotion-motivated
and emotion manager.

Where these contributions and the interpretative perspective of this chapter
agree is on a rejection of a rationalism which requires the recasting of the
vocabulary of organizational performance into a mechanistic systems vocabulary, or where it is assumed that the only valid description of organizational
action is in terms of an imputed systems teleology. The language of organizational practice is a multi-layered one, and its purposiveness does not emanate
from a single privileged source. 'Knocking ideas around', 'shaping up a job',
'defending your patch', 'giving someone a dressing down' refer to practices
which exist as the negotiated, ever reconstructed, everyday reality of organizational life. All such practices consist of a varying mix of the ingredients of
rationality, emotion and tradition. In sum they constitute a complex culture.
Analytical approaches which seek to suppress the contribution that any one of
these makes to that complexity distort reality and mislead their customers. For
too long the recognition of organizational emotions has suffered from the re-

pression exerted by rationalistic models of organization, even after those models have lost the esteem they once had.

The Weber to whom we return for a reanimated organizational analysis is not the exponent of ideal types and rationalistic methodology. He is the historian and empirical social researcher, the sociologist of religion and interpreter of world-views. In this guise his work examined the facticity of rationality, its origins and influence. Elsewhere I have described his approach as anti-foundationalist, determined to take a hold on a commonsensical social reality (Albrow 1991) and I have argued that his concern for social facts was quite the equal of Durkheim's (Albrow 1990: 277–9). The consequence for the study of organizations is a firm insistence on their empirical embeddedness in society, on their being sociologically determined.

If this is a different Weber from the one who customarily appears in association with bureaucracy, the explanation has to be that his work was many-sided, and that different orientations often co-exist uneasily within it. The case for giving one of them primacy is never easy to make, but my justification for giving pride of place to the empirical thrust is that Weber himself also wrote of bureaucracy in a vein closer to his more general historical and interpretative approach. His extended note on charisma, party and bureaucrats (Weber 1968, 2: 1130–32) and on the defects of bureaucratic power in Germany (ibid.: 1393–442) are decisive corrections to the view that he was in thrall to his rational ideal type. The contention here is that the context into which we have to set his work on organizations is as broad as the frame of reference for his work as a whole, namely that identified by Schluchter (1979) Kalberg (1980), Whimster and Lash (1987) and many others: the rise of modern Western rationalism. It is a frame which can give us radical distance and perspective on any number of the fashions in organizational analysis that have come and gone in the seventy years since Weber wrote. It equally must involve as broad and comprehensive a retrieval of the problem of the interplay of rationality and emotion as was involved in Weber's study of Protestantism and of religion in general.

NOTE

*   This chapter has been written at the invitation of the Editors as a sequel to the paper '"Sine Ira et Studio' – or Do Organizations have Feelings' (Albrow 1992) which was originally delivered to the BSA Weber Study Group Conference at Lancaster University, 17–18 April 1991. Their useful comments and also the help of Steven Groarke, Roehampton Institute, are gratefully acknowledged.

    Especial thanks are due to Robert Merton who sent generous and detailed comments on the earlier paper and thus assisted greatly in the writing of this chapter.

REFERENCES

Albrow, Martin (1968) 'The Study of Organizations – Objectivity or Bias?', in *Penguin Social Science Survey*, Harmondsworth: Penguin, 146–67.

Albrow, Martin (1970) *Bureaucracy*, London: Macmillan.

Albrow, Martin (1972) 'Weber on Legitimate Norms and Authority: a Comment on Martin E. Spencer's Account', *British Journal of Sociology* 23: 483–7.

Albrow, Martin (1975a) 'Legal Positivism and Bourgeois Materialism: Max Weber's View of the Sociology of Law', *British Journal of Law and Society* 2: 14–31.

Albrow, Martin (1975b and 1976) 'Introduction to and translation of Max Weber, 'R. Stammler's "Surmounting" of the Materialist Conception of History', Part One', *British Journal of Law and Society* 2: 129–52. Part Two, *British Journal of Law and Society* 3: 17–43.

Albrow, Martin (1980) 'The Dialectic of Science and Values in the Study of Organizations', in G. Salaman and K. Thompson (eds) *Control and Ideology in Organizations*, Milton Keynes: Open University Press, 278–96.

Albrow, Martin (1987) 'The Application of the Weberian Concept of Rationalization to Contemporary Conditions', in S. Whimster and S. Lash (eds), *Max Weber, Rationality and Modernity*, London: Allen and Unwin, 164–82.

Albrow, Martin (1990) *Max Weber's Construction of Social Theory*, London: Macmillan.

Albrow, Martin (1991) 'Societies as Constructed Facts: the Weberian Approach to Social Reality'. Paper delivered to the 12th World Congress of Sociology, 1990, Madrid translated as 'Las sociedads como hechos construidos: el enfoque de Weber de la realidad social'. *Estudios Sociologicos de el Colegio de Mexico* 9: 339–56. Separately translated and published in *Sociologia: Unidad y Diversidad* edited by Teresa Gonzalez de la Fe, Madrid: Consejo Superior de Investigaciones Cientificas, 75–92.

Albrow, Martin (1992) '"Sine Ira et Studio" – or Do Organizations have Feelings?', *Organization Studies* 13: 313–29.

Andrzejewski, S.L. (1954) *Military Organization and Society*, London: Routledge.

Bittner, E. (1965) 'On the Concept of Organization', *Social Research* 32: 239–55.

Blau, Peter (1955) *The Dynamics of Bureaucracy*, Chicago: Chicago University Press.

Burns, Tom and Stalker, G.M. (1961) (1966 edition) *The Management of Innovation*, London: Tavistock.

Burrell, Gibson (1988) 'Modernism, Post Modernism and Organizational Analysis 2: The Contribution of Michel Foucault', *Organization Studies* 9: 221–35.

Cooper, Robert (1989) 'Modernism, Postmodernism and Organizational Analysis 3: The Contribution of Jacques Derrida', *Organization Studies* 10: 479–502.

Cooper, Robert and Burrell, Gibson (1988) 'Modernism, Postmodernism and Organizational Analysis 1: an Introduction', *Organization Studies* 9: 91–112.

Crossman, Richard (1976) *The Diaries of a Cabinet Minister, Volume 2*, London: Hamish Hamilton and Jonathan Cape.

Fiedler, F.E. (1962) 'Leader Attitude, Group Climate and Group Creativity', *Journal of Abnormal and Social Psychology* 65: 308–18.

Fine, Gary A. (1988) 'Letting off Steam? Redefining a Restaurant's Work Environment', in M.O. Jones, M.D. Moore and R.C. Snyder (eds) *Inside Organizations*, London: Sage.

Flam, Helena (1990) 'Emotional "Man": I. The Emotional "Man" and the Problem of Collective Action', *International Sociology* 5: 39–56; and 'Emotional "Man": II. Corporate Actors as Emotion-Motivated Emotion Managers', *International Sociology* 5: 225–34.

Friedrich, Carl J. (1952) 'Some Observations on Weber's Analysis of Bureaucracy', in R.K. Merton *et al.* (eds) *Reader in Bureaucracy*, Glencoe, Ill.: The Free Press, 27–33.

Goffman, Erving (1956) (1971 edition) *The Presentation of Self in Everyday Life*, Harmondsworth: Penguin.

Gouldner, Alvin (1955) *Patterns of Industrial Bureaucracy*, London: Routledge.

Harré, Rom (ed.) (1986) *The Social Construction of Emotions*, Oxford: Blackwell.

Hassard, John (1990) 'Ethnomethodology and Organizational Research: an Introduction', in John Hassard and Denis Pym (eds) *The Theory and Philosophy of Organizations*, London: Routledge, 97–108.

Hearn, Jeff and Parkin, Wendy (1987) *'Sex' at 'Work'*, Brighton: Wheatsheaf.

Hobbes, Thomas (1651) (1955 edition) *Leviathan*, ed. Michael Oakeshott, Oxford: Blackwell.

Hochschild, A.R. (1983) *The Managed Heart: Commercialization of Human Feeling*, Berkeley: University of California Press.

Holgate, Nicholas (1992) 'Same Building, Different Department', *Chequerboard: the Treasury Staff Magazine* 4: 7, 9.

Kalberg, Stephen (1980) 'Max Weber's Types of Rationality: Cornerstones for the Analysis of the Rationalization Process', *American Journal of Sociology* 85: 1145–79.

Katz, Daniel and Kahn, Robert L. (1966) *The Social Psychology of Organizations*, New York: John Wiley.

Kets de Vries, Manfred, F.R. and Miller, Danny (1985) *The Neurotic Organization*, San Francisco: Jossey Bass.

Luhmann, Niklas (1985) *A Sociological Theory of Law*, London: Routledge.

McGregor, Douglas (1966) *Leadership and Motivation*, Cambridge, Mass.: MIT Press.

McLuhan, Marshall (1964) *Understanding Media*, London, Routledge.

Merton, Robert K. (1940) 'Bureaucratic Structure and Personality', *Social Forces* 17: 560–68.

Morgan, Gareth (1986) *Images of Organization*, London: Sage.

Parker, Martin (1992) 'Post-modern Organizations or Postmodern Organization Theory', *Organization Studies* 13: 1–17.

Patterson, M., West, M. and Payne R. (1992) 'Collective Climates: a Test of their Socio-psychological Significance', (Centre for Economic Performance Discussion Paper 94), London: London School of Economics.

Pauchant, Thierry C. (1991) 'Transferential Leadership. Towards a More Complex Understanding of Charisma in Organizations', *Organization Studies* 12: 507–27.

Parsons, Talcott (1947) Introduction to Max Weber, *The Theory of Social and Economic Organization*, Glencoe, Ill.: The Free Press.

Peters, Gangolf (1988) 'Organisation as Social Relationship, Formalisation and Standardisation: A Weberian Approach to Concept Formation', *International Sociology* 3: 267–82.

Reed, Michael (1985) *Redirections in Organizational Analysis*, London: Tavistock.

Robbins, Lionel (1935) *An Essay on the Nature and Significance of Economic Science*, London: Macmillan.

Schluchter, Wolfgang (1979) (1985 edition) *The Rise of Western Rationalism: Max Weber's Developmental History*, Berkeley: University of California Press.

Schwartzman, Helen (1989) *The Meeting: Gatherings in Organizations and Communities*, New York: Plenum Press.

Tagiuri, R. and Litwin, G.H. (1968) *Organizational Climate: Exploration of a Concept*, Cambridge, Mass: Harvard Business School.

Tonnies, Ferdinand (1887) (1974 edition) *Community and Association*, London: Routledge.

Trist, E.L., Higgin, G., Murray, H. and Pollok, A. (1963) *Organisational Choice*, London: Tavistock.

Weber, Max (1947) *From Max Weber*, edited by H.H. Gerth and C.W. Mills, London: Routledge ('Politics as a Vocation', 77–128; 'Science as a Vocation', 129–58).

Weber, Max (1968) *Economy and Society*, trans. G. Roth and C. Wittich, 2 vols, New York: Bedminster.

Whimster, Sam and Lash, Scott (eds) (1987) *Max Weber, Rationality and Modernity*, London: Allen and Unwin.

Chapter 5

Max Weber on individualism, bureaucracy and despotism: political authoritarianism and contemporary politics

Bryan S. Turner

The debate about the fact-value distinction in Max Weber's *Wissenschaftslehre* is probably the most misunderstood and misleading feature of Weberian sociology. Rather than seeking to terminate political debate, Weber's philosophy of social science sought to establish the scientific grounds on which sociologists could enter into political controversy. Weber's philosophy of social science and his political views about capitalism were in fact closely related (Löwith 1982). If Weber is worth reading, then his political sociology ought to be relevant to modern circumstances.

In the period 1989 to 1992, we witnessed some of the most significant changes in the social structure and politics of the global order to have taken place in the twentieth century. A series of major political events – Chinese steps towards democratization leading to the Tiananmen killings, the break-up of the Soviet Union, the collapse of communism as an organized form of politics, the reunification of Germany and the beginnings of the erosion of apartheid in South Africa – transformed international relations. Of course, the naive enthusiasm and optimism over the global processes of democratization have been tempered by the eruption of ethnic violence in Eastern Europe. It is, however, evident that these global transformations were not adequately anticipated by sociology and that, as a consequence, academic sociologists will be forced to rethink much of the conventional sociological paradigm with which we have operated in the last fifty years. The simple dichotomies of capitalism and socialism, communism and liberalism, despotism and liberalism no longer appear relevant as frameworks for understanding the course of contemporary events. Recent debates about the end of organized capitalism, deregulation, post-Fordism and postmodernism are well intentioned but probably inadequate attempts to reorganize the intellectual map by which modern societies are to be sociologically conceptualized.

The contemporary uncertainty over the intellectual value of the classical tradition of sociology ought to be fairly considerable, because conventional sociology has operated too comfortably within the narrow confines of the concept of society, where 'society' is treated as equivalent to the nation state. Thus, the current debate about globalization and the idea of a global society are welcome moves towards liberating sociology from its nineteenth-century preoccupations with the nation state paradigm (Turner 1990a). However, in attempting to think about such issues as citizenship and human rights in the context of contemporary political problems surrounding the Gulf crisis, the democratization of Eastern Europe, and the struggle for human rights by stateless communities such as the Palestinians and the Kurds, one is conscious of the severe limitations of the conceptual baggage of classical sociology. These social and political changes have forced sociologists to rethink their relationship to the classical legacy of sociology, especially their relationship to writers like Max Weber. In this chapter, I attempt to defend certain aspects of Weber's political sociology, because his analysis of the tensions between bureaucracy and democracy, between a rational social order and creative individualism, between traditional cultures and modernization, has anticipated many of the contemporary debates about the fate of modernity. In particular, Weber's critical views on authoritarianism in Russian political culture and his anxieties about Islamic values are uncannily relevant to the anxieties of the post-Cold War era. Although I am concerned to defend the relevance of Weberian sociology, I am nevertheless highly critical of the anti-democratic dimension of Weber's political philosophy.

Although the necessity to rethink social theory is urgent and obvious, one is nevertheless haunted by the continuing relevance of Weber's political sociology to the problems of our time. For example, Weber's critical view of the problem and limitations of reform within Russia and the prospect of liberal politics in the aftermath of the Russian revolution are strangely insightful and prescient, given the recent history of *glasnost* and *perestroika* during the Gorbachev period. His analysis of superpower rivalries, his view of the role of the Baltic states, and his sense of the danger of East European subordination to Russian imperialism have all proved only too accurate (Weber 1988). In trying to rethink the relationship between scholarship and politics, in particular between sociological knowledge and political action, Weber's writing on science as a vocation and politics as a vocation enjoyed a remarkable longevity and relevance (Lassman and Velody 1989). In addition, Weber's criticism of socialism as a strategy for a planned economy appears to have been only too well borne out by the failure of centralized communist economies as alternatives to free-market capitalism. Weber's fears about the stultifying consequences of bureaucratic regulation also appear to have borne fruit in the case of the virtual destruction of civil society in the communist countries of Eastern Europe. As a consequence, I do not wholly share Anthony Giddens' view (Giddens 1990) that much of classical sociology should be abandoned because it failed to provide an adequate understanding of high modernity, and that it remains hopelessly locked within the narrow conceptual framework of the nation state (Turner 1990a). Weber's philosophy of social science was specifically designed to avoid any reification of the concept of 'society'; Weber was concerned to understand social processes and relationships in terms of a theory of social action. In his political sociology, he was exercised above all with the analysis of power relations, and inter-state rivalries rather than an internal analysis of the institutions of the nation state (Turner 1992a).

Although one could list contemporary developments in politics at some length in order to pinpoint the continuing relevance of Weber's political sociology to modern problems, there have obviously been significant changes in world politics since Weber's death which have radically transformed the broad political and cultural contours of the global scene. In this chapter I am specifically interested in the growing importance of religious fundamentalism such as 'militant Islam' as a new factor in global politics. The point of this chapter is to see contemporary global political events through the framework of Weber's political sociology, especially in terms of the Nietzschean values of Weber's Freiburg inaugural address of 1895 (Weber 1989). From the context of German power politics, Weber clearly feared the impact of Russian reactionary imperialism on European development, but he did not anticipate the political vitality of Islamic fundamentalism and its growing importance in European politics. Weber's sketchy, incomplete and negative view of Islam becomes, as a consequence, more rather than less interesting for those sociologists who are concerned to understand the broad pattern of international relations and global struggles in the twenty-first century. Like most of the major nineteenth-century sociologists of religion, Weber anticipated the secularization of religious values and the decline of the authority of religious metanarratives (Turner 1991: 82). One task for contemporary sociological theory is to address the phenomenon of religious revivalism, so the role of fundamentalist Islam in shaping the late twentieth century is of paramount sociological interest.

I want in addition to examine Weber's ambiguous views on liberalism and individualism in the context of his critical discussion of the place of bureaucracy in capitalism, militarism and religion. Weber's endorsement of an authoritarian form of politics conflicted with his personal commitment to individuality, but he remained a permanent critic of the possibilities of destructive rationalization. Locating these issues within his political sociology, Weber's rather hostile analysis of state socialism has been largely supported by recent developments in what was the Soviet Union. These macro-political changes should lead both socialists and sociologists to rethink their basic assumptions. However, Weber was also hostile to certain forms of religious fundamentalism, and his negative views on Islam are only too well known (Turner 1974a). For some commentators (Gellner 1981), there is a strong possibility that Islam, unlike Christianity, will survive both communism and capitalism. In this discussion of Weber I want to provide a sociological reflection on the ambiguity of Islam's place in the development of European politics.

WEBER AND THE ANALYSIS OF ISLAMIC CULTURE

In trying to rethink the nature of sociological analysis as a framework for comprehending global political events, it is perhaps an ideal opportunity critically to reassess Weber's commentary on Islamic culture. Broadly speaking I am now more rather than less sympathetic to Weber's critical analysis of the contribution of Islam than I was in the 1970s when I published *Weber and Islam* (Turner 1974a).

It is possible to identify two rather separate Weberian arguments. First, there is Weber's view of Islam as a warrior religion which had produced values and cultural standards inimical to the emergence of liberal capitalism. In Weber's sociology of religion, the social carriers of the various world religions were held to have made a lasting impression on the entire cultural outlook of these religions. The pristine carriers of Buddhism (mendicant monks) and Confucianism (the literati) were clearly contrasted, in terms of long-term consequences, with the nomadic warriors whom Weber identified as the original carriers of triumphant Islam. However, Weber appeared to have been simply wrong about the carriers of Islam, who were in fact not tribal warriors but trading groups. Merchants rather than warriors seem to have been crucial in the spread of Islam as a world religion; Koranic morality, with its concern for balances and accounting, reflects this trading culture rather than the values of a feudalistic warrior class. Weber had a second argument, which was about the consequences of patrimonial bureaucracy on the development of Islam. In this argument, which considered the role of state structures rather than foundational cultures, the absence of autonomous cities, the underdevelopment of institutions of private property, the absence of an indivi-dualistic culture, the insecurity of social life under patrimonialism from centralized power and the absence of a bourgeois class were regarded as consequences of a particular pattern of state formation. These social features were crucial to the underdevelopment of civil society in Islamic history. This particular type of state was closely associated in Weber's historical sociology with differences in military organization, namely the contrasting importance of infantry and cavalry in decentralized political systems. In short, it was not the religious values of Islam which constrained the development of capitalism but social stationariness (Turner 1974b) resulting from the dead weight of oriental bureaucracy. It was the burden of bureaucracy which limited entrepreneurial activity and restricted the emergence of an urban, ascetic, bourgeois class. To put this argument in terms Weber did not use, it was the peculiarly weak development of civil society in Islam which accounted for its traditionalism, and not the residue of the values of a warrior class which trapped Islam in its subsequent medieval inertia.

Weber and Islam was critically received by a number of anthropologists and sociologists who were associated with the loosely constructed 'Hull School' which had formed around such scholars as Sami Zubaida, Talal Asad, Roger Owen, Michael Gilsenan, David Waines and Fred Halliday. Within the Marxist academic culture of the 1970s, my use of Weber to provide an analysis of Islam and capitalism was criticized on the grounds that it merely reproduced a par-ticular type of discourse or ideology in which the polarity between East and West was characterized by an absence of private property, secularity, guilds, middle classes, and entrepreneurship. Traditional patterns of large-scale bureaucratiz-ation in patrimonial and prebendal empires were seen, within a Weberian paradigm, to be inimicable to radical social change towards either democracy or *laissez-faire*, competitive capitalism. My interpretation of Weber was thus seen to be merely a reproduction of a particular orientalist view of the contrast between a dynamic West and stationary East.

Many attempts to correct this 'orientalist problem' (Turner 1978) were at that time significantly influenced by the work of the Marxist scholar Louis Althusser, who had become a significant force in the development of sociology in Britain. One can accept much of the Marxist critique of liberalism and orientalism, but still argue that there was nevertheless an important parallel between Marxist conceptions of the Asiatic mode of production and Weber's notions of prebendalism and patrimonialism. The Althusserian critique of Weber's philosophy of social science and Weber's sociology of action also failed to understand the structuralist and objective character of Weberian sociology (Turner 1977). In general terms, these attempts to contrast Marx and Weber have given way to the opposite tendency to regard Marx and Weber as complementary theorists of capitalism, underdevelopment and modernity (Bakker 1988; Sayer 1991).

In fact, both Marx and Weber could be criticized for their orientalist reconstruction of Islam as a historical problem, namely as a deviation from the revolutionary character of Abrahamic prophetic religions. In characterizing oriental societies as stationary and incapable of achieving internal reform, Marx and Weber have implicitly, and occasionally explicitly, provided a historical legitimation of Western imperialism and colonialism. In the case of Marx, it was obvious that the only way in which Chinese and Indian stagnation could be undermined was through the destructive importation of Western commodities, transport systems, army discipline and newspapers (Turner 1974b). However, both Weber and Marx underestimated the importance of scientific cultures within Islam itself, treated Islamic philosophy as merely a derivation from Greek sources, and regarded Islamic religion as parasitic on Judaeo-Christian monotheism (Turner 1987).

These paradigms for the analysis of East/West relations, especially in terms of Islamic cultures, in the social sciences in the 1970s were heavily influenced by underlying ideological battles. There was in the sociology of development and the sociology of religion a marked reluctance to criticize the governments, social institutions and cultures of developing societies, and an equally marked readiness to criticize all forms of Western aid and Western models of development as forms of imperialism. There was a general reluctance to consider the possibility of a myopic 'occidentalism' as the parallel of a pernicious orientalism. The moral reluctance to criticize political authoritarianism and totalitarianism in non-Western societies has fortunately been replaced by a more honest attempt to take a balanced view of anti-democratic regimes regardless of their historical or spatial locations. At the time, my criticisms of Marx's own orientalism in *Marx and the End of Orientalism* (1978) were openly and deliberately provocative, especially in the context of Marxist objections to Weber as a bourgeois sociologist. Of course, these ideological undercurrents had their origins in much earlier debates. In retrospect therefore, it is interesting to take note of the fact that

Western scientific analysis of oriental society and Islam in the 1970s neglected the earlier work of Karl Wittfogel, whose *Oriental Despotism* (1957) had provided a powerful critique of political authoritarianism within both oriental cultures and contemporary communism. In Wittfogel's treatment of Russian history, Stalinist authoritarianism was merely the contemporary manifestation of an age-old Asiatic power system. The critical reception of Wittfogel's work was shaped by the Cold War ideologies of the period. For example, in the same period, radical sociologists had been equally critical of Talcott Parsons, whom they dismissed as a conservative, despite Parsons's overt condemnation of both fascist and communist versions of totalitarianism. Parsons's historical account of the origins of modern societies (Parsons 1971) had given a privileged position to Western societies in the development of a global system and he was condemned as merely a representative of Cold War politics. It is only recently that an adequate appreciation of Parsons's contribution to democratic theory has begun to surface (Robertson and Turner 1991; Sciulli 1992).

It is now over a decade since the publication of Edward Said's *Orientalism* (Said 1978), which had a profound impact on the humanities and to a lesser extent on social science approaches to the study of Asia and the Middle East. The 1970s debate about orientalism can now be seen retrospectively as part of a general academic trend towards self-critical evaluation of sociological perspectives on 'other societies'. It is perhaps an appropriate time to assess how relevant that orientalist critique is to the contemporary political context.

Another major influence on these intellectual developments came from the social theory of poststructuralists like Michel Foucault. The impact of Foucault on the orientalist debate was located in two areas. In showing how any extension of knowledge was always an extension of power, Foucault (1974) helped to undermine the notion that scientific knowledge was intrinsically innocent. For example, the development of enlightened views on madness was intimately bound up with the development of confinement and the professionalization of medical services (Foucault 1971). Furthermore, the development of the enlightenment both produced and domesticated Otherness, by creating and controlling that which fell outside Reason and reasonableness (Boyne, 1989). These ideas had a very obvious application to the growth of oriental sciences and to the creation of Islam as Otherness.

While the critique of orientalism was appropriate and necessary in the 1970s, the radical character of Foucault's social theory has been somewhat eroded over time. In particular, Foucault's radicalism has been turned on its head in the context of debates about Islam. It has proved relatively easy to translate Foucault's radical critique into a defence of traditionalism. This inverted form of Foucault assumes the following form. If Western views of Islam are biased by an orientalist discourse, then they are false. The problems associated with oriental bureaucracies in so-called hydraulic societies, that is societies in which political life was shaped by central regulation of water supplies, in the work of Weber, Wittfogel, Eisenstadt or Bendix were in fact reflections of European political problems. By contrast, 'our' own indigenous account of Islam is not contaminated by this discourse, and consequently it is true. Therefore, there is no need for an internal critique because this indigenous non-Western culture is morally and politically correct. Self-description, based on local knowledge, has a privileged access to the truth and self-criticism is not necessary, because Western radicals have themselves condemned Western cultural perspectives as imperialist and distorted. This inverted orientalism has allowed Islamic intellectuals to treat the values of liberty as a Masonic ideology, secularization as a Jewish plot and the doctrine of equality as a challenge to the authority of God (Al-Ahnaf *et al.* 1992).

In contemporary debates about the place of Islam in Western values and institutions, inverted-orientalism or the inverted-Foucauldian argument is often combined with a version of postmodernism to develop a defence of indigenous, local knowledge . If we define postmodernism as 'incredulity towards metanarratives' (Lyotard 1984: xxiv) and furthermore if those metanarratives are firmly located in the origins of Western capitalism in the seventeenth century, then in a paradoxical fashion we can see how both Third World opposition to capitalism and feminist criticism of patriarchal ideology can be associated with postmodernism. Because Islamic culture has been a target of both Western capitalism and orientalist critique, one can well appreciate the temptation to see Islam and postmodernism in an alliance against the Western metanarratives of industrialism, modernism and secularism (Ahmed 1992). However, to adopt this apparently radical position, Islamic intellectuals have to forget or disguise the fact that in many respects Islam has traditionally claimed to be not merely a metanarrative but The Metanarrative; for example, the Koranic message has historically claimed that the divinely inspired words of the Prophet replace all hitherto existing religious accounts (Jewish and Christian) of reality. The claim that 'There is no god but God' cannot easily be reworked as a postmodern proposition.

These problems in the debate about postmodernism and orientalism find a parallel issue in the question of Marxism. It is now clear that the Marxist critique of bourgeois legality and individualism has been cynically used to negate the idea of human rights as merely a bourgeois device. Marx's critical analysis of rights in the so-called 'Jewish question' was specific to the peculiar circumstances of the Jewish communities of Europe in a period of liberal reform; these arguments have been generalized to suggest that any discussion of human rights is merely part of bourgeois ideology. Within the centrally organized societies of the communist bloc, grass-roots movements for social change which mobilize the idea of individual rights were often castigated as reactionary and bourgeois. In the period of post-communist reform this situation has once more been turned on its head, with reformers celebrating the values and virtues of bourgeois civility against the old and discredited public virtues of the Party. Where Party values came to be identified with crass cynicism and hypocrisy, dissident intellectuals returned to individualistic values of privacy, honesty and intimacy (Szelenyi, 1988).

Given these conservative ideological developments after Marxism and Foucault, the political sociology of Weber appears to be both intellectually and morally persuasive. It is possible to return to a more sympathetic interpretation of Weber's aims and achievements, especially in the analysis of religion and politics (Turner 1992b). For example, in *Max Weber on Economy and Society* (Holton and Turner 1989) Holton showed the necessary relationship between Weber's epistemological arguments and his economic sociology. Basically Weber was a methodological individualist, but this did not require him to rule out the existence of institutional constraints or cultural imperatives or the unintended consequences of action. However, it does mean that the individual is privileged in terms of the subjective definition of needs and rights. Weber's methodological individualism had important implications not only for his approach to economics, but also in his criticism of socialism as a means of rational planning and production. In Weber's economic sociology the market-place is the most effective means for the satisfaction of economic wants, because the subjective needs and wishes of individual consumers can never be known adequately by a centralized planning institution. In fact, the real problem for Weber is to explain the existence of society at all. Because Weber insisted on the incommensurability of values, he has considerable difficulty in explaining intersubjectivity and the existence of shared goals and means. The explanation of intersubjectivity is a very important step in the defence of any theory of rights (Ferry 1990). The second problem with Weber's argument from the point of view of this particular chapter is that, while he believed the market to be the most successful means of delivering values in economic terms, he did not fully extend this argument into the political sphere where the classical theory of liberal democracy is that democratic representation is a necessary condition for satisfying political wants. Weber's idea of plebiscitary democracy was a concession to the belief that the economic and military power of Great Britain and the United States was based on the fact that their governments had popular legitimacy. The leadership of Germany required leaders who had a popular, however limited, mandate.

But Weber's criticism of socialism on the grounds that it requires an extensive rationalization of life to achieve an equitable distribution of goods remains a powerful objection to the idea of centralized economic planning. In retrospect, it now seems that the remarkable growth patterns in the Soviet Union and East European socialist societies in the early years of the post-war period were dependent upon an endless supply of cheap labour, the presence of raw materials in abundance and the lack of any independent labour organizations which would have been able to push up wages. These socialist economies have fallen behind the capitalist societies in recent years for a great variety of reasons, but the exhaustion of cheap labour and the absence of significant entrepreneurial activity and technological change combined with inefficient management have produced significant economic decline, major environmental pollution and a severe shortage of consumer goods. I have argued elsewhere (Turner 1990a) that Preobrazhensky's *The New Economics* (1965) provided a convincing analysis of the problems of economic growth under socialist conditions. Whereas capitalism had found the iron heel of primitive accumulation in colonial exploitation, economic growth under socialism is normally denied the availability of colonial markets and instead must resort to the internal exploitation of the existing class system, which it has inherited from pre-socialist conditions. Preobrazhensky, noticing that the Russian bourgeoisie was relatively small and economically rather insignificant, argued that Soviet socialism would have to exploit its own peasantry in order to produce the necessary primitive capital accumulation for future investment and growth. However, as Soviet socialism matured, these avenues for internal accumulation have been slowly but steadily closed off.

If Weber believed that socialism was a less rational form of economic life than capitalism, he was even more critical of communism as a form of traditional, communal social relationship (*Vergemeinschaftlung*). Weber identified a number of types of communism (Breuer 1992) in his articles on the Russian revolution ('Zur russischen Revolution von 1905') and on the new German order ('Zur Neuordnung Deutschlands') in his *Gesamtausgabe* (Weber 1988). Communism derived from pre-modern forms of communal relationship in the household, the army and the local community. Domestic communism has been undermined, according to Weber, by the partial erosion of patriarchal power as household and economy become differentiated. The communism of the army and the religious order are based on charisma, which is not a stable form of power. Weber regarded Russian communism as based on three specific sources: the comradeship of rebellious soldiers, the utopian mentality of intellectuals and the revolutionary aspirations of the peasantry. It was on the basis of this sociological analysis that Weber came to the conclusion that Bolshevism was a military dictatorship which, in the absence of any widespread normative legitimacy, would soon collapse.

For the time being at least, the threat of Cossacks on the plains of Europe – a threat which constantly exercised Weber's political and strategic imagination – appears to have receded and Weber's argument that the independence of the Baltic states was a necessary precondition for a successful foreign policy in Eastern Europe has come true. The spectre of a centralized despotic bureaucracy in a communist Eastern Europe, which had been the central fear of German nationalists, has largely disappeared, but, within a Weberian view of foreign affairs, a new threat arises: the encirclement of Europe by fundamentalist Islam. Weberian fears for the future of Europe in response to Soviet expansion have been put to rest, but is there, again within a Weberian framework, an equally powerful counterforce to European Christendom in the dominance of Islamic authorianism? Perhaps we could pose this question rather differently by asking whether, from within a Weberian view of social change, Islam can be regarded as regressive? Weber's own answer was, of course, that Islam as a warrior religion had been converted entirely to a traditionalist and feudal form of religion, thereby precluding the possibilities of a secular, individualistic soteriology.

Weber's sociology of religion provides us with an inadequate assessment of the origins of Islam. Furthermore, if you accept Weber's definition of modernization in terms of ascetic discipline, anti-magical practices, a textually based rationalism, the existence of rational procedures for making and finding legal guidelines, and the application of rational science to everyday practices, then both Calvinistic Protestantism and fundamentalist Islam are modernist. That is, there is nothing in the history of Islamic values which would rule out the possibility of an Islamic breakthrough into rationalist modernism. So Islam is not, in cultural terms, essentially anti-modern, because its attachment to ascetic disciplines and the simplicity of textural rationalism combined with a prophetic religious code and a law-based morality obviously favour modernization, at least in Weberian terms as anti-magical world mastery. However, unlike Christianity, Islam seems to be politically more overtly committed to the principle of equality rather than to individualism, liberty and dissent. The unitarian doctrine in Islam, that the greatest sin is to imply that God has equals, would be one source of this pristine egalitarianism. Trinitarianism and Maryology, in the Catholic theological tradition, by contrast, open up a space for associates. Differences in approaches to sainthood are also relevant (Turner 1974b). The argument is that the more radical the monotheism, the more radical the egalitarianism within the community of faith. The political radicalism of Islam seems to favour the values of fundamental equality of humanity before God rather than the sanctity of the individual and the legitimacy of dissent (Berque 1984). This commitment to equality, which seems to stem from Islamic theodicy, has often led commentators to observe a similarity between socialist and religious egalitarianism. Ali Shariati (1980) was correct in arguing that, while equality was a value shared by both Islam and Marxism, Islam derived it from transcendental religious assumptions about relationships between God and Man, and not from materialism. While Islam has a universalist commitment to equality, it necessarily places less emphasis on the idea of the right of individual opposition. Radical Protestantism, by contrast, seems to be more tolerant of inequality (as in the Calvinist doctrine of the salvation of an Elect), while giving greater scope to the idea of individual autonomy. Weber's own moral outlook, with its emphasis on personality, choice and autonomy, was derived from a Kantian reading of the Christian gospels (Löwith 1993). For Weber the main threats to individual autonomy came from the growing importance of bureaucracy in the rational management of modern societies (of which socialist planning was simply one example) and from centralized despotic political power in patrimonial empires.

ORIENTAL DESPOTISM AND STATE BUREAUCRACY

Wittfogel's analysis of oriental despotism (1957) is one of the classic texts of political science and yet his 'comparative study of total power' has been a popular target for left-wing criticism for many decades. The problem with Wittfogel's thesis about absolute power was not so much his attempt to demonstrate that there were pre-industrial forms of totalitarian social control, but his historical study of the rise and fall of the concept of the Asiatic mode of production in Soviet communist theory. In short, Wittfogel argued that the Marxist concept of Asiatic society which had questioned the legitimacy of the

Soviet regime, had been suppressed by Stalin and others because it was an embarrassment to Soviet power. For Wittfogel, Stalinism was merely the restoration of Asiatic authoritarianism, since the Soviet state reproduced precisely the centralized regulation of pre-modern hydraulic society. Wittfogel's concern with the history of the Asiatic mode of production in the Soviet Union was seen as an example of his 'obsessive anti-communism and anti-Sovietism' (Hindess and Hirst 1975: 207) and at a theoretical level his thesis was criticized as a functionalist explanation which involved an unacceptable teleology. It was also a tautological argument: large-scale irrigation for agriculture required the existence of the powerful state, while the existence of the state presupposed an irrigation agriculture as its foundation.

In retrospect, much of this criticism now appears somewhat implausible, formalistic or irrelevant. Wittfogel, who himself spent time in a concentration camp where he had, as it were, studied totalitarianism at close quarters, was deeply influenced by the intellectual legacy of Weber, especially his theory of bureaucracy and the state. Wittfogel's main intention was to produce a critique of state power based upon a monopoly of public utilities. In particular, he was critical of bureaucratic state power in the Soviet Union from 1917 onwards, and this was the real origin of his treatment of the Asiatic mode of production. Furthermore, Wittfogel was not in any strict sense an orientalist: hydraulic power was seen to be an issue in Hawaii as much as in China. He rejected any unilinear view of history, but hydraulic government within what he called an agro-managerial bureaucracy was a distinctive pattern of power, quite separate from the more differentiated and localized feudal system. He did not really approve of the concept of 'oriental despotism', preferring to talk about hydraulic societies and conditions. One final feature of Wittfogel's sociology which we should remember was that he had been a member of the Frankfurt School prior to his migration to America. Wittfogel joined the Institute for Social Research at Frankfurt, where Carl Grundberg had agreed to supervise his dissertation. His early work was on science and bourgeois society, but he became famous for his studies of China and Asiatic conditions. He was not a member of the inner circle of the Frankfurt School (Jay 1973: 15) and Kolakowski (1978, III: 343) describes him as not 'a typical representative of the Frankfurt School'. However, Wittfogel's basic interest – the consequences for political life of the interaction of environment (nature) and culture – clearly continues to be a central issue in modern political theory.

It appears that Wittfogel has been neglected and that his critique of centralized bureaucratic power, which was modelled on Weber's political sociology, has been more than justified in the recent history of the erosion of bureaucratic power in the Soviet Union and Eastern Europe. Furthermore, enthusiasm for macro-political analysis in contemporary social sciences has often ignored Wittfogel's earlier contribution. For example, Roberto Unger's *Plasticity into Power* (1987) in many ways reproduces the arguments of Wittfogel, especially in the idea of conditions for reversion from a money to a natural economy in agrarian society.

Unger's enthusiasm for the idea of institutional plasticity can be seen as the reverse of Wittfogel's conception of total power.

THE SOCIOLOGY OF LIBERALISM

Marxism as an intellectual force cannot easily escape from or simply ignore the collapse of organized socialism in Eastern Europe and the Soviet Union. Marxists who claim that organized communism in Eastern Europe have nothing to do with socialism or Marxism are rather like Christians who argue that the obvious corruption and hypocrisy of the organized churches has nothing to do with Christianity; their faith is happily immune to the trials of reality. At the very least, there is a case to be answered and it is difficult to believe that the entire erosion of Marxism-Leninism in the Soviet Union can be regarded by socialist intellectuals in Western Europe with complete indifference or even disdain. One has to have considerable sympathy for Ernesto Laclau (1990: xii) who has argued that ' above all else there must be no wishful thinking in terms of a hypothetical Marx whose discourse has been left intact by the subsequent deformations of "Marxism". However, while Laclau proposes to rethink socialism from the perspective of discourse analysis, an alternative strategy could be a Weberian attempt to revitalize a set of concepts which had their origins in Western liberalism, such as the notion of citizenship, the pluralist theory of the state, human rights and individual autonomy.

As a general rule, sociology has been highly critical of the claims of liberalism, and one might argue that in fact sociology developed as an alternative to and critique of classical nineteenth-century liberal thought. Marx and Durkheim in very different ways provided a profound critique of liberalism, especially in its utilitarian form. Liberalism has often been regarded as the dominant ideology of capitalism, and certainly it is normally argued that liberal capitalism requires and presupposes individualism, which in turn is regarded by Marxist critics as a cynical defence of private property. Marx condemned writers like J.S. Mill and Jeremy Bentham as liberal ideologues of competitive capitalism who provided a moral defence of the inequalities of the market-place under the ideological umbrella of individual rights, private property and free markets. The classical criticism of liberal individualism was presented by C.B. Macpherson in his famous account of the theory of possessive individualism (1962). Here he showed that the liberal individualistic tradition from Hobbes to Locke assumed a possessive character in which the grounds for individual rights were in fact private property ownership. With its emphasis on privacy, property and rights, liberalism, according to Marxist theory, disguised the social nature of property and legitimized the inequalities of the market-place through the doctrine of individual responsibility and achievement.

While Marxists have criticized liberalism as a capitalist ideology, in the work of Emile Durkheim we find a critique of Spencerian individualism in which he condemned the egotism of utilitarian liberalism as a cause of anomie in modern

society. Durkheim's political sociology envisaged the growth of corporate institutions which would link the individual to the state in an organic relation; this
would mitigate the negative consequences of egoistic individualism (Durkheim
1992).

For various reasons this conventional characterization of liberalism as the
dominant ideology of capitalism no longer appears so compelling or relevant.
First, it is in fact very difficult to provide an adequate account of why a *specific*
ideology or belief system is a necessary requirement of capitalist production
(Abercrombie *et al.* 1980). Capitalism as an economic system appears to thrive
on or alongside a great diversity of belief systems and cultures. For example,
monopoly capitalism in Germany and Japan in the first half of the twentieth
century appears to have been more compatible with Fascist, nationalist and racist
ideology. Capitalism in Portugal, Spain and South Africa appears to have an
equally authoritarian system of belief rather remote from the individualistic
tradition of liberalism. In fact, *laissez-faire*, liberal and individualistic cultures,
which have been characteristic of what one might call the Anglo-Saxon version
of capitalism, may be the exception rather than the rule. Secondly, most explan-
ations of liberalism have failed to provide an adequate differentiation of types of
individualism in relation to liberal doctrine. It is important to distinguish between
individualism, individuation, individuality and the concepts of the individual in
attempting to specify the historical development of individualism in relation to
capitalism (Abercrombie *et al.* 1986). Individuality is a doctrine closely
associated with the romantic and conservative reactions to the growth of urban
industrial capitalism, and romantic individuality as an ideal is rather remote from
the more bourgeois conceptions of individual rights to property in the works of
writers like Hobbes and Locke. In short, liberalism is not a necessary ideology of
capitalism but it may be particularly relevant to questions of democratic pluralism. Furthermore, Marxist caricature of the concept of the individual in Bentham
and Mill is an inaccurate description of the genuine doctrine of individualism
which one finds in the work of J. S. Mill. The liberal concept of the individual
does not have to assume an anti-social, egoistic, rational and utilitarian form. In
fact, of course, Mill rejected precisely the rationalistic and positivist tradition of
individualism and liberalism in the work of his father, and it was on the basis of
the subjective definition of happiness that he eventually rejected the whole
legacy of utilitarianism. For Mill, poetry was definitely better than the game of
pushpin. Finally, the Marxist view that the doctrine of rights can *only* assume an
individualistic form has been broadly criticized by recent developments in the
theory of rights, especially the development of a communitarian tradition
(Freeden 1991; Sandel 1982). The development of an adequate sociological, as
opposed to philosophical and political, theory of human rights is thus a pressing
concern of contemporary sociology.

One criticism of conventional liberalism which may continue to have relevance is that many classical liberal writers had a rather limited or restricted
conception of democracy. Locke and many nineteenth-century liberals adhered

to a very confined conception of democratic participation in which it was implicitly assumed or explicitly stated that certain social groups (especially women and the lower social orders) would be excluded from full political participation. Citizenship within this early liberal tradition was restricted to a set of minimal legal rights and minimal political requirements for full social participation. Similarly, J.S. Mill retained a fundamental fear of the full participation of the uneducated working class in the emerging parliamentary system. His fear that democracy would produce a Chinese stationariness (Turner 1974b) was reinforced by the publication of Alexis de Tocqueville's *Democracy in America*, which contained a negative view of the possibility of a genuine democratic revolution in America.

Weber's version of liberalism was equally complex and problematic. On the one hand, it is obvious that Weber thought that the growth of bureaucracy under capitalist conditions would severely limit the possibility of authentic individuality and constrain the full flowering of personality. Rational capitalism produced a world of mindless bureaucrats and soulless experts, 'specialists without a spirit and sensualists without heart' (*Fachmenschen ohne Geist und Genussmenschen ohne Hertz*) as he said in the conclusion of the *Protestant Ethic* essays (Weber 1930: 182). On the other hand, Weber feared that general mass democracy would produce weak leadership and directionless politics. He also felt that in Germany in particular the weakness of democracy was associated with the continuing importance of the Junker class and the inability of the middle classes to develop genuine political autonomy and leadership. The failure of the 1848 revolution in Germany, the inadequacy of socialism and the underdevelopment of the working class, the legacy of Bismarckian centralized bureaucracy and the dominance of state structures were a set of conditions which precluded, in Weber's view, the emergence of *laissez-faire* capitalism and a liberal middle class. To counteract the impact of British industrial democracy, Weber felt, Germany required some minimal political legitimacy in order to function adequately on the international scene, and this minimal democratization would be best achieved through the development of the plebiscitary principle.

CITIZENSHIP AND LIBERAL DEMOCRACY

There are various ways in which, from a sociological perspective, liberalism might be defended against conventional criticism. For example, liberalism is not a necessary doctrine of capitalist society. Individualism does not require an anti-social conception of the individual (Holton and Turner 1989: 14–29). However, liberalism has been particularly weak in providing an adequate theory of democracy, precisely because it has concentrated on the conception of individual rights and obligations, but it is possible to develop a more collective or communitarian view of liberalism which would overcome some of the Robinson Crusoe assumptions of classical seventeenth-century liberalism in the writings of Hobbes and Locke.

The theory of citizenship can be seen as an attempt by later liberal philosophy to plug this gap in classical liberalism, that is to develop a theory of those social institutions which are necessary to protect the individual and individual rights. Liberalism was successful in providing a philosophy of individual rights and the institutions to protect individual rights, but it failed to provide an account of how the inequality of the market-place could be counteracted. It is within this framework that we might see the work of D.H. Marshall on citizenship (1950) as a late liberal attempt to develop a notion of citizenship, which was conceptualized as a counterweight to market inequalities.

There is no need at this stage to provide an elaborate description of Marshall's well known theory of the emergence of citizenship (see Turner 1986). For Marshall, citizenship was a bundle of rights which had emerged in three stages. In the seventeenth century, legal citizenship had emerged in terms of the right to a fair trial, the jury system and habeas corpus. In the eighteenth and nineteenth centuries, political citizenship had developed through parliament, which embodied the principles of universal franchise, competitive parties and a secret ballot. In the nineteenth and twentieth centuries, citizenship had expanded with the creation of the welfare state in which rights associated with social insurance, employment and health benefits were institutionalized. For Marshall, these institutions of citizenship stood in opposition to the inequalities of the market-place, and provided the individual with some respite from the naked impact of economic processes. Although Marshall has been heavily criticized, his conceptualization of the relationship between capitalist economy, liberalism, citizenship and civil society has produced an important framework for the analysis of the complexity of political democracy in capitalist society. At the very least, Marshall's approach is a starting point for the analysis of the problem of citizenship under capitalist conditions.

One problem with Marshall's account of citizenship is that it offers a narrow English conception of the historical development of the institutions of citizenship. In particular, it is important to distinguish between citizenship which develops from below as the consequence of radical struggles to enhance and develop rights, and those forms of citizenship which develop from the state downwards as a process of pacification. The other significant variable in the development of citizenship is cultural: the conception of public and private space within a society. In societies where the public realm is perceived as a potential moral danger to the individual, we can expect rather limited forms of state-down citizenship rights which limit the public space open to the individuals. Where there is a special emphasis on the moral primacy of the private, we can expect rather limited forms of citizenship institutionalization. By putting these two variables together, we can develop four types of citizenship: passive, radical, liberal and authoritarian (Turner 1990b). Weber's political sociology is based precisely on this limited conception of authoritarian citizenship in which the freedom of the individual can only be guaranteed by the strength of state institutions. This conception of political life is clearly very different from the tradition of liberal democracy in Britain and America or radical democracy in the French revolutionary tradition. We are now in a position to study the implicit sociology of citizenship which is housed within Weber's historical sociology of political institutions.

Weber identified three broad historical conditions for the emergence of modern citizenship. The first is the growth of autonomous urban associations in the Western city; here Weber wanted to make a contrast between the organic development of the city-state in medieval Europe and the emergence of the city as military centre within Islamic and Asian cultures. In the medieval city, a set of immunities emerged against the invasion of feudal power, and it was this autonomy which was eventually guaranteed by the emergence of urban militia. Secondly, urban Christianity provided an ideology which was very much suited to the development of political democracy, because Christianity undermined the tribalistic affiliation of previous communities in which blood ties were the basis of social solidarity. Christianity was eventually able to provide a universalistic doctrine based on faith and organized by a celibate priesthood whose descendants could not claim special privileges on the basis of a blood relationship. Christianity provided one origin of the idea of a universalistic brotherhood uniting people together on the basis of their belief rather than familial tribal or kinship relations (Gierke 1990). Finally, Weber was specifically interested in the emergence of rational law-making as a stable base for procedural rules of adjudication. Disputes could be collectively resolved by appeal to publicly known norms of procedure rather than depending upon *ad hoc* law-making through magical devices. These three conditions – the autonomy of the city, the universality of faith and the stability of rational law – were historical circumstances in which a universalistic notion of citizenship might ultimately emerge.

However, this optimistic view of the historical emergence of citizenship was in Weber's sociology counteracted by a number of extremely pessimistic views of the possibilities of participatory democracy. This view of democracy developed by reference to two issues. The first concerned the iron law of oligarchy, where Weber embraced the negative view of democratization which had been developed by his friend Robert Michels (Mommsen, 1987). The rationalization of mass party democracy would eventually undermine the possibility of adequate representation and political accountability. The second issue related, as we have seen, to the specific class circumstances of politics in Germany at the beginning of the twentieth century: the dominance of the Junkers, the weakness of the middle class, the absence of effective national leadership, and the immaturity of the working class. In short, Weber's pessimistic view emerged firstly from his analysis of the problem of the bureaucratization of politics under mass party conditions, and secondly from his analysis of the specific configuration of social classes in the context of international rivalries. Weber's commitment to the ideals of individualism and liberalism was always circumscribed by his political sociology, and by the master theme of rationalization (Löwith 1993).

CONCLUSION: POSTMODERNISM, ISLAM AND POLITICS

In this discussion of Weber's combination of the normative framework of liberalism with a pessimistic view of bureaucratization, I have been specifically concerned with an analysis of Weber's political sociology of international rivalries. I have considered his criticisms of socialist bureaucracy and patrimonial (Islamic) bureaucracy as a context for expounding his political anxieties. In his seminal lecture at Freiburg in 1895 Weber (1989: 198) self-consciously adopting the language of Nietzsche, bitterly commented that 'Our successors will not hold us responsible before history for the kind of economic organization we hand over to them, but rather for the amount of elbow-room we conquer for them in the world and leave behind us.' In this chapter I have indicated two inter-related features of modern European politics on which we could expect Weber to have taken a decisive and controversial position: the decline of Soviet communism, and the rise of militant Islam. Weber was a persistent critic of East European bureaucratic authoritarianism on both liberal and nationalist grounds. One can only assume that he would have enthusiastically welcomed the demise of the bureaucratic and authoritarian features of the Soviet state. In addition, given Weber's anxieties about the ethnic diversification of Germany east of the Elbe, he would have observed the development of Muslim communities in Germany, and more generally in Europe, with some degree of horror.

These contradictory developments in the political map of Europe make the traditional issue of orientalism especially problematic. Here I have indicated my dissatisfaction with the sorts of solution in social science which were common in the 1970s. On the one hand, Islamic apologists have often been able to embrace a peculiar combination of orientalist critique and postmodernism to make Islamic authoritarianism immune to rational criticism. On the other hand, Weber's own conception of liberal democracy was particularly sceptical and limited. However, if we adopt Weber's plea for political realism, then we can say that the real test of European liberalism will be to defend both full democracy and cultural pluralism in a period of global economic recession. In this test, the unification of Germany and the growth of 'European Islam' will be crucial ingredients. It is difficult to remain too optimistic about what kind of 'elbow-room' will be possible in these global circumstances.

REFERENCES

Abercrombie, N., Hill, S. and Turner, B.S. (1980) *The Dominant Ideology Thesis*. London; Allen and Unwin.
Abercrombie, N., Hill, S. and Turner, B.S. (1986) *Sovereign Individuals of Capitalism*. London: Allen and Unwin.
Ahmed, A.S. (1992) *Postmodernism and Islam*. London: Routledge.
Al-Ahnaf, M., Botiveau, B. and Fregosi, F. (1992) *L'Algérie par ses Islamistes*. Paris: Karthala.
Bakker, J.I. (1988) 'Patrimonialism, involution, and the agrarian question in Java: a

Weberian analysis of class relations and servile labour', pp. 279–301 in J. Gledhill, B.Bender and M.T. Larsen (eds) *State and Society. The Emergence and Development of Social Hieararchy and Political Centralization*. London: Unwin Hyman.

Berque, J. (1984) *L'Islam au temps du monde*. Paris: Sindbad.

Boyne, R. (1989) *Foucault and Derrida*. London: Unwin Hyman.

Breuer, S. (1992) 'Soviet communism and Weberian sociology', *Journal of Historical Sociology*, 5(3): 267–90.

Durkheim, E. (1992) *Professional Ethics and Civic Morals*. London: Routledge.

Ferry, L. (1990) *Political Philosophy 1. Rights – the New Quarrel between the Ancients and the Moderns*. Chicago: University of Chicago Press.

Foucault, M. (1971) *Madness and Civilization: A History of Insanity in the Age of Reason*. London: Tavistock.

Foucault, M. (1974) *The Order of Things: an Archaeology of the Human Sciences*. London: Tavistock.

Freeden, M. (1991) *Rights*. Milton Keynes: Open University Press.

Gellner, E. (1981) *Muslim Society*. Cambridge:Cambridge University Press.

Giddens, A. (1990) *The Consequences of Modernity*. Cambridge: Polity Press.

Gierke, O. von (1990) *Community in Historical Perspective*. Cambridge: Cambridge University Press.

Hindess, B. and Hirst, P.Q. (1975) *Pre-Capitalist Modes of Production*. London: Routledge and Kegan Paul.

Holton, R.J. and Turner, B.S. (1989) *Max Weber on Economy and Society*. London: Routledge and Kegan Paul.

Jay, M. (1973) *The Dialectical Imagination. A History of the Frankfurt School and the Institute of Social Research 1923–1950*. London: Heinemann Educational Books.

Kolakowski, L. (1978) *Main Currents of Marxism*. Oxford: Clarendon Press. 3 vols.

Laclau, E. (1990) *New Reflections on the Revolution of Our Time*. London: Verso.

Lassman, P. and Velody, I (eds) (1989) *Max Weber's 'Science as a Vocation'*. London: Unwin Hyman.

Löwith, K. (1993) *Max Weber and Karl Marx*. London: Routledge.

Lyotard, J.-F. (1984) *The Postmodern Condition: A Report on Knowledge*. Manchester: Manchester University Press.

Macpherson, C.B. (1962) *The Political Theory of Possessive Individualism: Hobbes to Locke*. Oxford: Oxford University Press.

Marshall, T.H. (1950) *Citizenship and Social Class and Other Essays*. Cambridge: Cambridge University Press.

Mommsen, W.J. (1987) 'Robert Michels and Max Weber: moral conviction versus the politics of responsibility', pp. 121–38 in W.J. Mommsen and J. Osterhammel (eds) *Max Weber and his Contemporaries*. London: Allen and Unwin.

Parsons, T. (1971) *The System of Modern Societies*. Englewood Cliffs, New Jersey: Prentice-Hall.

Preobrazhensky, E. (1965) *The New Economics*. Oxford: Clarendon Press.

Robertson, R. and Turner, B.S. (eds) (1991) *Talcott Parsons, Theorist of Modernity*. London, Sage.

Said, E.W. (1978) *Orientalism*. New York: Pantheon Books.

Sandel, M. (1982) *Liberalism and the Limits of Justice*. Cambridge: Cambridge University Press.

Sayer, D. (1991) *Capitalism and Modernity. An Excursus on Marx and Weber*. London: Routledge.

Sciulli, D. (1992) *Theory of Societal Constitutionalism. Foundations of a non-Marxist Critical Theory*. Cambridge: Cambridge University Press.

Shariati, A. (1980) *Marxism and Other Western Fallacies*. Berkeley: Mizan Press.

Szelenyi, I. (1988) *Socialist Entrepreneurs: Embourgeoisement in Rural Hungary*. Oxford: Blackwell.

Turner, B.S. (1974a) *Weber and Islam, a Critical Study*. London: Routledge and Kegan Paul.

Turner, B.S. (1974b) 'The concept of social "stationariness": utilitarianism and Marxism', *Science and Society*, 38 (1): 3–18.

Turner, B.S. (1977) 'The structuralist critique of Weber's sociology', *British Journal of Sociology*, 28 (1): 1–16.

Turner, B.S. (1978) *Marx and the End of Orientalism*. London: Allen and Unwin.

Turner, B.S. (1986) *Citizenship and Capitalism. The Debate over Reformism*. London: Allen and Unwin.

Turner, B.S. (1987) 'State, science and economy in traditional societies: some problems in the Weberian sociology of science' *British Journal of Sociology*, 38(1): 1–23.

Turner, B.S. (1990a) 'The end of organized socialism?', *Theory Culture and Society*, 7(4): 133–44.

Turner, B.S. (1990b) 'Outline of a theory of citizenship', *Sociology*, 24 (2): 189–217.

Turner, B.S. (1991) *Religion and Social Theory*. London: Sage.

Turner, B.S. (1992a) 'Weber, Giddens and modernity', *Theory Culture and Society*, 9 (2): 141–6.

Turner, B.S. (1992b) *Max Weber, from History to Modernity*. London: Routledge.

Unger, R.M. (1987) *Plasticity into Power*. Cambridge: Cambridge University Press.

Weber, M. (1930) *The Protestant Ethic and the Spirit of Capitalism*. London: Unwin University Books.

Weber, M. (1988) *Gesammelte Politische Schriften*. Tübingen: J.C.B. Mohr (Paul Siebeck).

Weber, M. (1989) 'The national state and economic policy', pp. 188–209 in K. Tribe (ed.) *Reading Weber*. London: Routledge.

Wittfogel, K. (1957) *Oriental Despotism: a Comparative Study of Total Power*. New Haven, Conn.: Yale University Press.

Chapter 6

Commerce, science and the modern university

Keith Tribe

For reasons too diverse to elaborate upon here, British social history has been propagated as a discourse on social movements, rather than social institutions. The social history of crime, for example, is perceived primarily as a history of changing perceptions of criminality and criminal behaviours; where historians drew upon sociological insights, it was the work of Becker and Cicourel that they found of most relevance. Comparatively little attention is given to the institutional dynamics of law as a social process, the organization of policing, the creation and articulation of formal and informal codes of public morality, not to mention the means of financing the whole enterprise. This would smack too much of Foucauldianism, of a kind of late twentieth-century recapitulation of systems theory in which the person disappeared under the abstractions of systems functionality and dysfunctionality.

This might seem an eccentric point from which to begin a chapter on Max Weber and the modern university, but it serves to emphasize a point about the nature and scope of social history. For if, in what passes for the history of education in Britain, one were to adopt the standpoint of social history, then it would be to talk of the social background of those passing through the schooling process, and of the nature of class control in the classroom. Curriculum design, school and college architecture, transition points, examination systems, finance – none of these really seem to belong in a social history, this is the stuff of administrative history, which is not a popular or a highly regarded sub-discipline. The educational system is treated as an administrative entity, not as a social institution serving identifiable, sometimes contradictory, ends. This is unfortunate, for we need serious critical histories of educational systems, in order to gain perspective on the reshaping of school and university, and to challenge the rhetoric of reform. In the absence of such challenge, educational reform becomes simply an instrument of power. This phenomenon was noted some years ago by historians studying the movement for educational reform in late nineteenth-century France, in which 'reform' was primarily an instrument of inter-ministerial competition; it was therefore an unending process, rather than a struggle to achieve an improved condition.

The fate of science and scholarship in the modern university is consequently something which is left to the administrators – or rather, the management. It is not something on which informed public discussion takes place, in part because it is actually quite difficult to become very well informed about it, if this means moving beyond casual empiricism to a balanced understanding of the dynamics involved. There is, for instance, no serious account of the development of the British schooling system from the later nineteenth century, nor is there one which deals with the various levels of post-school education – colleges, vocational training, adult education, and universities. What literature exists is either extremely limited in scope, or recapitulates past or present prejudices. If we are to gain insights into the development of our educational system, its original purposes and the manner in which it evolved to the structures that surround us today, a fresh perspective is required. Here, as elsewhere, the work of Max Weber can be of use.

In November 1917 Weber gave a lecture to a meeting of the Munich Federation of Free Students on the theme 'Science as a Vocation'. Over a year later he delivered a second, complementary lecture, published under the title 'Politics as a Vocation'.[1] Both derive their argument from the Burg Lauenstein lecture 'Personality and the Life Orders', which had been presented in the autumn of 1917;[2] and this common source accounts for the manner in which Weber treats the problems of science and politics from the standpoint of personality – what it means to be a scientist, scholar or politician in the modern world.

As Hennis points out, about one quarter of 'Science as a Vocation' is taken up with the external conditions of an academic occupation, comparing university systems and career structures in Germany and America. At issue is the problem of science and scholarship in the modern university – for by 'science' Weber means scholarly activity in general, rather than a narrow focus on specific disciplines. He adopts at first the stance of the 'pedantic economist', considering how a student would enter a scientific career; but his principal objective was to focus upon the personal qualities required of the scientist working within the institutions of the modern university. Before he could broach these qualities, it was necessary to elaborate on the nature of the modern university as the institutionalized form of scientific knowledge and its reproduction.

This is effected by contrasting the German university system with that of the United States. The former had been widely regarded in the later nineteenth century as the model for science and teaching: it had fostered significant advances in the natural sciences, humanities, and social sciences, and had also played an important role in the education of a new educated bourgeoisie, the *Bildungsbürgertum*. In many respects, the new universities created in France, Britain and the United States in the later nineteenth century looked to Germany as the exemplar of the modern university as an institutional combination of teaching and research. The work of the 'old' universities had focused on the transmission of established knowledge to a professional elite, in which scholarship meant first, the preservation, and second, the dissemination, of a given body of knowledge. By the late nineteenth century this conception of scholarship as a work, essentially, of conservation had altered, and a new conception of knowledge as the product of constant research and discovery was taking hold. It was in this context that the universities came to combine research and teaching functions, in which teaching was conducted across a broader spectrum of disciplines, themselves defined in terms of the new research ethos. The result was a new institutional structure, the modern university, in which research and teaching existed in a symbiotic relationship. The German university system was itself overtaken by these developments, however, and Weber argued that by the first decades of the twentieth century the authority of the 'plutocratic' German model was being displaced by a 'bureaucratic' American model. He then proceeded to analyse this American bureaucratic form in the new terminology of the modern capitalist enterprise, in which workers were separated from the means of production, the principle of the division of labour governed internal organization, and the whole was subjected to rational, bureaucratic management. The imperatives of a world based upon individual scholarship and science was giving way to the mechanisms of the market, directed from the one side by the demands of students, and from the other by the growing need for certification from employers. Squeezed in this way, how could scientific and intellectual development survive an apparently unrelenting pressure to mould scientists and scholars into the 'uninventive specialists' anticipated in the closing pages of Weber's *Protestant Ethic and the Spirit of Capitalism*? This was the issue to which Weber directed the attention of his student audience in 1917.

Wilhelm Hennis has demonstrated at length that this issue takes us to the heart of Weber's central concern with the nature of human personality, and the manner in which it is moulded by the institutional conditions of existence under which humans live and work. It is not my intention to recapitulate these arguments, which have been adequately exposed by Hennis in a number of essays; instead, I wish to direct attention to a more prosaic question concerning the genesis and provenance of Weber's account of the modern university. Given the general line of argument that Weber advances, it might seem curious that his account of the German university system is almost entirely negative, whilst that of the United States is decidedly positive. And yet this apparent paradox has gone unremarked. Weber saw modernity as an iron cage, in which the incremental development of bureaucratic domination eradicated individual personality and creativity; surely, therefore, he would seek to defend the German university model against the new American prototype? On the contrary: despite the international regard accorded the German university, he saw that its time of pre-eminence was past, that it provided no workable model for the future. Given the general purpose of Weber's argument, why then did he choose to frame it in this manner, treating the American system as the system of the future? What effect does this choice have upon the broader implications of his manifest argument, that the development of the sciences depended upon the personal dedication of scientists and scholars within an increasingly impersonal and fragmented institutional environment?

Two substantive issues need to be clarified if we are to provide some kind of adequate response to these questions. First, some understanding of the development of the German and American university systems is called for, so that we might establish the nature of Weber's perspective upon them – which elements he sought to emphasize, which elements he neglected. Secondly, once the nature of Weber's contemporary understanding of these systems is clearer, we can turn to consider Weber's own engagement with educational policy and the university. This in fact reaches back to the mid-1890s, while his interest in the American system seems to have first been prompted during his visit to the United States in 1904. Between 1908 and 1912 there are 29 items listed in Martin Riesebrodt's bibliography of Weber's writings[3] devoted to various aspects of university policy, and consisting chiefly of newspaper articles and conference contributions. An early outline of his analysis of the American university system can be found in a contribution to discussion at the Conference of German University Teachers in 1911; in this limited sense, then, the comparison of German and American universities made in 'Science as a Vocation' was nothing new. However, the use which Weber made in 1917 of the contrast between German and American universities differed from that made in 1911. An examination of the circumstances in which arguments regarding the nature of purpose of modern universities were first expressed should cast fresh light upon more familiar aspects of Weber's concerns.[4]

The various newspaper articles and conference contributions of Weber in the period 1890–1912 focus on two aspects of the contemporary German university system: the Althoff System, and the manner in which students of the new commercial colleges were aping the worst aspects of the university student fraternities, the *Burschenschaften*. The more general issues thereby raised were, respectively: the power of patronage in making appointments to professorial positions; and the treatment of educational institutions as means for the acquisition of social status, rather than for the transmission and development of knowledge. Weber had personal experience of both. He had been brought up in a political household in the Prussian city of Berlin, but spent the entirety of his professional life working outside Prussia and beyond the reach of its Ministry of Culture and the patronage that it had first offered him; and while a young student in Heidelberg in the early 1880s he had been a member of a fraternity, drinking large quantities of beer and gaining the obligatory duelling scar, a scar which earned him a clip round the ear from his mother and which was later concealed by his beard.[5]

Friedrich Althoff was the Prussian Minister of Culture, using to the full his power to influence appointments to Prussian universities. Weber had come to his attention in the early 1890s, and indications were made that, if Weber were agreeable, an appointment to a chair in law at the University of Berlin would be possible. The talk was of a chair in commercial law, but Weber did not want the kind of patronage that would dictate the shaping of his career. Instead, when in July 1893 a chair of economics was offered to him at the University of Freiburg in Baden, Weber accepted. Althoff immediately intervened, and informed the

Baden Ministry directly that Weber had a brilliant legal career in front of him and would only use the Freiburg appointment as a springboard from which he could start an academic career. This spoiling manoeuvre caused the round of negotiations to falter, until in January 1894 the Freiburg faculty drew up another list, once more placing Weber first out of three candidates.[6] Weber accepted once again in April, and moved to Baden in the autumn of 1894. He taught here until moving, in the summer of 1897, to the University of Heidelberg, likewise in the state of Baden, where he taught economics until his nervous collapse in May 1898, after which he continued with only occasional teaching duties to 1903, when he finally resigned his Heidelberg chair.

The university system within which Weber worked was organized along lines not dissimilar in structure to those prevailing in Germany today. The university was a state institution under the control of the relevant state ministry,[7] and not governed, as in Britain, by its own professors and administrators in conjunction with a Court and a Council. Senior appointments were therefore made only on the recommendation of a faculty through the presentation of a ranked list to their ministerial rulers; no independent right of appointment existed, the ministry reserving for itself in addition the right to alter a proposed ranking of candidates. The university as a whole, together with its full professors, was financed out of a state educational budget just like the local schools and colleges, with only a small contribution being made to costs by student fees. Students with the appropriate school-leaving certificate were free to register by the semester wherever they chose, paying a tuition fee and following specific lecture courses, sitting their final examination where and when they chose. This final examination qualified them for entry into their chosen profession. Full 'ordinary' professors constituted an academic core of paid state employees who, once appointed to a post, were expected to teach the full range of material associated with that post. They were assisted in this by 'extraordinary' professors – aspirants who were in some cases paid, but in all cases possessed doctorates and in addition had successfully passed their *Habilitation*, which was a condition of appointment to an ordinary professorship. Tutoring and occasional lecturing were carried out by those on the lowest rung of this ladder, the *Privat-Dozenten*, unpaid assistants qualified to teach by possession of a postdoctoral qualification, but who lived on tutoring fees.

Weber was aware that this division of responsibility for teaching and research was undergoing change. In 1908 an article reviewing the situation in various disciplines was published in the journal edited by Weber, the *Archiv für Sozialwissenschaft und Sozialpolitik*, and this seems to have drawn Weber's attention to emergent problems in some disciplines with regard to the future succession to professorial posts – in medicine and the natural sciences for example there was a significant surplus of eligible candidates, while in law there was a deficit, raising the issue of how such discrepancies might be best dealt with. The author, Eulenburg, argued on the basis of his data that the traditional three-tiered distinction, representing distinct stages in the academic career and reflecting different degrees of commitment to the university and hence the state, had become reduced to two tiers. There was no longer any effective distinction between the *Privat-Dozent* and the extraordinary professor, attenuating the graduations of academic status in the formation of the senior professoriate, and sharpening the distinction between the paid, state-employed core of full professors, and the unpaid fringe of aspirants who were the source of new research and the pool from which new professors would be drawn.[8] The problem here was that while the scholarly activity of these aspirants was free of state direction, only those who conformed were likely to find themselves assimilated into the Professoriate. The developments outlined by Eulenburg carried therefore implications for the vitality of the research ethos, and for the quality of the future professoriate.

The German universities were ancient foundations, with some exceptions such as the universities of Halle and Göttingen. These were 'new' universities of the late seventeenth and early eighteenth centuries respectively, while the University of Strasburg, had been founded as part of the educational incorporation of Alsace, following the victory over France in 1870. All these institutions had been based upon the four faculties of theology, medicine, law and philosophy, in which the last was chiefly responsible for preliminary teaching of students passing on to other studies. Although the number of students in each faculty varied from university to university, so that the relative importance of each faculty differed, it was expected that a flourishing university would maintain capable professors in each of the four faculties. The classical role of the university was therefore the training of lawyers, doctors and priests, the primary professions of early modern Europe. This was not dissimilar in principle to the prevailing situation in England, where Oxford and Cambridge were until late in the nineteenth century chiefly concerned with the training of an Anglican clergy.

Teaching was by lecture, complemented by the private study of the student. There was therefore little direct contact between students and teachers. This was altered in the early nineteenth century by the addition of the seminar – an institution in which professors and advanced students met on a regular basis, and which provided a forum for the training of doctoral students. The development of the seminar was prompted by the need on the part of the Professoriate to build research teams, and the complementary need on the part of the students to gain supervision and patronage from professors who would then, once their work was completed, possibly assist them in the development of their careers. This introduced a clear distinction between the *Brotstudenten*, those students concerned only with completing the minimum work necessary to pass the examinations needed for a professional career; and students who sought an academic training and thus embraced the research ethos embodied in the seminar. In the humanities and the natural sciences the development of the seminar and the research laboratory was perceived internationally to be the chief merit of the German university, although as far as the Germans themselves were concerned the primary function remained that of professional training.

In this system, it was usual for the more academically oriented students to move from university to university, studying under different professors until they were ready to sit their final examinations, in the process taking advantage of studying with the most eminent names in the field. It was important that universities appointed full professors of reputation – for this was one of the factors that attracted numbers of good students. Such students as took advantage of this opportunity also required the resources to study at two or three universities before sitting their state examinations, placing a natural financial constraint on this academic path to a university education. Since entry into a professional occupation was exclusively via university qualification, any prospective lawyer or doctor or teacher had to possess the relevant university qualification, although in this case the vocational path did not necessarily require movement between universities on the part of students. In general, the importance of the linkage between qualification and professional grouping meant that the university structure as a whole had to move in step with the dynamics of the labour market, producing enough students of the right kind and with an appropriate academic education. From the later 1890s a steadily increasing proportion of qualified school-leavers went on to attend university, creating pressures within the university system and raising questions about the likely long-term effects on the labour market. One response to an increased demand for vocational qualifications was the foundation of the business colleges, beginning with a joint venture between Leipzig university and the Leipzig Commercial College in 1898. This was quickly followed by new, independent colleges in Cologne, Frankfurt and Berlin, all of which conferred a diploma on their graduates after two years' study. Initially, the intake to these new colleges was a mixture of *Abiturienten* (qualified school-leavers) and qualified apprentices; by 1920, however, they were recruiting almost entirely from the pool of qualified school-leavers, and the introduction of an economics diploma into universities in 1923 was part of a convergence between the new, independent colleges and the existing university system.

The American university system was, by contrast, not originally developed as a means of training doctors and lawyers. The small colleges that existed before the Civil War taught a curriculum founded almost exclusively on classics and mathematics, and possessed no research function at all. In post-bellum America this became perceived as a national problem, for educational institutions had an important part to play in the modernization and development of the United States. Private and state funds became available for the foundation of new universities and colleges; the existing colleges likewise entered a period of significant expansion. One major feature of this process was a desire to model the development of the university system on that of Germany, by which the Americans meant an institution of higher learning and research, not a professional school. While more than adequate financial resources for this development were available, the existing college system could not by itself generate the intellectual and organizational base necessary for the creation of a modern university system. Consequently, during the 1870s a growing stream of students travelled to German universities to study at an advanced level and gain in this way the intellectual qualifications for appointment to positions in the new American universities.[9] The experience that such students gained of the German system was naturally focused on the seminar and research laboratory, ignoring the role of professional training, which was of little relevance to them. In this way German universities provided graduate training for a whole generation of American scholars and scientists, whose own experience of the German university was heavily weighted towards its research activities. Germany had provided the only practical and imitable institutional form of higher learning; 'European' standards meant German standards, but in adopting them individually and institutionally Americans themselves contributed not a little to the identification of a 'German' model as the foundation for modern university organization. Colleges in the United States disseminated a general education by classical means; they were not part of a system of vocational education, and there was consequently no direct link between certification and employment, as in the German system. The 'German' model as the exemplar of the modern university therefore came, for the Americans, to focus on its research, rather than its training functions. European universities, fewer in number than in America, and of a higher average academic standard, embraced an educational philosophy which emphasized the symbiotic relationship between teaching and research. However, the greater degree of qualitative variance in the American system promoted the development of elite institutions in which research tended to have a higher priority than was customary among their European counterparts. Significant national variations were thereby introduced into what was understood as the 'German' model for the modern university, and an appreciation of this variation in perception of the nature of the modern university is important to our understanding of Weber's points about specialization, and the problem of securing an intellectual environment in which knowledge of all kinds can be advanced.

The classical curriculum of American colleges had been broken up by the introduction of the elective system of study, in which students were permitted to select those courses that would be best suited to their future needs. Cornell when it opened in 1868 offered instruction to any person in any subject; and in 1869 Harvard adopted the elective system. The propagation of this student-led form of instruction involved a renunciation of the traditional function of the college as a medium for the transmission of established knowledge, and the adoption of a culture directed towards the dissemination of specialized knowledge. This naturally had repercussions for the training and selection of teaching staff, since generalists were incapable of effectively developing specialized knowledge.

In responding to this, American universities adopted the PhD from Germany, but transformed it into a certification of specialization directed towards the reformed college teaching system, which was the primary market for graduates with higher qualifications.[10] In the German context the doctorate was as much a qualification within a staged career structure as it was a mark of academic achievement. This career culminated in the post of full professor, who would then be formally obliged to cover in his teaching whatever was laid down for the post which he represented. The German 'ordinary' professor was in a sense the personification of the field assigned to him, and was surrounded by apprentices and assistants to whom he could delegate specific areas of work. The American professor, on the other hand, emerged by the later nineteenth century as a member of a department that covered a discipline through the combination of the special-ities of its staff; junior members became senior members by the elaboration of their specialism.[11] By contrast, advancement in the German system presupposed that such specialization was at a severe discount. The discrepancy between Germany, where 'Professor' remains a title reserved for senior academics, and the United States, where all are professors of one sort or another, reflects a genuine difference in the organization of knowledge, and not simply a dilution of academic rank.

The rapid pace of innovation in the United States towards the end of the nineteenth century was not without its problems. For one thing the proliferation of degrees had led to wide variations in quality, which began to cause concern during the 1890s. As a consequence of debate on these and related issues the Association of American Universities was founded in 1900 with the objective of introducing greater uniformity among PhD requirements, achieving foreign recognition of the American doctorate, and a general raising of standards among the weaker institutions. This organization quickly assumed the role of a national coordinating council for academic standards, establishing a framework within which institutions and the qualifications that they issued could be compared.

Mechanisms for the financing of universities and colleges likewise exerted a standardizing pressure. The first wave of post-bellum foundations were facili-tated by land grants and the gifts of wealthy individual benefactors who lent their names to the institutions they funded – Cornell, Vassar and Johns Hopkins are just three of the most well known today.[12] By the turn of the century, however, organized benefaction on the part of philanthropic foundations began to displace individual generosity. Chief among these were the General Education Board founded in 1902 with $1 million from Rockefeller, and the Carnegie Foundation for the Advancement of Teaching established with an endowment of $10 million in United States Steel Corporation bonds in 1903.[13] The Board instituted a programme aimed at improving the standard of American university education by selective aid, only those which were already well-funded receiving significant assistance. Then as now, wide variations in standards characterized the American university system; but at the turn of the century a new hierarchy was increasingly firmly established, at the top of which were to be found institutions of inter-national eminence. Tradition was no guarantee of supremacy; the leading institutions were those which had adopted the features of the modern university, and among such institutions were new foundations (such as Chicago) and old (such as Harvard). Nor did the distinction between private and state universities indicate the standing of an institution, since state universities were by definition recent foundations, whereas among the private foundations were both recent and old-established colleges. The benefactions of the General Education Board and of the Carnegie Foundation were blind to the state/private distinction, funds being directed to any qualifying institution, no matter what its status. The growth and increasing differentiation of the American university system in the early part of this century was not characterized by any clear distinction between state and private universities – constraints and objectives were common to both.

Some of the consequences of these developments were discussed by Veblen in a work which, like Weber's 'Science as a Vocation', analyses the university as a capitalist enterprise. Originally drafted in 1904 as a response to developments in the University of Chicago, *The Higher Learning in America* finally appeared in 1918 and presented an indictment of the subversion of learning by business ethics, based upon a firm belief in the centrality of research as the *raison d'être* of the modern university. Veblen defined the objective of the university as the quest for knowledge – in fact a very modern definition and, as argued above, not one that coincided with the established features of German and English universities. The primary, central purpose of a university was the advancement of knowledge, Veblen argued; such instruction as was given should be compatible with this objective, and not interfere in any way with its realization:

> Training for other purposes is necessarily of a different kind and is best done elsewhere; and it does not become university work by calling it so and imposing its burden on the men and equipment whose only concern should be the higher learning.
>
> The lower schools (including the professional schools) are, in the ideal scheme, designed to fit the incoming generation for civil life; they are therefore occupied with instilling such knowledge and habits as will make their pupils fit citizens of the world in whatever position in the fabric of workday life they may fall. The university on the other hand is specialized to fit men for a life of science and scholarship; and it is accordingly concerned with such discipline only as will give efficiency in the pursuit of knowledge and fit its students for the increase and diffusion of knowledge.[14]

The management of American universities had recently shifted from the clergy to a laity composed chiefly of politicians and business, argued Veblen; and the latter naturally viewed the university as a form of business in which investment had to be made and turnover assessed. The 'Captains of Erudition', the new heads of these institutions, were increasingly obliged to exercise a capacity for business in their management of the institutions in their charge, treating faculty members as paid employees hired to produce the business's product.[15] The general prestige of an institution governed by such principles meant prestige with the laity, not with the scholarly classes. This makes it easier to pass off as erudition that which would not pass the scrutiny of scholars. Veblen goes on:

> Competitive business concerns that find it needful to commend themselves to

a large and credulous body of customers, as, e.g., newspapers or department stores, also find it expedient somewhat to overstate their facilities for meeting all needs, as also to overstate the measure of success which they actually enjoy.[16]

When combined with the sound business principle that it is bad policy to offer better quality than that which is demanded, 'particularly to customers who do not know the difference', departments are prevented from confining their activities to what they do best. The business ethos, and the application of business principles to the modern university, results, according to Veblen, in a diversion of university activity from its central purpose – the promotion of learning and scholarship – and towards a diffuse involvement in recreational activities of uncertain quality.

Veblen's analysis of the American university system was formulated at almost exactly the same time that Weber was developing his critique of the German system. In fact, as we shall see, there is much in Veblen's analysis of the American system that coincides with Weber's own discussion of German conditions – the increasing domination of commercial interests, and the dilution of the purpose of the university within a system more concerned with status than scholarship. Weber's position, like that of Veblen, is not a simple expression of conservatism: Veblen was defending the modernizing aspiration of the university against tendencies that conspired to undermine it, while Weber had from the first shown a great interest in public education and its development. In the mid-1890s he had participated in several popular educational initiatives, one of which involved the presentation of a course of lectures in a programme that was to provide the inspiration for the foundation of the Mannheim Business College in 1907.

Weber's later hostility to the business colleges turned on the manner in which their student body increasingly aped the less desirable qualities of their university counterparts. He was not opposed to the colleges in principle, and soon after his appointment to Heidelberg he delivered a course of lectures in Mannheim. The course was presented during the winter of 1897–8 at the invitation of the local Chamber of Commerce, and the four lectures were given the general title 'The Course of Economic Development'. As can be seen from the themes of the individual lectures,[17] the purpose was to provide a general introduction to economic history, placing the structures of the capitalist economy in the context of earlier systems of economic organization. The numbers attending these lectures surprised the organizers, and they quickly followed up with another course on trade policy, delivered this time by Schulze-Gävernitz, Weber's former colleague in Freiburg. These lectures were intended by the organizers for 'businessmen and industrialists, and those of their older employees in possession of the requisite general education; they are to be continued in a systematic manner next year.'[18]

Three separate lecture courses were accordingly presented during the winter months of 1898–9: the first on railways and railway rates; then in early 1899 a course on the stock exchange, Weber's own speciality, delivered by Gothein,[19] who in 1903 was to be Weber's successor at Heidelberg, and who had also recently been closely involved in the creation of the Cologne Business College; and a third on commercial law, given by a local lawyer. The Chamber sought to institutionalize these lectures but encountered difficulty in finding suitable speakers; this prompted them to petition the Baden government requesting the establishment of a second chair in political economy in Heidelberg (alongside the one occupied by Weber), it being made conditional upon both Heidelberg incumbents to regularly deliver fifteen lectures during the winter months in Mannheim. The second chair was indeed established, but no direct link was made with Mannheim until the arrival of Gothein in 1903, who was able, on the basis of his recent experience in Cologne, to advise those in Mannheim planning the creation of a local business college.

Weber had therefore both direct and indirect connections with the local movement for business education, which in the light of his other engagements in the service of popular education during the 1890s was unremarkable. There are reasonable grounds for supposing that, if it had not been for his illness and subsequent retirement in 1903, he could well have played a more central role in the business college movement, especially as his colleague on the *Archiv für Sozialwissenschaft*, Werner Sombart, was appointed Professor of Economics at the Berlin Business College in 1907, moving only later to a chair in the University of Berlin. As it was, Weber's engagement in academic politics during the years 1908–11 was from the outside, writing articles in newspapers and making speeches at Congresses. What then engaged his attention?

In 1908 Weber published six pieces on academic freedom in daily newspapers. The first two addressed issues raised by the so-called Bernhard Affair, the appointment of a young 'operator' (as Weber called him) to a chair of economics at the University of Berlin. This was at the insistence of Althoff, and in the absence of any consultation with the Berlin faculty involved. What Weber chose to emphasize in the affair was the manner in which Bernhard deemed it unnecessary to seek the confidence of his new colleagues. He was, as Weber said, a 'compliant mediocrity', a new type of academic that was on the rise and of which there were now many in Berlin. Since the appointment of mediocrities to positions of prominence led to their appointing newer mediocrities in their turn, argued Weber, the die was cast for the decline of Berlin as a centre of scholarship. This would benefit those universities in the provinces who chose not to go down this route, since eminent scholars and scientists would choose to build their careers there.[20]

The line of attack on university politics was altered in the autumn of the same year, in remarks made in connection with the second meeting of the Conference of University Teachers, whose theme was academic freedom. Here Weber highlighted the manner in which Michels had been informed that he would not be admitted for the second degree of *Habilitation* (enabling him to put himself forward for a professorship), on grounds of his political activities (he was a

Social Democrat) and also on account of his 'disordered domestic relations' – he had not permitted his children to be baptized and so, it had been said, he was not capable of assuming a position of academic authority. Weber concluded from this that 'freedom of science' (*Lehrfreiheit*) in German universities, a condition widely associated with the achievements of German scholarship and sciences, went only as far as that which happened to be politically acceptable at the time. Academic freedom was freedom to do anything, so long as it did not offend the authorities.[21]

Another aspect of this was raised in a series of three articles which took as their point of departure the nature of the freedom of expression enjoyed by professors in their lectures. Schmoller had successfully sued a student who had publicized remarks made in the course of a lecture, which were privileged and not intended for the public. This privilege was constrained by the requirement that a professor should be loyal to the state, i.e. he should be obedient and disinclined to use his office as a vehicle for any kind of criticism. On the other hand, the professor was free to say anything he pleased that did not impinge on his loyalty to the state.[22] The result of this was as follows:

> The fact that teaching, especially at a high level, has become a matter of state business, is the product of a quite specific cultural development – on the one hand the result of a process of secularization, on the other the centuries-long severe poverty of the nation which ruled out the emergence of those powerful private foundations upon which so many excellent universities are based in Anglo-Saxon lands. Today this development is for us a fact which we must confront, and to whose account . . . should be placed significant positive values, for the extent to which material means have been made available is such that they could only have been provided by the state. Nonetheless, this does not answer the question of the manner in which we should evaluate this development of the material foundations of our university structures in the totality of their effects.[23]

The implication of this relationship between state and university was a definite limitation of academic freedom, although in itself university teaching should be neither for nor against the state – universities are not institutions concerned with the propagation of beliefs, argued Weber, they are there to analyse facts and real conditions.

These and related remarks were directed to the capacity of the German university as an institution in which the condition of scientific and educational progress – academic freedom to research and to teach, free from official proscription and direction – could be developed. It is perhaps no accident that the problem emerged at this time,[24] when the foundation of the Second German Empire had passed into an established fact and the internal tensions and uncertainties of the subsequent Wilhelmine era were growing. In 1911, addressing the Conference of University Teachers, Weber took as his theme a comparison of American and German universities; but this mainly turned out to be an excuse to launch an attack on the business colleges which focused attention on the function of these colleges in the status system of modern Germany.

Weber had already made remarks in passing some years before, to the effect that the new institutions did not serve in the first instance a demand for knowledge, but rather a demand for participation in the status of university education. This remained his general position right through to 1919, at the time of the upgrading of the Cologne Business College to the University of Cologne, a development of which he evidently disapproved.[25] His manifest objective in 1911 was to compare German university administration with that governing the American system, but he also moved on to make some general remarks about student society and life. His argument was here made more difficult by the fact that, as he recognized, American student fraternities bore a striking resemblance to their German counterparts, limiting the utility of a comparison between the two systems. Nevertheless, the principal section of his address was directed to his own experiences of the 1890s in relation to Althoff, and the nature of the independence within the German university system conveyed by the state-based system of financial support. Whereas the American system was quite differentiated and competition between institutions derived from the quite major differences that could thereby arise, the principal differentiating element in the German system was that of the state supporting particular institutions. Saxony and Baden were singled out for praise in their pursuit of an enlightened and disengaged policy, whereas Prussian universities all bore the stamp of state administration. Moreover, the predominance of Prussia within the new Germany had lent the university system the form of a cartel – just like the German railway system, noted Weber – in which Prussia determined the general course of development that all would take. The scope for real competition between universities in Germany was therefore more restricted than would at first sight appear.[26]

Reaction to his remarks was first directed against the disparaging comments on Althoff, but soon Weber found himself picked upon by leading representatives of the business colleges, who vehemently denied that student fraternities of the kind Weber was criticizing existed. As it happened, there was a fraternity, albeit not officially recognized, in Berlin,[27] and the plans for the new Cologne Business College included a duelling room. Weber's comments were well founded, in fact, although the phenomenon that he selected was quite peripheral to the general development of the business colleges. The hysterical tone of some of the attacks on Weber did not assist clarification on this, and Weber had to make repeated statements in the press, finally composing an explanatory statement on the business college question not intended for publication.[28] As a consequence, the comparison of German with American universities was diverted first into a somewhat personalized attack on Althoff, and then into a peripheral aspect of the business school movement, which in turn provoked a lengthy and fruitless exchange with some of its proponents.

When in 1917 Weber returned to the comparison of German and American universities he managed to avoid becoming ensnared in the way that he had been in 1911. In dealing with the American universities, he once more laid emphasis on the competition between institutions and the independence that this gave them. Seen in the light of his comments on the Althoff System, it becomes clearer that he viewed the German system as centrally controlled – Prussian control, in effect, since in Germany Berlin occupied a leading role in cultural politics. There were, as noted above, some features of the German university system which would prompt provincial universities to seek out the best candidates when making appointments; but this was overlaid by the power of the state and the inherent conservatism embodied in the German version of academic freedom exposed by Weber. American universities, by contrast, competed vigorously with each other; although they might in themselves contain bureaucratic elements, the lack of a direct relationship between university and state bureaucracy, and between student career and qualification, were major advantages. When combined with the autonomy lent academics by the departmental system of disciplinary specialization, such that responsibility for academic decision-making lay with academic specialists, the American system of university education and research based on a competitive, dispersed foundation was less constrained than the German system as it entered the twentieth century.

None the less, it is striking that the initial sections of 'Science as a Vocation' relate most closely to the American emphasis on the research university, rather than on the more numerous institutions where a form of general education was the basis of the curriculum. It is here that we might once again note the convergence with Veblen, who likewise treated the modern university strictly defined as an institution dedicated to the research ethos, but which also taught – a strictly American view at that time. It therefore made a great deal of sense for Weber to frame his discussion of the future of science and scholarship in terms of the structure of the American university. Veblen argued that the colonization of the research university – a creature barely two decades old at the time he originally wrote – by the business ethos threatened its survival as an institution capable of extending scientific knowledge, and so much of his account focuses on the more negative aspects of the American universities. Both Veblen and Weber, of course, make use of the metaphor of the factory, the new capitalist enterprise which is also, at exactly this time, achieving its definitive twentieth-century form. The modern corporation, as charted in the works of Alfred Chandler, overcame the problems of size and control, and developed structures which, over the following thirty or forty years, permitted organizations to reap the advantages of scale without losing their ability to adjust or innovate. A similar adaptive response is evident in university systems, confronted with sometimes conflicting pressures, but where research and scholarship at worst co-existed with the demands of teaching.

It is ironic, of course, that at the end of the century the terminology of business organization should be introduced into public policy on higher education, authoritatively recapitulating those very assumptions concerning the objectives of university education that Veblen's businessmen had made at the beginning of the century. But the manner in which Weber poses his question – what is to become of science and scholarship in a modern university whose characteristics are increasingly those of a business enterprise? – is perhaps even more open now than it ever has been. We cannot expect to find in the writings and concerns of Max Weber a solution to present dilemmas; but what we can discover there are well-posed questions, and insights into structural features and constraints. Such insights and questions are notably absent in current educational policy-making; at the very least, they could help us formulate a new conception of the role of education, research and scholarship that relied neither on a narrow elitism, nor on the blind and bureaucratic imposition of a management rhetoric derived from an obsolete model of American industrial organization.

NOTES

1 Delivered on 28 January 1919 – see W. Schluchter, 'Wertfreiheit und Verantwortungsethik. Zum Verhältnis von Wissenschaft und Politik bei Max Weber', in his *Rationalismus der Weltbeherrschung*, Suhrkamp Verlag, Frankfurt am Main, 1980, p. 238.

2 See the account in W. Hennis, *Max Weber. Essays in Reconstruction*, Allen and Unwin, London 1988, pp. 70–1.

3 As printed in the prospectus to the *Max Weber Gesamtausgabe*, J.C.B. Mohr (Paul Siebeck), Tübingen, 1981.

4 Wilhelm Hennis has discussed some of this material in his article, 'The Pitiless "Sobriety of Judgement": Max Weber between Carl Menger and Gustav von Schmoller – The Academic Politics of Value Freedom', *History of the Human Sciences* 4 (1991) pp. 39–48. His object is however to expose the meaning of 'value freedom', rather than evaluate the manner in which Weber assesses university institutions.

5 See the account in H.N. Fügen, *Max Weber*, Rowohlt, Reinbeck bei Hamburg, 1985, pp. 31–2.

6 The details of the Freiburg appointment can be found in F. Biesenbach, *'Die Entwicklung der Nationalökonomie an der Universität Freiburg i.Br. 1768–1896'*, Dissertation, University of Freiburg, 1968, pp. 200–2.

7 That is, subordinated to the government of Prussia or Baden or Saxony, rather than to the central government in Berlin.

8 F. Eulenburg, 'Der "akademische Nachwuchs"', *Archiv für Sozialwissenschaft und Sozialpolitik,* 27, pp. 808–25.

9 It was not the international reputation of the Humboldtian university that drew American students, despite evident language barriers; but the fact that secular advanced study was not available at this time in England, and the French university system remained unreformed until the 1890s.

10 An account of the transformation of the college institution to a modern university can be found in R.L. Geiger, *To Advance Knowledge. The Growth of American Research Universities, 1900–1940*, Oxford University Press, New York, 1986. R.E. Kohler, 'The Ph.D. Machine. Building on the Collegiate Base', *Isis* 81 (1990), pp. 638–62 deals in detail with the role of the PhD qualification in this process.

11 J. Higham, 'The Matrix of Specialization', in A. Oleson and J. Voss, *The Organization of Knowledge in Modern America, 1860–1920*, Johns Hopkins University Press, Baltimore, 1979, pp. 11–12.

12 Others would be Brown University, named after Nicholas Brown; Clark University, after Jonas G. Clark; Duke University, after Washington Duke; and Stetson University, after John B. Stetson, hat manufacturer.
13 M. Curti and R. Nash, *Philanthropy in the Shaping of American Higher Education*, Rutgers University Press, New Brunswick NJ, 1965, pp. 212–20. Rockefeller allocated $118 million to the General Education Board between 1902 and 1920.
14 T. Veblen, *The Higher Learning in America. A Memorandum on the Conduct of Universities by Business Men* [1918], Augustus M. Kelley, New York, 1965, pp. 19–20.
15 Ibid., p. 92.
16 Ibid., p. 107.
17 The topics were as follows: (1) The emergence of private property and the agrarian foundation of the European economy; (2) Feudalism and urban economy in the Middle Ages; (3) The development of the economy and the mercantile system; (4) The historical position of modern capitalism. *Jahresbericht der Handelskammer für den Kreis Mannheim für das Jahr 1897 T.1*, Verlag der Handelskammer für den Kreis Mannheim, 1897, p. 153.
18 Ibid.
19 *Jahresbericht der Handelskammer für den Kreis Mannheim für das Jahr 1898 T.1*, Verlag der Handelskammer für den Kreis Mannheim, 1899, p. 179.
20 M. Weber, 'The Bernhard Affair', *Minerva*, 11 (1973) pp. 575–6. This has been reprinted, together with related articles by Weber on academic politics, in E.Shils (ed.) *Max Weber on Universities*, University of Chicago Press, Chicago, 1974.
21 'The Alleged "Academic Freedom" of the German Universities', *Minerva*, 11 (1973) pp. 586–7.
22 'Die Lehrfreiheit der Universitäten', *Saale-Zeitung*, 553 (25 November 1908) p. 1.
23 'Die Lehrfreiheit der Universitäten II.', *Saale-Zeitung*, 554 (25 November 1908) p. 1.
24 In the 1830s for example the Brothers Grimm had been part of the Göttingen Seven, who were dismissed from their posts for their liberal views; the conception of academic freedom articulated by Weber is not, once more, one related to an ancient freedom, but is closely associated with his view of the modern university as an institution combining teaching with research, a form of modern apprenticeship in scientific reasoning and development.
25 In a general attack on the aspiration to status among the German middle classes Weber noted in the 'Agrarstatische und sozialpolitische Betrachtungen zur Fideikomirβage in Preußen', *Archiv für Sozialwissenschaft und Sozialpolitik*, 19 (1904) p. 572 fn.1, that the *Handelshochschulen* were becoming simply a means of advancement – see A. Hayashima, 'Max Weber und die deutschen Handelshochschulen', *Kwansei Gakuin University Annual Studies*, 35 (1986) p. 146.
26 'American and German Universities', *Minerva*, 11 (1973) p. 596. In fact for this reason Weber might have been led to support the business colleges, none of which were directly under state control; but he never commented on this aspect of their organization, concentrating instead on a minor issue, that of student fraternities.
27 See A. Hayashima, 'Die deutschen Handelshochschulen und ihre Kritiker', in *Zur Geschichte der ökonomischen Lehre und Forschung in Berlin*, Wissenschaftliche Schriftenreihe der Humboldt-Universität zu Berlin, Berlin, 1987, pp. 136–48.
28 Reprinted in Hayashima, 'Max Weber und die deutschen Handelshochschulen', pp. 168–72.

Chapter 7

Max Weber and the dilemmas of modernity

Larry J. Ray and Michael Reed

This chapter is concerned with the intersections between debates about 'post-bureaucratic' styles of organization; interpretations of Weber's sociology; and more generally, assessments about the 'fate' of modernity. This latter concern locates the discussion within the framework of the Weberian legacy, even if the analysis draws in addition on more recent sources (notably Habermas, 1984 and 1989). Issues of bureaucracy, rationality, resistance and democratization are explored with reference first, to the crisis of communist bureaucratic regimes, and secondly to the debate about post-Fordist flexible specialization. We argue that despite their divergent natures, the unravelling of two systems of control, state socialism in the 'east' and Fordist accumulation in the 'west', illustrate some general themes concerning the limits of organizational performance. In the case of state socialist systems, bureaucratic management paradoxically generated its opposite, in the form of de-bureaucratized informal social spaces, in the 'second society'. We suggest, however, that these were not aberrations, but on the contrary were required by the system in order to continue functioning at all. In a different way, the crisis of Fordism encountered limitations of hyper-differentiation which prompted a reversion to 'earlier' modes of integration that had none the less adapted to an era of high technology (e.g. the electronic cottage). Thus both transformations illustrate how bureaucratic organization encounters limitations of complexity, the management of which leads towards new forms of flexibility, de-centralization and horizontal integration.

To what extent do these new forms of integration run counter to Weber's analysis of the dynamics of bureaucratization? In part, the answer to this question depends upon which aspects of Weber's writing are being emphasized. Certainly recent developments call into question the ubiquity and inevitability of the classical 'iron cage' thesis, although, as several foregoing chapters indicate, a more nuanced reading of Weber's rationalization thesis is possible. It is often assumed that the state socialist bureaucracies for example, represented the epitome of rationalization, although one could argue on the contrary that these were in many ways highly un-Weberian systems, and that attempts to convert the Party's rule into a *Rechtstaat* was a catalyst for their disintegration. If this was the case, then formal rationalization might erode rather than consolidate bureaucratic power, and it might be possible to identify, alongside the iron cage, an emancipatory potential within rationalization. Further, perhaps there is an *ambiguity* in the world-historical process of rationalization, opening up alternative possibilities for the emergence of organizational forms, and those described by Weber might represent only one of a number of possible constellations.

It would be naive, however, to assume that the crisis of either Fordism or of state socialism was about to lead unproblematically to more rational, participatory organizational forms. On the contrary, transitions are dangerous and risk only partial completion or even reversion to earlier forms. Moreover, a crucial question is whether the fragmentation of vertically integrated organizational forms does indicate an incipient democratization of social life, or on the contrary the birth of more sophisticated technologies of control? This possibility is considered with reference to debates about the significance of flexible specialization and its potential to create new types of work organization. Towards the end of the chapter two possible outcomes of ongoing restructuring of organizational forms are elaborated in terms of 'participatory' and 'repressive' modernity. It is argued that both potentialities can be recovered from Weber, which lends his sociology a particular pertinence amidst a play of promise and danger across the world stage.

REREADING WEBER

We claim in this section that it is possible to read Weber in a way that suggests a more open and nuanced conception of rationality and modernity than that implied by accounts focusing on the iron cage.[1] Of course, there are already many readings of Weber. Robert Merton took what he understood to be Weber's idealist explanation of the rise of capitalism as a model for his own idealist account of the effect of Puritanism on the rise of science. For Bendix and Roth, Weber was a political theorist and idealist historian; whilst for Gerth and Mills he was a kind of multi-dimensional Marxist. Talcott Parsons' Weber was the cornerstone of functionalism, although Jeffrey Alexander has recently construed him as a multi-dimensional Parsonian. Schluchter, in company with Eisenstadt has read Weber as the evolutionist of world-historical rationalization. Again, there is Weber the methodological individualist, the relativist (Sprinzak, 1972), the phenomenologist (Schutz 1972) and even postmodernist. There are 'left' and 'right' Weberians, and so on. Randall Collins (1985) comments that 'the ghost of Max Weber, torn limb from limb, has spread over the landscape and now is almost coextensive with the warring states of current sociology'.

Why then undertake yet another dissection of the Weberian corpse? A poor reason for doing this would be the hope that our claims about the current state of society might be accorded posthumous legitimacy by having been prefigured in the work of the founding father. Perhaps more justifiably though, it is worth explicating tensions in Weber's thought for at least two reasons. First, because Weber's analysis of rationalization, loss of meaning (*Sinnverlust*) and the process of cultural differentiation does still constitute a crucial starting point for theorizing modernity and organizations, which is indicated by the other chapters in this volume. Secondly, the development of a nuanced conception of rationality is an important counterweight to theorists (discussed below) who claim that we now encounter post-Weberian organizations in both the post-socialist and capitalist sectors of modernity. In the process we hope that this discussion will not simply dismember Weber's ghost even further, but will contribute to understanding the dilemmas confronted by the modern world.

The iron cage thesis, which has been influential both in analyses of bureaucratization and more global critiques of modernity, [2] elaborated Weber's famous claim that 'The future belongs to bureaucratization . . . [and] is distinguished from other historical agencies of the modern order of life in that it is far more persistent and "escape proof".' Again Weber says,

> [t]he performance of each individual worker is mathematically measured, each man becomes a little cog in the machine and aware of this, his one preoccupation is whether he can become a bigger cog . . . it is horrible to think that the world could one day be filled with these little cogs, little men clinging to little jobs, and striving towards bigger ones . . . . . this passion for bureaucracy is enough to drive one to despair.

(1978 II: 1401)

Weber discussed rational action in terms of the two well-known concepts of formal goal-rationality (*Zweckrationalität*) and substantive, value-rationality (*Wertrationalität*). He restricted the notion of rationality proper to matters of calculation, the corollary of which was the ultimate irrationality of all substantive values. Purposive rationality was institutionalized especially in economic and bureaucratic life, where it presupposed a shift from communal to associative social action, accompanied by calculability, authenticity and freedom from illusions. This disenchantment of everyday life, as is again well known, led to the erosion of ultimate systems of meaning, elaborated into his thesis of substantive meaning loss in modern society. Thus the dominant process of rationalization pointed towards the iron cage, which would be broken only by non-rational charismatic movements (and then only temporarily), an attitude known as 'technological-organizational fatality' (*Sachzwang*).

However, we are suggesting that the 'other Weber' actually counterpoised the iron age to the expansion of formal reason, and thereby implied that rationalization was a multi-dimensional process, even if he feared that purposive rationality (*Zweckrationalität*) would win out in the end. Even so, Weber did suggest that state bureaucracies might be constrained by an informed and active public and press, combined with rights of Parliamentary Inquiry on the British model (1978 II: 1416ff.). Perhaps formal rationality was not only an iron cage, but also opened up possibilities for the rational negotiation of values and beliefs in differentiated and post-traditional societies?

Formal-rational legitimation (rule through consent) was actually judged by

Weber to be more durable than *either* traditionalistic *or* instrumental types of domination, a claim which runs counter to the thesis that the future belongs to bureaucratization. For example,

> [a]n order which is adhered to from motives of pure expediency is generally less stable than one upheld on a purely customary basis through the fact that the corresponding behaviour has become habitual . . . But even this type of order is in turn much less stable than an order which enjoys the prestige of being considered binding, or as it may be expressed of 'legitimacy'.
>
> (Weber 1976: 125)

In other words, 'pure expediency' is a less stable basis for social integration than custom, but both are less stable than consensual legitimation. In this volume Stuart Clegg notes that, 'At the base of any bureaucracy are its members' beliefs in the legitimacy of its existence, its protocols, its personnel and its policies.' However, bureaucratic authority is not necessarily consensual rule. For one thing, the dominant symbol-systems within an organization are usually accepted, with anything beyond minimal commitment, predominantly by those in the higher authority positions (Giddens 1990: 147).[3] Weber himself acknowledged that bureaucratic rule was not based on consent so much as on habitual loyalties, since the bureaucratic order 'impinges on the masses from the outside', and 'merely replaces the belief in the sanctity of traditional norms by compliance with rationally determined rules and by the knowledge that these rules can be superseded by others, if one has the necessary power' (Weber 1978 II: 1117).[4]

This suggests that bureaucratic domination might not be as durable as it first seemed. Weber suggested that 'the masses' experience bureaucratic domination in a quasi-traditionalistic way. Yet he was well aware that rationalized conduct, such as acquisitive work routines, rational accounting or bureaucratic organiz-ation required anchorage in the values and practices of everyday life, and this surely was one of the central points of the *Protestant Ethic* essays. Further, the claim that the future belongs to bureaucracy, predicated upon centralization and monopolization of organizational power, actually ran counter to Weber's broader view of modernity in terms of increasing differentiation and fragmentation, as shown in Figure 7.1. Modernity was understood as a process of differentiation of society (legitimate orders through which participants regulate their membership of social groups), culture (the stock of knowledge from which actors derive interpretations), and personality (competences that permit actors to reach under-standing and thereby assert an identity). Each of these further differentiated according to categories of experience and spheres of knowledge – the cultural value spheres of science, law/morality and art; economy from society; capital from the state; and the separation of ethics, belief and practical activity.

If this analysis was correct then one might actually expect modernity to *defy* monistic systems of organization for at least two reasons. First, because the sheer complexity of differentiated social orders actually renders bureaucratic manage-ment inefficient and counterproductive when it attempts to coordinate diverse

SOCIETY

CAPITAL
Household separate from production
Capital accounting
Commodity
Scientific knowledge
STATE
Centralized tax system
Military
Monopoly of legal force
Bureaucracy

CULTURE

Modern science – rationalization
Autonomous art (subjectivity freed from conventions)
Radicalized salvation (split of inner/sacred from external/objective worlds)

PERSONALITY

Radical repudiation of magic
Isolation of believers
Methodical conduct of life (vocation)
This worldly orientation
Methodical rigour

Figure 7.1 Occidental rationalism

and autonomous spheres of action. Excessive control might be counterproductive for the survival of the system of domination since advanced economies need to 'generate a wealth of ideas, including technological ideas, [so] the system has to allow not only scientific theories and hypotheses, but also socially odd ideas, non-conformist art, questionable art, questionable economic theories and even dissident ideologies' (Toffler and Toffler 1985). Secondly, the post-traditional moral order, within which the authority of bureaucratic systems must be accepted, is uncertain and fluid precisely because of the erosion of the spell-binding power of sacred worldviews.

To put this another way, legitimacy, as consent to authority, implies the possibility of agreement/disagreement and therefore of argument about competing validity claims, so cannot therefore be reduced to quasi-traditionalistic belief in the sanctity of bureaucratic decisions. Indeed, it could be argued that already implicit in his concept of procedural rationality was the way out of the impasse of *Sinnverlust*. Formal-rationality could actually offer a solution to the core problem of modernity, that is, how to coordinate action in highly differentiated post-traditional societies that had to integrate complex and largely impersonal relationships, without recourse to sacred worldviews or other totalizing frameworks of meaning. In post-traditional societies each belief becomes a validity *claim* which subjects are obliged to address with recourse only to rational arguments, which take on an increasingly procedural, formal nature.

If this argument is valid, then one could accept Weberian premises about the direction of rationalization, without accepting the conclusion that *Sinnverlust* and the iron cage are inevitable. Within each differentiated sphere (society, culture, personality) actors can potentially pose validity questions which can be addressed via formal procedures of rational agreement. Weber himself did not take the analysis this far, although he did gesture in this direction by setting up the polarity between formal-legal democratization and bureaucratic domination. Both, after all, were products of universalistic morality and legality yet pointed in quite different directions. This implied at least the possibility of two different outcomes, the iron cage on the one hand, and the expansion of discursive rational legitimation on the other. Rather than assume that the impulse to bureaucratize inexorably follows the democratization of social organization (e.g. 1978 II: 1417ff.) Weber could have followed through the consequences of his highly differentiated model of modernity, and treated the expansion of conditions for agreement separately from the more narrow process of instrumental calculation.

Weber's sociology could have moved in three directions: (1) analysing social movements like democratic revolutions which sought to institutionalize formal rationality; (2) outlining a cultural sociology of the new, more rationalized contemporary order; (3) describing the institutionalization of one subtype of rational action (purposive rationality) into systems of markets and bureaucracies, and how these became dominant organizational forms. Habermas (1984 and 1989) suggests that Weber took up only the third possibility, concentrating on the origins of instrumental capitalism and bureaucracy.[5] However, by mistakenly identifying calculability as modernity *per se*, Weber saw newly autonomous spheres of modern culture (science, morality, art) as doomed to irrationality and loss of meaning, since they eluded the procedures of instrumental validation.

Habermas' rereading of Weber arguably extrapolates what Weber might have said had he pushed this analysis of rationalization further, and complements Weberian sociology with his reconstruction of speech act theory (universal pragmatics).[6] Habermas develops a significantly modified typology of social action (see Figure 7.2) which pulls in insights from symbolic interactionism and phenomenology. The central Weberian concept *Zweckrationalität*, the basis for the iron cage, appears here as a limited case within a complex typology of social

ACTION TYPE	PRESUPPOSES	ORIENTATION	CRITERIA
Teleological/ strategic	Social actor	Goal directed to anticipation of others' decisions	Success/failure
Normatively regulated	Social group	Common values Complying with a norm	Legitimacy/assent
Dramaturgical action	Public	Reflexive presentation of self	Sincerity
Communicative action	Inter-subjectivity	Reach understanding Negotiation	Consensus validity

Figure 7.2 Typology of social action

action. *Zweckrationalität* is limited in that it presupposes an isolated social agent whose behaviour is directed towards successful anticipation of other actors' decisions. On closer examination, teleological action presupposes a world of meanings known to actors through beliefs and interpretations, which can at any time be called into question in the course of social interaction. This means that strategically acting subjects must be cognitively equipped to appropriate both decision-making systems and normative frameworks through which actions are legitimized, which in turn implies a common cultural heritage through which actors recognize interpretations (Habermas 1984: 100).

This normatively regulated action is orientated towards shared values within which two questions are opened up: 'does a subject's action accord with existing norms?' and 'do existing norms embody values that deserve assent?' These raise further questions of normative legitimacy which in a post-traditional period can be resolved only through appeal to discursive argumentation. Further, social action is orientated towards a visible public via the reflexively monitored present-ation of self. This dramaturgical action deploys attributes of style and aesthetic expression which address a common cultural heritage. Again though, the appro-priateness and sincerity of self-presentation is subject to validity-testing ('do actors mean what they say or are they only feigning?') which suggests that rather than accord formal rules quasi-traditional status, actors regard them with an attitude of irony and detachment.[7]

By drawing attention to normative and dramaturgical dimensions of action, Habermas believes that he has found a way out of Weber's *Sinnverlust*, since actors' communications presuppose the possibility of rational agreement in a way which *implicitly* coordinates action. Hence, 'we are concerned here with recon-structing a voice of reason, which we cannot avoid using whether we want to or not when speaking in everyday communicative practice' (Habermas 1991: 244). This tacitly presupposed potential for rational discourse is reconstructed in the concept of communicative action, which takes each of the other three types (strategic, normative, dramaturgical) into account. Further, with the disintegration of sacred worldviews, the argumentative functions of language are progressively opened up and claims to legitimate authority subject to challenge. Entering into dialogue about the validity of utterances involves a specific type of discussion (*Diskurs*) oriented towards examining or 'redeeming' consensus, a practice which is infinitely reflexive in that participants can objectify any utterance and attempt to repair the interruption in dialogue (Habermas 1984: 28).[8]

Such practices will be successful only if we assume equality of access to speech acts and freedom to move from level to level in *Diskurs*, since it is only under such conditions that consensus could be motivated by the force of better argument. This enables Habermas to introduce the 'general symmetry requirement' (also called the 'ideal speech situation') which is the core of his communicative paradigm. That is, if a consensus is to be reached guided only by the force of better argument then, *whether we recognize it or not*, we routinely assume certain conditions. Namely, that everyone has an equal chance to deploy, initiate and perpetuate speech acts; utterances are comprehensible; their propositional content is true; what is said is legitimate and appropriate; and that it is sincerely spoken.

Habermas is as aware as anyone else that these conditions of communicative competence are counter-factual and rarely present in actual speech, but it is precisely this which justifies two further claims. First, that the hermeneutic goal of normal communication is disturbed by power relations which intrude to prevent questions being raised or validity claims being tested. Secondly, that these constraints on communication are self-defeating since they contradict the underlying assumptions that make discourse possible at all. From this it follows that rationality can be measured by the degree of openness or closure in communication and that the goals of truth, freedom and justice are not after all substantively irrational, but are anticipated in structures of ordinary language communication.[9]

According to this view, the Weberian vision of modernity dominated by bureaucracies and instrumentality represented a one-sided, jagged profile of modernization which can be contrasted with 'knowledge of structurally anchored developmental trends that run in opposite directions'. (Habermas 1991: 260). This bipolar model enables us to speak of dominant (strategic) and suppressed (communicative) modernities. The iron cage of bureaucratization is contrasted with the 'universalistic foundations of law and morality that have been also incorporated . . . into the institutions of constitutional government, into forms of democratic will formation and into patterns of identity formation' (Habermas 1989: 113). Weber did not deny this of course, although he regarded democratic institutions as weak by comparison with bureaucratic organizations. However, by separating two impulses within modernity – purposive rationalization and communicative rationalization – we can begin to locate the basis of vibrant resistance to bureaucratization. We will suggest that the extension of systems of money and bureaucratic power into lifeworld contexts (the process that appears metaphorically in Weber's notion of the 'iron cage') actually meets with resistance and is moreover, ultimately self-defeating. Our intention though is not to trade an 'optimistic' Habermas against a 'pessimistic' Weber but to examine the play of communicative structures and strategies of control.

Social movements are important here, as carriers of new organizational forms structured by the polarity of dominant and suppressed modernity. Struggles for participatory social organization then are struggles for the expansion of communicative possibilities, for the realization of a democratic tendency, already implicit in modern consciousness, perhaps in proto-organizational forms that are released during periods of crisis. However, depending on the strength of the core system of domination *vis-à-vis* an organized alternative, some loosening up of control, or even radical de-regulation might be consistent with the survival of the core system.[10] Thus more flexible forms of adaptation which harness new energies, such as cooperative work practices, combined with participatory flows of decision making, might amount to admitting sufficient flexibility to offload systemic crisis while leaving mezzo-level bureaucratic structures in place, only weakly constrained by public spheres.

This section has elaborated a multi-dimensional Weberian control model which is set out schematically in Figure 7.3. Here the iron cage (global bureaucratization and meaning loss) encounters resistance arising from problems of over-complexity and the need to secure agreement, rather than blind agreement for modern authority structures. Thus one outcome of the present is that the iron cage gives way to more fluid and reflexive organizational forms that permit democratic structures of participation, an outcome that was anticipated by Weber, even if it was not a dominant motif of his theory. An alternative possibility is that through this very process of fluidization the iron cage is restored, in that disarticulated modes of organization permit a deep penetration of instrumentality into everyday life, through which the core system is reproduced in a more 'flexible mode'. This case would confirm the gist, if not the detail of Weber's more pessimistic prognosis of future organizational forms. In the following two examples, these points will be elaborated.

POST-SOCIALISM AND THE 'POST-WEBERIAN' STATE

This and the following section assess whether the iron cage is collapsing from over-extension and metal fatigue and considers the implications this has for our understanding of Weberian theory. Some commentators have suggested that the collapse of communism provides evidence for the crisis of the Weberian control model. In this volume for example, Bryan Turner argues that 'Weber's fears about the stultifying consequences of bureaucratic regulation also appear to have borne fruit in the case of the virtual destruction of civil society . . . in Eastern

IRON CAGE	RESISTANCE
Global bureaucratization Meaning loss Erosion of democracy	Problems of over-complexity Failure of bureaucratic domination

FLUIDIZATION	IRON CAGE RESTORED
Disintegration of the iron cage Reflexive modernization Open structures of participation Representative modernization	Deep penetration of instrumentality Reproduction of the core system in a more 'flexible mode' Repressive modernization

Figure 7.3 Multi-dimensional Weberian control model

Europe'. Others have further suggested that the irrationality of communist systems revealed something important about bureaucratic domination *per se*, a view suggested by Vaclav Havel (1988). He regarded Soviet-type systems as 'inevitable consequences of rationalism' which had broken with *Naturwelt* and an immediate pre-rational empathy with nature, and warns the West to understand itself through its reflection in the communist world. Again, Zigmunt Bauman (1992a: 166–7) says that

> [l]ike socialism . . . communism was thoroughly modern in its passionate conviction that a good society can only be a carefully designed, managed and thoroughly industrialized society . . . Communism was modernity in its most determined mood and most decisive posture . . . purified of the last shred of the chaotic, the irrational, the spontaneous, the unpredictable.

Similarly Murray (1992) writes of 'Soviet Fordism' as an application (and exaggeration) of the organizational forms of capitalist Fordism – the synchronization of production flows, gigantic scale, and product standardization.[11] These arguments suggest that Soviet communism was the apogee of the iron cage, in which case the crisis of communism was indicative of a more general crisis of rationalized types of organization.

Other writers, however, suggest that the Soviet system was not a 'Weberian' bureaucracy,[12] and emphasize the extent to which it was politicized, collectivist, authoritarian, geared to a utopian futuristic goal, and based on cadre rather than public recruitment. Talcott Parsons (1973) contrasted these features, typical of a 'universalism-ascription' orientation, to the alleged 'universalism-achievement' orientation of Western societies. Further, a number of writers claim that by contrast with pluralist democracies Soviet-type societies represented a form of domination *sui generis*, where power was loosened from its capillary moorings to become an end in itself. Fehér, Heller and Márkus (1984) for example described the system as a 'dictatorship over needs', the goal-function of which is a new type of domination (*Zweck der Produktion*) pursued as an instrument of the corporate ruling group. Gross (1989) described the Soviet state as 'unique in modern history, devoted primarily to making sure that no other social force can get things done. It is, so to speak a spoiler state.'[13]

Which approach is correct? Were Soviet systems instances of the Weberian nightmare realized, of the 'bureaucratization of the world'? In answering this question it is useful to distinguish between structure and process. A snapshot of the Soviet system at any point between 1917 and 1991 would reveal features at variance with the Weberian model. However, its underlying trajectory was arguably one of increasing approximation to a formal-rational system, a process that came to a head with *glasnost* and *perestroika*. Paradoxically, however, rather than indicate increasing closure of an iron cage, this process was one of increasing pluralization in response to fermenting crisis, illustrating the problems encountered by a command bureaucracy attempting to regulate a complex society. These issues will be developed with reference to the following points. First, Soviet-type societies were in essence not formal-rational but rather estate bureaucratic systems, and consequently represented a partial rather than completed modernity. Second, the over-extension of bureaucratic systems into socio-cultural reproduction (the lifeworld) actually prompted and sustained re-traditionalized adaptive responses (such as the second society) upon which Soviet systems became dependent. Thirdly, one can detect an underlying tendency towards rationalization in Soviet-type societies perhaps going back to the 1950s, but the more their organization approximated formal-rational systems the less effective were the established methods of domination, and the greater the degree of reliance on other institutional orders. Fourthly, the rapidity of the collapse of Soviet-type societies and the consequent crisis throws into relief the divergence between popular expectations of participatory rationalization, and the ability of the core system to survive in a more flexible form, a process which is illustrated by 'nomenklatura privatization'.

What was the relationship between the Soviet-type societies and Weber's concept of a modern bureaucracy? It is well known that Weber placed socialism within the already powerful tendency towards bureaucratic domination, arguing that,

> [s]tate bureaucracy would rule alone if private capitalism were eliminated. The private and public bureaucracies, which now work next to, and potentially against, each other and hence check one another to a degree, would be merged into a single hierarchy. This would be similar to the situation in ancient Egypt, but it would occur in a much more rational –and hence unbreakable – form.
>
> (Weber 1978 II: 1402)

However, he also distinguished between two types of planned economies

(*Plannwirtschaft*) – one which was state-regulated but where investment and profitability decisions were still made according to market criteria; another where market mechanisms had been superseded through complete socialization of the means of production (1978 I: 110ff.).[14] In 1919 the latter type did not exist anywhere, but in hindsight, drawing on the experience of the Soviet model, it is apparent that this system differed from formal-rational bureaucracy in more than just its scale of operations, and in many respects was not a very 'Weberian' organization. Even so, one must be careful to distinguish the structure and self-reproduction of the system from its underlying trajectory.

The central mechanism of recruitment to the elite was the Party List (nomenklatura) which regulated appointments to all significant decision-making positions. In the 1920s–40s this created a politicized bureaucracy not unlike Weber's 'plebiscitary democracy' (*Führer Demokratie*), a form of routinized charisma where the leaders' personal staff were recruited from 'able people of humble origin', creating a cadre stratum economically dependent on the regime (1978, I: 270). Whereas in the modern bureaucracy Weber anticipated 'dominance of a spirit of formalistic impersonality: "*Sine ira et studio*" without hatred or passion' (1978, I: 225), the Stalinist apparatchik was expected to display both hatred and passion, to denounce class enemies, saboteurs, 'Trotskyites', 'Zinovievites' etc., enthusiastically endorse the party line, and mobilize subordinates to do the same. It is true that after the purge of the 'Red Directors' (1936–8) recruitment to managerial positions placed more stress on technical expertise, but proletarian or peasant class background, proven loyalty to the Party, and patronage remained necessary for recruitment and promotion (Hough, 1969).[15] Further, the *vydvizhentsy*, upwardly mobile technical graduates, were likely to be loyal, having been schooled in Stalinism and too young (most were under 35) to have had political affiliations prior to the Stalin period (Hough 1969: 38).

However, after Stalin the Soviet system began a transition of *longue durée* from a plebiscitary to more formalized bureaucracy, in a way Weber would have appreciated, having argued that 'the more bureaucratization advances and the more substantial the interests in benefices and other opportunities become, the more surely does the party organization fall into the hands of experts . . . As a rule the party organization easily succeeds in this castration of charisma' (1978 II: 1131–2). Indeed, after the end of Stalin's purges, when tenure became secure, nomenklatura office holders formed a self-perpetuating bureaucratic elite usually appointed for life, (Getty 1985; Fehér and Arato 1989). Enmeshed within a complex system of patronage they were granted a 'fiefdom' in the form of responsibility for an administrative sector (Voslensky 1984: 70).[16] However, despite a tendency towards hierarchical centralization (*edinonachalie*) and functional specificity with clearly defined competences, Soviet administration still eluded central features of the Weberian model. It retained dual, rather than monocratic, structures of authority emanating from the Party and the ministries, along with complex subdivisions that were reproduced at local, regional, national and union levels. By the 1960s local party organs, whom Jerry Hough likens to French prefects, had acquired considerable latitude to deal with local officials, enterprise managers and government departments, and were not tightly locked into a command-action hierarchy (Hough 1969).[17] This gave scope for discretion and a degree of flexibility, but also created the opportunity for the consolidation of sectional interests and local networks of corruption. Flaherty (1992) describes the post-Stalinist state as governed by sectoral negotiations, or spontaneous decentralization, where a 'hollowed out' plan increasingly reflected the demands of dominant sectors rather than central regulation of the economy. Concealment of productive capacity, inflated reports in return for a guaranteed share of allocation, informal connections at all levels, approximated the 'informal handshake' mentioned in the Introduction. In this system, despite formal separation from ownership of the means of administration, the line between disposal and ownership of resources became increasingly unclear as the nomenklatura became a distinct social stratum differentiated from other groups in Soviet society by their privileged access to consumption (Hill 1988; Hosking 1992: 294–5; Voslensky 1984).

This redistributive principle had implications for the range of variation that was possible in Soviet societies without challenging the reproductive capacities of the system. Our discussion of Weber and Habermas suggested that one of the central problems of modernity is coordinating anonymous complex interactions across differentiated value spheres. Yet an autarchic political entity, the Party, dominated and connected a set of semi-autarchic institutions such that there was no culture of impersonal measured action and little experience of impersonal procedures (Jowitt 1992). So long as Soviet-type societies could mobilize large populations through organizational charisma (such as the Stakhanovite movement) and pursue extensive economic development, annual growth was sustained.[18] But as Korosic (1988) argues, Soviet bureaucracies could accomplish only crude primitive accumulation based on labour mobilization, and were unable to develop functionally integrated economies of scale, confronted with which bureaucratic coordination was overloaded. Further, unlike the ideal-typical 'Weberian' bureaucracy, rule was not procedurally formalized but was rather 'control by exception', since regulations were departed from without formal revision (Fehér et al. 1984: 175; Staniszkis 1992: 11). Beneath the appearance of order (the rule of the Party, the planning mechanisms etc.) there was actually substantive disorder, manifest in systemic irrationalities, such as rising capital: growth ratios; excessive waste; and dependence on parallel circuits of the second economy.

So far then, Weberian theory has offered insights into the evolution of Soviet-type systems, but to understand the dynamics of post-Stalinism we need to deploy a more dialectical model which refers first, to the impact of system rationalization on the lifeworld, and secondly to the ways in which modes of lifeworld adaptation structure future outcomes. The transition to post-Stalinist control was driven by the routinization of charismatic mass mobilization and terror. However, post-Stalinist rule could have progressively abandoned the principles of the military-command economy, of *Zweck der Produktion*, and there *were* moves towards decentralization, local democracy, marketization and increased consumer production under Khrushchev, and later with the Kosygin–Agenbegyan–Lieberman reforms in the 1960s. However, eroding the mechanisms of central allocation might have threatened a system of stratification governed by privileged sectoral access to consumption of the accumulated surplus, and the reforms were short-lived (Fehér and Arato 1989). Unable radically to de-Stalinize, the system underwent a more limited, repressive rationalization in the form of Brezhnev's 'developed socialism'. This involved substantive legitimation through social security, income maintenance, housing subsidies, health and welfare (Márkus 1982).[19] The Brezhnev period saw the evolution of bureaucratic particularism or neo-patrimonial clientelism, that is, an essentially traditionalistic informal coalition between localized bureaucracies and the working class around values of redistribution and egalitarianism. This system created a kind of functional legitimacy where state control over allocative mechanisms rendered subjects dependent on state agencies for their material well-being (Staniszkis 1992: 101–2). Linda Cook (1992) describes this period as founded on a new 'tacit social contract' between the state and workers, and Bunce (1983) writes of a 'new mode of interest intermediation . . . [which] sought to minimize conflict and maximize productivity by incorporating dominant economic and political interests directly into the policy process, while cultivating the support of the masses through an expanding welfare state'. Zaslavsky writes of an 'organized consensus' based on recruitment of skilled workers to the closed cities, and the accumulation of power and patronage by leaders in the republics (Zaslavsky 1982). However, during this period the limits to bureaucratic domination were reached and the system began to fray into compromises based on repressive corporatism, weak labour discipline, tolerance of corruption and parallel circuits of exchange in the informal economy.

The long-term crisis of the Soviet system illustrates the inability of over-extended bureaucratic structures to coordinate action in complex societies. Habermas (1989: 384) suggests that systemic colonization is ultimately unworkable since once 'the administrative action system gains . . . autonomy in relation to the economic system' crises arise from 'self-blocking mechanisms in planning', where rational action orientations come into contradiction with unintended systemic effects. This can be seen most clearly in the way over-extension of bureaucratic control into social reproduction actually created re-traditionalized adaptive responses through the 'second society' which grew alongside substantive rationality. The second society had two dimensions: (i) self-provisioning (e.g. home-building to escape years of queuing for municipal housing) perhaps on the basis of non-monetary reciprocity; (ii) selling goods and services in an underground economy. Hankiss (1991: 310) points out that the terms 'official' and 'second' societies do not refer to two groups of people, but to two dimensions of social existence governed by different organizational principles that were none the less dependent upon one another in that the second society provided a degree of flexibility not permitted by the rigidity of the planning mechanisms. Over-burdened with demands for mobilization, adaptive social networks developed alongside the state, the key features of which were mechanical solidarity; informal networks ('shock absorbers' in private agriculture and intensified domestic exploitation of women); dissolving anonymity by eroding institutionalized trust; horizontal integration based on the particularism of family, friendship or ethnic group (Stark 1992).

The over-developed bureaucracy thus became dependent on adaptive re-sponses from the lifeworld, and for a time the second society served as a kind of crisis displacement mechanism. However, this symbiosis was only one of three possible relations between de-bureaucratized networks and official society. The second society could further have a corrupting effect, where bribes and em-bezzlement became part of everyday life and sapped resources and energies from the official sector, in which life became increasingly cynical and ritualized. Again, the second society could become system-threatening as informal net-works became the nucleus of oppositional movements and alternative channels supplanting official society. This occurred both in the political realm (e.g. with Solidarity) and in the economic, where informal trade became the effective economy (Sampson 1985–6). In other words, relationships between official and de-bureaucratized societies were precarious, partly because the second society was a form of both adaptation and resistance, indicating inherent limitations of the iron cage.

It was paradoxical perhaps that the underlying routinization of the system, which was made explicit by the Gorbachev reforms, also served to undermine the rule of the Party and bureaucracy. In the face of systemic failure combined with pressures from the world economy (Ray 1993 and 1994) the Gorbachev team pursued strategies of legalizing the state combined with increased reliance on the informal economy to provide steering capacities. The move towards a formal-rational mode of legitimation, Gorbachev's attempt to create a 'socialist legal state' (*sotsialisticheskoe pravovoe gosudarstvo*) like Andropov's efficiency drive in the early 1980s, aimed to de-politicize Soviet administration, which would henceforth pursue technical (*Zweckrationalität*) goals.[20] To this end the post-Brezhnev period saw strategies like tightening labour discipline (e.g. the anti-alcohol drive, or threatened dismissal for inefficiency), introducing money incentives, limited marketization, replacing soft budgetary constraints with harder ones, and importing Western technology and management styles.

However, *perestroika* undermined the principle of bureaucratic domination, since the more Soviet systems approximated formal-rational organizations, the more they undermined rather than strengthened bureaucratic domination. The more the Party sought to rule by consent the more it faced problems arising from chronic legitimacy deficit. Despite shifts in the social basis of Soviet control the justification of the rule of the Party *per se* remained dependent on what Staniszkis calls the 'myth of the vanguard' which was not capable of formal-rational legitimation. Yet abandoning the myth of the vanguard and placing rule on a legal foundation left few cultural reserves available to justify the Party's monopoly of power.[21] Reforms confronted the dilemma of either restricting themselves to increasing the efficiency of the existing system, or expanding into a 'reconstitution of civil society and the change of the agent of reform from 'above' to 'below' . . . to eliminate the primacy of discretionary power from several social spheres' (Fehér and Arato 1989: 7). Radical reform would have called into question the legitimacy of the whole system by opening up a civil society from below, on the basis of a legally constituted state.[22] Instead, the hitherto parallel society, the de-bureaucratized sphere, began to assume functions of coordination and regulation, in part attempting to follow the example of Hungarian 'market socialism'. The symbiosis that had evolved between the official and informal economies whereby planners relied on the ability of people to provision themselves via informal channels illustrated the paradox that an institutional order upon which the system was dependent was also a site of resistance.

One interpretation of the crisis of state socialism, then, is that a politicized estate bureaucracy was forced to evolve into a more 'Weberian' form, in the course of which it encountered irreconcilable contradictions. Since this process was brought about by a crisis that arose from the inability of an over-extended bureaucracy to anchor itself in the socio-cultural sphere, it is possible to speak of inherent limitations to the iron cage. Reform communists attempted to regenerate legitimacy resources through releasing popular movements and widening the basis of participation whilst preserving the core integrity of the system. This was unrealistic partly (as Fehér *et al.* argued) because of the incompatibility between popular demands and the survival of the nomenklatura in its estate form. Soviet systems could no longer generate even minimal acquiescence, and expectations of participatory modernization were evinced in legitimation crisis: masses took control of the streets, workers went on strike, work-place committees were formed, spontaneous political organizations appeared (Banac 1992; Hosking *et al.* 1992). Two points are relevant here. First, the appearance of ethical-charismatic movements was as much a symptom as a cause of the collapse of central authority. Secondly, a number of commentators have drawn attention to the suspicious ease as well as speed of the fall of communism. Comisso (1990) comments that in Hungary the 'militant reformist wing of the HSWP did more to destroy the party than did all the opposition groups together. The Bulgarian Communist Party abandoned its leading role before the opposition requested it. In Czechoslovakia the leaders were pushed by Moscow, likewise in the DDR after Hungary opened its borders.' The question is, then, why party elites undermined their own rule, possibly precipitously?

One answer to this question is to examine divergent opportunities released by the unravelling of Soviet systems, with reference to the duality of repressive and progressive rationalization outlined above. One possible future for post-socialist societies, which has shown some real potential in Hungary for example (Neumann 1992), is the evolution of flexible decentralization, self-management, the growth of regional and local markets, horizontal integration, the expansion of civil society, that is, sophisticated and open structures for managing complexity and impersonality. It is possible that the structures of the second society might provide the basis for horizontally integrated networks based on collegial and trust relationships. However, the evolution of these kinds of structures might be fettered by the process of 'spontaneous privatization' which enables former industrial managers to become owners, often by illegal conversion of assets, a situation where economic restructuring is subject to little regulation (Kowalik 1991; Hausner 1991; Levitas and Stralkowski 1990; Mandel 1991). Illegal divestiture of state property preserves the social power of the nomenklatura, which could no longer be guaranteed within an economic framework characterized by excessive rigidity (Voskamp and Wittke 1991) and high social welfare costs (Szalai, 1989). Indeed, Ivo Mozny (1991) and Hankiss (1990) have argued that in the communist period the nomenklatura had limited capacities for self-reproduction so long as their power derived from bureaucratic position rather than ownership, since bureaucratic privileges were neither alienable nor inheritable. To facilitate inter-generational transfer of capital, East European ruling elites permitted the political guarantees of public ownership to disintegrate while assisting the transition to a marketized economy. One consequence of this is the formation of private monopolies in which the old organizational structure remains more or less in place through a 'hollowed out' holding company run by the former nomenklatura. Further, the differentiation between economic and political subsystems generates increased systemic flexibility, as economic domination slips from view and creates the possibility of the new class ruling without governing.[23]

Thus the struggle for control of the post-communist transition centres around the poles of repressive and participatory rationalization. On the one hand, the core identity of the former system might reappear through the conversion of the political capital of the nomenklatura into economic capital through nomenklatura privatization. This possibility has been compared with a transition from feudalism to parasitic merchant capitalism where the latter remains for a long time dependent on the former (Burawoy and Krotov 1992). On the other hand, as Simon Clarke (1992) argues, post-socialist privatization is an uncertain process surrounded by class conflicts over control of the state industrial base. Successive privatization programmes in Russia have run into the ground partly as a result of opposition from workers and industrial managers, whose views tend to be represented in the Congress of People's Deputies by the Civic Union, the largest single grouping with around 40 per cent of the votes. Further, the process of nomenklatura-privatization has proved highly controversial and the State Property Committee has attempted to end it – though with how much success is a matter of dispute.[24] By July 1992 four privatization options crystallized: (i) purchase of a controlling interest by employees; (ii) employees receive 25 per cent of non-voting stock free and a further 10 per cent at 30 per cent discount; (iii) a minimum of one-third of employees form a partnership and buy the enterprise; (iv) the enterprise is auctioned but employees receive 30 per cent of the proceeds. Clarke suggests that these options amount to 'giving the controlling interest in enterprises to the workers free', and that it opens up a serious possibility of democratization from below rather than a transition to capitalism.

It should be noted, though, that there are countervailing tendencies to this prospect of participatory rationalization. First, Clarke might be overly dismissive of the prospect of nomenklatura-privatization as a central mechanism of asset transfer from the state to the newly constituted private sector. Alternative accounts in Mandel (1991), Filatotchev *et al.* (1992) or Ray (1994), for example, suggest that nomenklatura-privatization is a highly significant mode of new elite formation.[25] Secondly, once shares have been floated corporate buyers might not be prevented from moving in on labour cooperatives, something that might occur especially when firms attempt to re-capitalize. The Piyasheva-Selunin group of economists have argued that since the bulk of the population have no savings the real buyers of state enterprises will still be commercial organizations set up by the former nomenklatura.[26] Thirdly, whoever owns the enterprises, their future viability will depend upon the institutionalization of markets and their successful interlocking with other cultural practices.

This bears on a range of other difficulties. The illicit nature of much asset conversion hampers the process of embedding new economic relationships within a framework of civil law, and thus impedes the stabilization of the political system. Further, the adaptive responses of the second society created a traditionalistic culture, with a strong divide between 'public' and 'private' realms, in which economic exchange relies on kinship networks (Neumann 1992); cynicism about public life is widespread (Hausner 1992); and religiosity is increasing (Konstantinova 1992). Both the official and informal economies presupposed the uncosted and undervalued labour of women, since in relation to both the patriarchal household was the main unit for the supply of labour (Elson 1988). It appears now that patriarchal structures, sustained by the interplay of the formal and informal sectors, are becoming more firmly entrenched in a public sphere, while women are relocated within the 'private' domain (Pilkington 1992). These developments, combined with the problems of institutionalizing procedures for formal interest articulation and negotiation, increase the likelihood of a 'populist-authoritarian scenario' (Zon, 1992). This would involve state-regulated marketization and protection from the world market, heavy restrictions on trade unions, a weak bourgeoisie and nationalist-masculinist ideology (perhaps supported by the army) with a high probability of conflicts with neighbouring countries over borders and the treatment of minorities.

With the crisis of state socialism arises the paradox that whilst the over-extended state engendered rationality crises, it was the attempt of reform communist leaders like Gorbachev to further 'Weberianize' the systems, by legalizing the state and pluralizing the economy, that precipitated their final demise. The iron cage encountered rationalization limits in the form of resistance from lifeworld structures upon which bureaucratic systems became dependent, but which ultimately undermined them. On the one hand this illustrates that there are limits to the effectiveness of the iron cage, which might not constitute such an unbreakable form as Weber imagined. On the other hand, socio-cultural rationalization, as a critical process of validity questioning, might not be so grey and lifeless after all, but on the contrary might expand emancipatory horizons. However, systemic crisis creates a range of possibilities, one of which is that the former nomenklatura might convert bureaucratic power into capital, and privatize the state, rather than decentralize the economy. If this turns out to be the dominant mode of post-socialist transition, it would represent a repressive rationalization in which the system develops only sufficient flexibility and fluidity to reproduce itself and deploy hitherto underdeveloped cultural learning potentials, such as monopolistic markets. Against this limited rationalization, however, it is suggested that the transition is also a site of struggle for a broader and participatory rationalization which expands structures of ownership and democratic pluralization. This remains a potential, but it is too soon to say what the outcome might be.

POST-FORDISM AND THE 'POST-WEBERIAN' ECONOMY

The idea of a uniform process of rationalization, which has been questioned above, echoes the 'theory of convergence' (Kerr *et al.* 1960) which dominated the sociology of industrial societies and organizations throughout the 1950s and 1960s, as well as reappearing under a different theoretical guise in the post-industrialism literature which became increasingly influential from the 1970s onwards (Kumar 1978). Both convergence theory and post-industrial analysis suggested that there was an underlying evolutionary dynamic at work within modern societies that would necessarily push the latter in the direction of increased administrative centralization, economic concentration and political regulation (Leggatt 1985). This view took its inspiration from conventional readings of Weber's work on bureaucratic rationalization which indicated that an unstoppable 'organizational juggernaut' would inevitably terminate in the iron cage of externally imposed bureaucratic control and the internalized culture of self-discipline (Jacoby 1973). More recently, this evolutionary logic of organizational structuring has been most clearly identified in analyses of Fordist production regimes and regulative systems which are seen to be founded on the principles and rationales associated with rational bureaucratic control exemplified in Weber's ideal type of legal rational domination (Ritzer 1992). In each case, in relation to convergence theory, post-industrialism and Fordism, the trajectory of long-term socio-economic and political development in the West is seen to be dependent on a core set of organizing principles which regards the Weberian vision of bureaucratic domination and control as a technical or functional necessity.

However, more recent analyses (DiMaggio and Powell 1983) of changes in the political economies and social structures of advanced capitalist societies suggest that both the dynamics and direction of institutional development might be very different from the bureaucratic 'iron cage' anticipated by Weber, or the evolutionary trajectory of irreversible bureaucratic centralization anticipated by the theorists of industrial and post-industrial society. Contemporary research indicates that a series of technological, economic, socio-political and cultural disruptions are occurring within advanced capitalist societies, the effect of which is to erode the core ideological frameworks and organizational structures characteristic of modernity. These ruptures reverse the underlying dynamic of Weberian rationalization (Offe 1985; Lash and Urry 1987; Castells 1989; Harvey 1989; Jessop 1991; Crook *et al*. 1992) and generate a process in which the logic and structure of centralized control gives way to the pragmatics of an 'organizational smorgasbord' on which 'organization becomes the art of deconstructing organizations that can re-organize themselves' (Stark 1991: 57).

These structural transformations destabilize and marginalize the regulatory capacity and managerial effectiveness of 'neo-corporatist' or Fordist regulative regimes which dominated capitalist societies from the mid-1940s to the mid-1970s (Williamson 1989; Jessop 1991). The ability of bureaucratized systems of socio-economic and political management to deliver the ideological coherence, social stability and economic advance which Weber[27] and evolutionary theorists tended to take for granted has been directly challenged by contemporary analyses of 'post-Fordism', 'Disorganized Capitalism' and 'Postmodernism' which predict the end of the 'organized society' (Reed 1991). Economic globalization, technological rationalization and political deregulation are seen to attack the very foundations of modern social systems which depend on instrumental rationality and bureaucratic organization as their directive strategy and mechanism. Weber's assumption that the cognitive, ideological and organizational power of bureaucracy would be unrivalled is increasingly untenable in the light of the alleged organizational 'disorganization' of advanced capitalist societies.

This argument revolves around four structural developments: the unpredictable and uncontrollable disruptions to standardized methods of organizational management caused by more sophisticated information technologies (Castells 1989; Mulgan 1991; Scarborough and Corbett 1992); the centrality of expert knowledge and power within the much more decentralized and dispersed corporate forms emerging in the 'information mode of development' (Castells 1989; Sabel 1991); the extreme economic fragmentation and segmentation which these socio-technical changes generate (Piore and Sabel 1984; Lipietz 1992); and the 'hyper-differentiating' cultures which are both cause and consequence of these transformations in the material base of advanced capitalist economies (Crook *et al*. 1992). Taken as a complete package, these changes are seen as entailing a falsification of Weber's prognosis concerning the inevitable advance of bureaucratic rationalization and the dominance of bureaucratic structures of administrative coordination and control within the political economies of all modern capitalist societies. For Weber, it is argued, the indestructibility of bureaucratic mechanisms of coordination and control, and the administrative and political power which flows from them, is underwritten by the universal and irreversible demand for maximum formal rationality and efficiency which can be met only by the technically superior methods that the former make available. However, once this guarantee is no longer valid and is replaced by a much more complex and differentiated set of demands, then the trend towards bureaucratic domination looks much less inevitable. The possibilities of a post-bureaucratic or post-Weberian organizational world are apparent in contemporary capitalist systems where the complexity and volatility of socio-technical and political-cultural developments outrun the control systems made available by rational bureaucracy.

Each of the four structural changes referred to earlier – information technology, knowledge/expertise, economic restructuring and cultural 'hyper-differentiation' – needs to be discussed in more detail before a more informed evaluation of the continuing relevance and significance of Weber's analysis of bureaucracy and bureaucratization in Western political economies can be formulated.

Information technology and de-bureaucratization

Advances in information technologies and their impact on socio-economic and political structures has been a leitmotif in social and organizational analysis which received added impetus from the debate over 'post-industrialism' and its implications for the future development of (post)modern societies (Bell 1973; Lyon 1988; Lyotard 1984; Smart 1992). This literature has challenged Weber's prognosis of an unstoppable trend of bureaucratization,[28] to the extent that the development and implementation of more advanced information technologies are seen to create a new 'technological paradigm' (Castells 1989). A fundamental organizational characteristic of these more advanced information technologies, it is argued, is the shift from centralized bureaucratic organizations in the economy, state and culture to decentralized networks or 'adhocracies' in which rigid hierarchies of coordination and control are replaced by much more flexible systems of management in which 'informality' and 'collegiality' become the norm (Mulgan 1991). Information technology offers a capacity for exercising effective and efficient 'control at a distance' in which the standardized strategies and practices of bureaucratic discipline can to a large degree be dispensed with (Zuboff 1988; Clegg 1990; Cooper 1992). Indeed, these present a strategy and apparatus of control in which the Foucauldian nightmare of 'total control' becomes realizable insofar as they facilitate the internalization of self-discipline as the guiding feature of organizational life and management in 'post' or 'late' modernity (Giddens 1985; Burrell 1988; Dandeker 1990). The supervisory 'gaze' of the foreman, guard, clerk and teacher gives way to more unobtrusive, subtle and indirect forms of surveillance and control which are no longer dependent on rules or visible human intervention but rely on the automatic and continuous disciplining of thought and behaviour made available by the 'information panoptican' (Zuboff 1988). The latter offers the promise of certain knowledge based on the totality and invisibility of observation and monitoring that it affords. But it also opens up a more attractive possibility for enhanced intellectual learning and development throughout the organization; the nurturing and maturing of a 'knowledge base' which encourages a greater degree of involvement, commitment and responsibility at all levels within the organization:

> The relationships that characterize a learning environment thus can be thought of as posthierarchical. This does not imply that differentials of knowledge, responsibility and power no longer exist; rather, they can no longer be assumed. Instead, they shift and flow and develop their character in relation to the situation, the task, the actors at hand. Managing intricacy calls for a new level of action-centred skill, as dialogue and inquiry place a high premium on the intuitive and imaginative sources of understanding that temper and hone the talents related to 'acting with'. The dictates of the learning environment, rather than those of imperative control, now shape the development of such interpersonal 'know-how.'
>
> (Zuboff 1988: 401–2).

Whether viewed through the theoretical prism of a 'Foucauldian nightmare' of total control or a 'Zuboffian dream' of learning environments, developments in information technology seem to make the Weberian prognosis of the encircling 'iron cage' of bureaucratic domination and control outmoded. This is the case insofar as the latter is premised on crude or primitive control rationales and mechanisms which are long past their organizational 'sell by' date. Developments in information technology also highlight the strategic centrality of knowledge and expertise to the organization and management of collective action in post-bureaucratic societies.

Expert knowledge and power

Within the more fragmented and decentralized organizational structures resulting from the diffusion of advanced information technologies, the strategic importance of highly specialized knowledges and skills to long-term corporate viability and competitiveness becomes absolutely central (Pettigrew and Whipp 1992; Nelson and Winter 1982). To the extent that knowledge-based sectors and organizations emerge as the economic engine room of long-term material growth and development within modern societies (Machlup 1980), then the specialized personnel and repertoires that provide the competitive edge within an increasingly globalized and unstable economy emerge as the *key resources* (Reich 1991; Lipietz 1992). This development might cast the technical necessity and managerial practicality of the Weberian control model into further doubt in the sense that it pushes and/or pulls organizations and institutions into 'deviant' structural arrangements that call into question the relevance and fitness of imperatively coordinated forms of collective action (Reed 1992).

This deviation is most clearly expressed in the form of work organizations that cede a much higher and more meaningful degree of task-related autonomy and policy influence to expert or professional workers than that envisaged by the standard Weberian control model (Hinings *et al.* 1991; Starbuck 1992). More specifically, the increasing centrality of knowledge-intensive organizations and workers to corporate competitiveness and national economic success is seen to require a virtual 'bonfire' of bureaucratic regulations and constraints normally associated with machine bureaucracy (Starbuck 1992; Mintzberg 1989). This is deemed necessary because of the underlying conflicts between expert/ professional modes of work and collegiate organizational culture on the one hand, and externally imposed management and regulation on the other (Raelin 1991). This contradiction is reinforced by socio-technical trends which make the contribution of 'knowledge workers' (Blackler *et al.* 1993) to the mediation of uncertainty or extremely complex problem/puzzle-solving even more important in conditions where the link between environmental demands and organizational survival becomes increasingly dependent on the interpretations and evaluations that specialists provide. To the extent that experts provide the vocabularies, languages and techniques – even myths (Morgan 1992) – through which external threats can be propitiated and potential opportunities exploited, then they establish a knowledge base and resource potential that management has to take into account in both strategic and operational decision making (Pahl and Winkler 1974; Reed 1989). This 'taking into account' is likely to result in organizational designs and related control systems in which the dependence of 'dominant coalitions' (Child 1972, 1973) on middle- and lower-ranking experts becomes even more pronounced and destabilizes institutionalized power structures in which formal position within the established authority hierarchy was once the overriding consideration (Pettigrew 1973; Lash and Urry 1987). Thus, the capacity of rational bureaucratic control systems to exercise effective and efficient organizational coordination and surveillance is further called into question by economic and technological changes in which highly specialized knowledge, and the competitive advantages that it delivers, becomes central. In combination with developments in information technologies that destabilize and erode bureaucratic structures, the increasingly strategic value and relevance of 'expert work' within an expert division of labour – which is itself increasingly differentiated and fragmented into highly specialized occupational categories and groups (Reed 1992) – further undermines the coherence and cogency of the Weberian control model.

Economic restructuring

The neo-Fordist perspective suggests that a new regime of 'flexible accumulation' (Harvey 1989; Whitaker 1992) is emerging out of the breakdown of Fordist production regimes and corporatist regulative structures in advanced capitalist societies. This breakdown is explained in terms of the inherent rigidities in and limitations of Fordist/corporatist structures as they struggle to come to terms with the discontinuities and dislocations resulting from the globalization of capitalism in general, and 'finance capital' in particular (Lash and Urry 1987; Aglietta 1979; Offe 1985; Jessop 1991). The globalization of capital movements, production regimes and technological innovation creates a control crisis within conventional Fordist/corporatist systems in that the latter are simply unable to cope with the demands for temporal adaptability, spatial flexibility and informational portability which the former create (Harvey 1989). While the overall logic of capital accumulation remains as the driving force of economic, political and social change, the institutional configurations and organizational forms through which it is to be secured undergo a dramatic transformation in which Fordism/corporatism can no longer handle the spatial and temporal displacements produced by globalization:

It was primarily through spatial and temporal displacement that the Fordist regime of accumulation resolved the overaccumulation problem during the long postwar boom. The crisis of Fordism can to some degree be interpreted, therefore, as a running out of those options to handle the overaccumulation problem . . . The crisis of Fordism was, therefore, as much a geographical and geopolitical crisis as it was a crisis of indebtedness, class struggle or corporate stagnation within any particular nation state. It was simply that the mechanisms for controlling crisis tendencies were finally overwhelmed by the power of the underlying contradictions of capitalism.

(Harvey 1989: 185–6).

Harvey's analysis of a new regime of 'flexible accumulation' suggests that the transition from Fordism will entail a mix of highly efficient Fordist production regimes in some sectors and regions with flexible technologies and organizational forms that provide the socio-technical, economic and administrative capacities that globalized capitalist competition demands, particularly in the finance, service, high-tech, knowledge-intensive sectors.

The 'post-Fordist' interpretation of economic restructuring and its organizational consequences is very different to that provided by those commentators who have drawn on the work of the 'Regulationist' school to provide a 'neo-Fordist' analysis of structural change in advanced capitalist societies (Hyman 1991). The post-Fordist case suggests that an 'epochal redefinition of markets, technologies and industrial hierarchies' (Sabel 1982: 231) is taking place which entails a fundamental shift towards a system of flexible specialization that breaks with the major institutional and organizational forms associated with Fordist production regimes (Piore and Sabel 1984; Murray 1989; Rustin 1989; Lipietz 1992). Within the post-Fordist mode of analysis, it is market saturation/fragmentation and technological innovation – rather than a crisis of over-accumulation – which are identified as the primary economic changes generating radical transformations in institutional and organizational forms. The combination of market saturation in mass consumer goods, the segmentation of product markets into much more specialized and discriminating 'niches', the potential for greatly enhanced flexibility and decentralization made available by new technology, and the substantially reduced need for the integrating function traditionally provided by industrial bureaucracy seems to spell the death-knell of the Fordist production

regime. The latter, it is argued, is in the process of being superseded by production regimes which reject markets and hierarchies as the primary coordinating
and control mechanisms in advanced industrial societies (Piore and Sabel 1984:
275). Not only is the iron cage of bureaucratic centralization and control being
rusted away by the corrosive agents of economic and technological change, but
it is also unravelling as a rationale for institutional governance and organizational
design under the extreme pressures exerted by socio-technical and cultural forces
which push in the direction of diversity, fragmentation and disorder (Sabel 1991).

Neo-Fordist and post-Fordist analyses of long-term institutional change (Wood
1989; Whitaker 1992; Sayer and Walker 1992) generally agree that the dynamic
and trajectory of economic development both entail a dramatic movement away
from the highly centralized and rationalized administrative regimes characteristic
of Fordism/corporatism. In this respect they concur in their joint belief that the
Weberian control model is becoming increasingly dysfunctional and obsolete
within a set of macro and microeconomic conditions which largely remove the
need for the hierarchically based coordinating and integrative mechanisms that
were previously found in the organizational core of Fordism. These latter tasks,
they argue, can now be carried out through technical, organizational and social
structures which radically depart from the logic of bureaucratic coordination and
control.

Cultural hyper-differentiation

The argument that Weber's analysis of rational bureaucracy and his prognosis
concerning the inevitability of bureaucratic rationalization were both premised
on a theory of cultural development which no longer holds has attracted growing
support in recent years. Indeed, Weber's belief in bureaucratic rationalization and
domination as the inevitable organizational fate of modernity is thought to be
premised on a 'metaphysical pathos' which takes extreme cultural standardization and homogenization for granted (Gouldner 1959; Clegg 1990). For Weber,
it is argued, the indestructibility of bureaucratic mechanisms of coordination and
control, and the administrative and political power that flow from them, is
guaranteed by the universal and irrevocable cultural imperative for maximized
formal rationality and substantive efficiency within modern societies (Mommsen
1992; Scaff 1989). However, we have seen that this assumes a degree of cultural
'homogenization' and standardization within modern societies which is incom-
patible with the cultural differentiation associated with late or postmodernity.
Crook *et al.* argue that the

> [p]ostmodernization of culture proceeds through a hypercommodification
> which finally erodes the distinction between commodified and non-
> commodified regions, through a hyper-rationalization which fragments the
> 'problem-solving' thrust of modernism, and through a hyperdifferentiation in

which cultural fragments transcend categorical boundaries and produce the effect of dedifferentiation.

(Crook *et al*. 1992: 221).

At one level this may be interpreted as being in line with Weber's analysis of the rationalizing processes and tendencies. However, viewed at another level Crook *et al*.'s analysis suggests a reversal of the Weberian drive towards rationalized art, literature, communication, music etc., insofar as the former envisages a degree of cultural pluralism and fragmentation which slows and then reverses the impetus of cultural homogenization and standardization. This has its institutional and organizational correlates in the form of a 'disorganizing' dynamic which arrests or slows the logic of bureaucratic rationalization (Crook *et al*. 1992: 228–9). Thus, the universal cognitive norms and cultural principles that Weber identified as providing the normative foundations for bureaucratic rationalization are now recontextualized within a radically different socio-political and cultural framework in which 'destandardization' – in all institutional domains – is the dominant leitmotif (Beck 1992: 139ff.). An irreversible organizational trend towards enhanced structural differentiation and fragmentation is directly linked to a process of radical cultural transformation in which the universalization of normative imperatives associated with rationality and control is replaced by a 'pluralizing' dynamic which destabilizes and relativizes all value systems. We thus see again how Weber's vision of a future iron cage is reinterpreted as one possible (and probably self-limiting) version of a postmodern world in which cultural diversity, ambiguity and contingency have become the norm. The dystopian vision which flows from them is an increasingly partial guide to the alternative organizational futures available to late/postmodern societies.

Taken as a whole, the four developments reviewed in this section suggest that Weber's analysis of the direction and outcome of long-term institutional and organizational change within the political economies of advanced capitalist societies can no longer be sustained. Combined with the analysis of the collapse of the Soviet-style iron cage in the previous section, they present an indictment of Weber's position – at least if this is understood as a form of historical determinism and cultural pessimism. A more subtle and sensitive appreciation of Weber's contribution to our understanding of the dilemmas of modernity, and the continuing significance and relevance of that contribution to contemporary sociological and organizational analysis, will now be attempted.

THE DILEMMAS OF MODERNITY

The Habermasian rereading of Weber developed in the second section of this chapter provides the theoretical and normative basis for the re-evaluation of Weber's contribution to our understanding of the dilemmas of modernity developed in this section. This rereading of Weber offers us a more nuanced interpretation of the inherent tensions and contradictions that Weber highlights as integral to the process of modernization and the contested discursive arenas and related organizational forms that it reproduces.

Our analysis of institutional and organizational restructuring in Soviet-style command economies and Fordist production regimes in Western capitalist societies suggests that the evolutionary premisses that informed a great deal of industrial and post-industrial convergence theory have to be fundamentally rethought. This is so to the extent that the latter was grounded in a logic of sociotechnical rationalization which inevitably resulted in bureaucratized institutional structures and organizational forms that would become universally dominant within the world system (Kerr *et al.* 1960; Kumar 1978; Leggatt 1985). However, accounts of the dynamics and trajectories of institutional and organizational change in both socialist and capitalist political economies indicate that convergence theory provides a grossly oversimplified analysis of the inherent complexities of socioeconomic transformation within modern industrial societies. These accounts also suggest that the evolutionary, not to say teleological, predilections of convergence theory traded on a highly questionable interpretation of Weber's analysis of bureaucratic rationalization which cannot be sustained if a less deterministic evaluation of his iron cage thesis is allowed to emerge.

We need to develop a more sophisticated appreciation of Weber's writing on bureaucracy and bureaucratization and its implications for the way in which we interpret and assess his 'rationalization thesis'. As Beetham has argued, Weber's analysis of bureaucracy contains three major aspects: as a system of administration that approximates to the rational control model; as a separate 'social force' within society that provides a mode of administrative and, potentially, political domination; and as an instrument of class power and domination (Beetham 1985, 1991). The first of these analytical perspectives predominates in Weber's 'sociological' writing on bureaucracy, while the second and third approaches are much more influential in his 'political' writings. Once we move beyond the more methodological or technical aspects of Weber's writings on bureaucracy and bureaucratization, then alternative pathways of organizational and institutional development are opened up which cannot be contained within the rationalization thesis and its inevitable termination in the iron cage of totalitarian control. This also sensitizes us to the strategic role of expert knowledge within Weber's theory of bureaucratic rationalization and the countervailing forces which inevitably challenge and modify established control structures – whatever the nature of the wider political, economic and cultural setting in which the latter develop.

This broader reading of Weber's work on bureaucracy begins to make available a more realistic and grounded assessment of the *inherent limitations* of purposive rationality and the opportunities for communicative rationality to emerge as a much more powerful force within the long-term development of modernity. This is so to the extent that the efficient operation of bureaucratic control systems necessarily demands their supplementation and elaboration by political and cultural modifications that inevitably undermine the integrity and

coherence of their organizational functioning. This over-extension of bureaucratic systems of coordination and control unavoidably produces 'gaps' or
'fissures' which can be exploited by subordinate groups to their advantage. The
actual operation of bureaucratized systems of surveillance and control is shaped
by the interventions of superordinate and subordinate groups who subject, in
various ways and to varying degrees, hierarchical structures and expert cultures
to communicative critique. In this way, over-rationalized control systems generate their own, inherent, tensions and contradictions; they respond to control
failures by the re-imposition and extension of more complex and elaborate
control mechanisms, which simply extends the possibilities for a more discursive
rationality to take hold (Reed 1985). As Weber clearly recognized in his less
technical writings on bureaucracy, modern organizational forms have within
them the 'seeds' of a 'dialectic of control' (Giddens 1985, 1991), which makes
the prospects for effective bureaucratic domination dependent on the contingent
outcome of demands for greater openness and wider involvement in decision-
making processes rather than on the inexorable workings of historical, structural
or historical 'laws' of socio-economic development. Thus, the analytically pure
control model which Weber develops as a vital component of his 'theory' of
bureaucratic rationalization has to be substantially qualified (Beetham 1985,
1992). Weber's political writings open up the possibility of more contested and
'participatory' forms of communication and action in which institutionalized
power structures cannot simply 'have their way' in collective decision making.
This implies that bureaucratic control systems have to modify and adapt to the
changing conditions in which they operate.

Our analysis of institutional and organizational change in the East and West
provides ample illustration of the way in which bureaucratized systems of coordination and control can become so over-extended, as in the case of Soviet-style
systems, or so operationally inflexible, as in the case of Fordist-type regimes in
the West, that they are no longer equipped to cope with the demands of their
respective environments. In both cases, the failure of centralized bureaucratic
control regimes to deal with very different challenges and opportunities that
deep-seated socio-economic and political change presents casts serious doubts on
the organizational capacity of rational bureaucracy to 'deliver the goods' – in
terms of the efficient and effective regulation of collective action – which
Weber's more technical analysis assumes. The incapacity of Soviet organizational structures to cope with the complexity of a differentiating economy and
society, as well as the adaptive forms of lifeworld resistance, and the failure of
Fordist regimes to adapt to the globalization of capitalist production and exchange, both stand testimony to the plurality of organizational logics that shape
the actual practice of 'organizing' in the extreme diversity and unpredictability
characteristic of 'late modernity'.

Reinterpreted in this light, the incipient erosion of bureaucratized control
systems in the East and West can be seen as making available opportunities for
more democratic and participatory organizational forms to emerge and take root

in very different socio-economic and political soil. These developments might offer real chances for more participative and communicative discourse to become established within the flexible and decentralized organizational forms increasingly characteristic of Western capitalist economies and Eastern political systems. But the extent to which the enhanced cognitive power and increased personal and social autonomy made available by the ongoing 'destandardization' of organizational control systems (Beck 1992; Crook *et al*. 1992) can be mobilized to effect real and lasting transformations of established power structures is itself a very open, and highly controversial, issue. Beck's anticipation of a 'reflexive modernization' that, in Habermas' terms, facilitates the resolution of social conflicts through the expansion of communicative rationality, and the participatory linguistic/organizational forms through which it is to be practised, has to be set within a more developed analysis of 'expert' power and control within late/postmodernity (Giddens 1991; Bauman 1992b). Rather than the gradual rusting away and eventual collapse of the iron cage, we may be witnessing the bureaucratization of the socio-psychological textuality of everyday life. The iron cage is no longer 'out there', located within relatively visible and identifiable social structures and mechanisms, but 'in here', locked away within self-disciplining routines and practices (Foucault 1979; Rose 1991). The power of externalized bureaucratic structures gives way to – or is at least modified by – more sophisticated and unobtrusive control regimes in which the discourse of the expert or professional becomes dominant (Burchell *et al*. 1991). As DiMaggio and Powell have argued in their critical elaboration of Weber's analysis of bureaucratic rationalization:

> The foci and motive force of bureaucratization have changed since Weber's time. But the importance of understanding the trends to which he called attention have never been more immediate.
>
> (DiMaggio and Powell 1983: 158)[29]

Any significant analysis of the increasingly subtle and uncertain dialectic of control within the organizational designs and institutional configurations constitutive of late or postmodernity will require a theoretical framework that is adequately equipped to deal with the complex interaction of power, discourse and practice as they shape the endemic struggle between 'repressive' and 'reflexive' forms of modernization. The capacity of institutionalized forms of class, bureaucratic and professional power to resist or corrupt the more open, reflexive, sceptical and participative rationality carried forward by post-Fordist organizations or 'post-bureaucratic' social movements should not be underestimated. The development of more genuinely pluralistic decision-making systems based on communicative, rather than purposive, rationality *might* become more likely and practical as the inherent contradictions and limitations of the standardized 'Weberian' control model accumulate. The limited capacity of bureaucratized control systems to deal with the escalating economic, scientific, technological, environmental and political risks inherent within late/postmodernity is quite apparent. Nevertheless, a naive optimism or progressivism may not be the most appropriate theoretical or normative basis for analysing contemporary restructuring and its long-term consequences (Sayer and Walker 1992). We should remain alert to the simultaneous potentialities for very different institutional and organizational outcomes contained within the same set of initial socio-economic, political and economic conditions.

Weber never lost sight of the fact that a weakening of the control exercised by powerful classes and elites within societies or organizations does not mean that they are necessarily forced to relinquish their overall domination of decision-making agendas. Indeed, Beck's prognosis may be reworked within a neo-Weberian problematic and framework to provide a more realistic assessment of the shifting balance between 'repressive' and 'reflexive' modernization as it shapes the organizational forms through which social change is advanced and managed. Such an assessment may indicate that the line between the demise or closure of the bureaucratic iron cage is very fine indeed; this becomes even more difficult to judge in a context where the proliferation of control systems and practices seems to be literally 'out of control'.

REPRESSIVE AND PARTICIPATORY MODERNITY

Weber's theory of bureaucracy was most popular during the period of organized capitalism, but it is now less clear whether 'the future belongs to bureaucratization' or indeed whether organizational behaviour is as routinized as Weber imagined. This chapter has addressed the unravelling of two systems of control – Soviet socialism and Fordist capitalism – that have been dominant for the best part of the twentieth century. What are the implications of this for our understanding of Weber's theory of organization? The account developed in the first section suggested (drawing on Habermas) that Weber was overly concerned with teleological and strategic forms of social action, and preoccupied with the aspect of modernity institutionalized in bureaucratic and market structures. However, against the iron cage control model it is possible to reconstruct a more subtle Weberian analysis that is sensitive to the importance of consent as a basis for authoritative commands. This is a dialectical view of a modernity that, since it embodies multiple possibilities, is never closed. Moreover, the fate of the Soviet-type systems indicates not only that they encountered limits to rationalization, but also that the crisis was precipitated by the very process of rationalization itself, which suggests that the process is more complex and contradictory than at first it seems.

Further, Weber's understanding of modernity as the differentiation of cultural value spheres militated against the viability of monolithic bureaucratic structures, since one would expect these to encounter both resistance from the lifeworld and problems of over-complexity. This is so in at least three senses. First, the differentiation of spheres of validity (science, morality and law, and art) along with boundaries between society, culture and personality entails a fragmentation of worldviews. Totalizing and heroic systems of meaning, like Marxism-Leninism, can be upheld only at the cost of massive *de*-differentiation. Secondly, modernity involves coordination of relationships of anonymity and impersonality, what Giddens (1990) calls 'disembedding social systems' or Habermas 'steering media' of money and expert systems. In order to successfully coordinate actions, however, these systems are dependent upon institutional relations and cultural practices such as trust. Here again, the kind of colonization represented by Weber's bureaucracy, where commands have quasi-traditionalistic status, is unlikely to remain embedded in post-traditional value systems. Third, action coordination is premised on the possibility of what Habermas, following Kohlberg and Piaget, calls 'post-conventional' communications which presuppose formal-rational grounding of authority in the argumentative power of language. Whereas Weber drew the pessimistic conclusion that *Sinnverlust* was the inevitable fate of modernity, a grey-on-grey future, this procedural concept of rationality allows us to envisage open communicative structures through which difference might be negotiated.

Against this background it might be possible to speak of the contemporary crisis of mono-organizational forms, illustrated here with reference to problems of post-communism and post-Fordist flexibility, as opening the possibility of democratizing modernity. This would entail the evolution of structures that permitted a resolution of conflicts through expansion of communicative rationality. From this point of view, the disarticulation of organizational structures is a moment of uncertainty which opens up the possibilities for communicative critique of expert cultures and closed circuits of decision making. This disarticulation further creates space for social movements which experiment with alternative lifestyles and permit a fluidity of communications and work practices. One could cite as evidence for this both the diverse social movements attending the collapse of communism and contemporary global movements such as ecology and feminism which embody new identities and power configurations as proto-organizational forms.

Resolution of the problems of late modernity then would presuppose the institutionalization of autonomous public spheres, and new types of legitimacy grounded less in substantive value systems and more in expanded capacities for agreement – potentials which are prefigured in the formation of post-traditional, differentiated social organizations. Habermas (1990) has described the collapse of communism as 'rectifying revolutions' in that, unlike classical revolutions that offered a vision of the future, these aimed at 'overcoming distance' between themselves and the level of modernity reached in the West. Complex societies are unable to reproduce effectively if they do not coordinate action through anonymous mechanisms of money and power, anchored in institutional orders of the lifeworld, which were largely absent from Soviet-type societies.

However, a crisis in the *ancien régime* creates opportunities, and no more than that, for progressive rationalization. Markets themselves, after all, are crisis-prone, and their extension into lifeworld settings will generate pathologies unless regulated by cultural institutions. Since there is no guarantee of this happening, the prospect of transition to the kind of participatory modernization indicated here should be tempered by more sober analysis. First, transitions are highly uncertain and become the site of struggle between a range of social forces, which was illustrated by the disputes over nomenklatura-privatization. New modes of economic integration themselves generate new stratification and conflict potential, such as ethnic and gender divisions in the labour market or those groups marginalized by flexible work systems. Secondly, the outcome of these struggles, and the alignment of social forces in late modernity, is in turn affected by the prior mode of development of lifeworld values and practices. People accustomed to cynicism about public life, for example, or clientelistic and patriarchal habits, might prefer the security of authoritarian politics to the risks of postmodern fluidity. Thirdly, just as there were limits to the extension of the iron cage, grounded in problems of unmanageable complexity, there might likewise be limits to the capacity for democratic participation in complex organizations. Niklas Luhmann argues that in functionally differentiated societies, vertical and horizontal differentiation are inescapable means of reducing what would otherwise be unmanageable complexity. Open participatory structures (of the kind envisaged by Habermas' communicative action) would 'degenerate into ciphers of indeterminate and unspecifiable complexity' – they are the 'future that cannot begin' (Luhmann 1982: 119–20). Despite his deep disagreements with Luhmann, Habermas himself acknowledges that some degree of systemic regulation is inevitable in modern society, and to imagine otherwise is to invoke the possibility of return to a 'nostalgically loaded, frequently romanticized past' (Habermas 1989: 342).

Whilst the classical version of Weber's thesis is untenable because of the complex differentiation of modern societies, it is still possible that flexibility itself will open up scope for a more effective instrumentalization of social relations and a deeper penetration of control mechanisms into everyday life. In this context flexible structures create the populist illusion of empowerment while in practice representing *more* tightly organized control through dispersal and flexibility, which enhance social visibility (Harvey 1989). In this way the core identity of the system is preserved in more differentiated organizational settings. Even so, this Foucauldian cage would not be a system without capacities for resistance – on the contrary the very penetration of control systems into everyday life would generate new sites of struggle and dimensions of emancipation.

NOTES

1 In contrast with Martin Albrow (in this volume) who is looking to open the iron cage through a less rationalized and more affective Weber, we are attempting to recover a more subtle rationalization process than that suggested by exclusive attention to the concept of purposive calculation.
2 For example, Burnham (1962); Rizzi (1985); Adorno and Horkheimer, (1944) or more recently Hickson and Lammers (1979).

3 See also Abercrombie, Hill and Turner (1980) who argue that 'ruling ideologies' at most provide a sense of cohesion within the ruling class and make little contribution to sustaining the loyalty of those outside.

4 This is not unlike Beck's idea that the tradition of industrial society itself replaces pre-modernity, but for Beck this was modernity in a truncated form, which is now undermined by reflexive modernization (1992: 153).

5 Here Weber's account focused on the Puritan sects whose theology had an elective affinity with capitalism, while ignoring two crucial developments: first, Puritanism's limited cognitive potential compared with that of other intellectual movements such as the Humanists, whose contribution to modern science was crucial; secondly, radical Reformation sects like the Anabaptists, whose egalitarian anti-acquisitive ethics pointed towards a subterranean critique of capitalist modernity which was later to surface in socialist movements. Both suggest multiple lines of potential development in the seventeenth century, of which the 'protestant ethic' and its 'spirit of capitalism' was but one.

6 Habermas proposes to 'radicalize' Austin and Searle's linguistic philosophy by shifting the centre of concern from the propositional content of language to validity claims which are raised implicitly. Since the latter are claims to authority and legitimacy they invoke power relations (Habermas 1984: 278).

7 Habermas is aware that dramaturgical action can take on strategic qualities, for example where the audience are opponents to be cynically managed. But even cynical self-presentation is dependent upon claims to subjective truthfulness: the confidence trickster is parasitic on naively assumed trust.

8 Similarly, David Sciulli refers to collegial, voluntaristic, social networks that institutionalize normative constraints on the arbitrary exercise of power through a 'lived anticipation' of the possibility of scrutiny. He believes that these collegial formations explain 'Weber's Dilemma', i.e. why did increasingly rationalized societies escape authoritarianism? The presence of collegial formations in civil society enables it to resist authoritarian systemic pressures (Sciulli 1992).

9 Habermas (1984: 123) deploys the notion of the lifeworld as 'pre-reflective background consensus', but departs from more conventional phenomenological notions, such as that of Gadamer, who in turn has insisted (*pace* Habermas) that we cannot escape embeddedness in tradition and any supposition that we can is 'objectivist dogmatism' (Gadamer 1976: 30). For Habermas this is unsatisfactory since the process of making the lifeworld available to public scrutiny changes its nature – it 'dissolves . . . before our eyes as soon as we try to take it up piece by piece . . . [and] loses precisely those characteristics by virtue of which it belonged to the lifeworld structures: certainty, background character' (Honneth *et al.* 1981).

10 A core structure of domination refers to a situation where one group is better able than others to bring about an allocation of inputs and products which extends their economic and extra-economic benefits and ensures continuity of appropriation in the future. This core structure might reproduce itself through various cultural and regulatory forms.

11 The Bolsheviks' well-known admiration for Taylorism resulted in an attempt to apply principles formulated for the enterprise to the whole society. Murray (1989: 54–64) does point out that unlike the capitalist version, Soviet Fordism lacked the 'pull' of monetary demand and the 'push' of the threat of unemployment. Further, for capitalist enterprises anticipated profit stimulates rationalized work organization, whereas Soviet enterprises were geared to fulfil physical planning targets, with results described below.

12 See Clegg, Chapter 2 in this volume, for an account of the key features of Weber's ideal-type bureaucracy.

13 This is an over-statement, however, since 'the' Soviet state was never a unified entity

but was rife with competing sectoral interests. From the Agenbegyan/Kosygin reforms of the 1960s, if not before, sections of the planning bureaucracies were attempting to release initiative 'from below' to break out of administrative inefficiency.

14 Not unlike the SPD leaders, Weber seems to have envisaged a gradual transition from capitalist to state bureaucratic forms, or perhaps something akin to Hilferding's 'organized capitalism'. However, at what point profit would be replaced by central allocation as a means of resource distribution is unclear. Even in a planned capitalist economy anticipated profit remains the stimulus to investment whereas in a post-capitalist economy production decisions are limited only by scarcity and technology (e.g. Rakovski [Kis] 1978; Mandel 1992).

15 The Red Directors, appointed after 1917 on the basis of political and organizational reliability but with limited technical education, were removed wholesale from key administrative posts in the Great Purges. There is not space here to detail the shifting balance between expertise and political criteria in appointment to the Soviet bureaucracy, but this is discussed by Hough (1969) and Fitzpatrick (1979).

16 The Soviet nomenklatura consisted of about 700 in 1918, 100,000 by the 1930s and by the 1980s 250,000 according to Voslensky (1984: 95) and 300–400,000 according to Mandel (1992: 83). That is, about 0.1–0.2 per cent of the population.

17 Recent studies (e.g. Getty 1985) have suggested that even in the Stalinist period the centre had limited control over local Party organs, and under the surface there was extensive organizational chaos, which at that time facilitated terroristic control.

18 Published GDP growth rates were often of course inaccurate. During the Gorbachev period percentage annual rates for the Soviet Union were published with a retro-spective inflation adjustment: 7.2 (1951–60), 4.4 (1961–65), 4.1 (1966–70), 3.2 (1971–75), 1.0 (1976–80); and 0.6 (1981–86). This declining curve is due in part to exhaustion of extensive development, rising energy costs, and poor work motivations in a system where there was little to consume with increased earnings (Walker 1987: 53ff.). Even so, during the Eighth and Ninth Five Year Plans (1966–75) steel output rose from 91 to 141 million tons pa; coal 587–710 million tons p.a.; petroleum 243–491 million tons p.a.

19 Weber describes substantive rationality as 'the provisioning of given groups of persons with goods . . . under some criterion of ultimate values, which are often geared to social justice' (Weber 1978: I 85). However, Weber described the concept as 'full of ambiguities' and never developed it into a dimension of legitimation comparable with traditional charismatic or rational types.

20 A very clear statement of these technical goals is found in Tanya Zaslavskaya's 'Novosibirsk Paper,' published in 1984 in the Andropov period, which caused amaze-ment at the time for its frank diagnosis of irrationalities and inefficiencies in the system. Both Zaslavskaya and her colleague at Novosibirsk, Aganbegyan, were later members of Gorbachev's New Team.

21 Gorbachev frequently invoked Lenin's New Economic Policy as the precursor of *perestroika*. But the NEP had been a temporary expedient after the Civil War, and after seven decades of communist rule was a rather weak claim to legitimacy.

22 Fehér and Arato (1989: 25) regarded the Gorbachev period as merely the third wave of elite change in Soviet history – the first being Stalin's terroristic 'revolution from above'; the second, Khrushchev and Brezhnev's closure of revolutions from above, extension of privileges and tolerance of corruption; whilst Gorbachev's technocratic strategy required Western aid and a brake on military investment.

23 This is not to suggest a simple continuity of rule from the former system to the present, since a new configuration of hegemonic groups will be worked out through alliances and struggles. However, former nomenklatura are likely to be key players in these new class formations.

24 Stanislav Shatalin (President of the Reform Foundation) for example has described Yeltsin's decree combating corruption as a 'fig leaf', creating only the illusion of struggle (*Izvestia* 28 April 1992).
25 Further, he insists on the importance of separating juridical ownership (which is changing) from the social relations of production (which he claims are not) but what are the latter if not rights of disposal inscribed into juridical relations?
26 L. Piyasheva (Deputy General Director, Moscow Mayor's Office); Members of Moscow Economic Council: A. Isayev (Dir. Institute of Economics Planning and Management of the Aircraft Industry), V. Selyunin (economist and public affairs writer), G. Lisichkin (economist), S. Khokhlov (adviser to Research Centre on Private Law), S. Alekseyev (member of Russian Academy).
27 The status of Weber as an 'evolutionist' has been the subject of considerable debate. Parsons (1966) understandably appropriates Weber as an evolutionist, while Giddens (1971) challenges this reading of Weber.
28 Mommsen (1992) provides a recent interpretation of Weber in these terms.
29 DiMaggio and Powell's (1983) rereading of Weber is located within the development of an 'institutionalist' perspective within organizational analysis as outlined in Scott (1985) and Clegg (1990).

REFERENCES

Abercrombie, N. Hill, S. and Turner B. (1980) *The Dominant Ideology Thesis*, London: Allen and Unwin.
Adorno, T. and Horkheimer, M. (1944) *Dialectic of Enlightenment*, trans. E. Cumming, London: New Left Books.
Aglietta, M. (1979) *A Theory of Capitalist Regulation*, London: New Left Books.
Banac, I. (ed.) (1992) *Eastern Europe in Revolution*, New York: Cornell University Press.
Bauman, Z. (1992a) *Intimations of Postmodernity* London: Routledge
Bauman, Z. (1992b) 'The Solution as Problem', *Times Higher Education Supplement*, 13 November.
Beck, U. (1992) *Risk Society – Towards a New Modernity*, trans. M. Ritter, London: Sage.
Beetham, D. (1985) *Max Weber and the Theory of Modern Politics*, London: Allen and Unwin.
Beetham, D. (1991) *Bureaucracy*, Milton Keynes: Open University Press.
Beetham, D. (1992), *The Legitimation of Power*, London: Macmillan.
Bell, D. (1973) *The Coming of Post Industrial Society*, New York: Basic Books.
Blackler, F., Reed, M. and Whitaker, A. (1993) 'Knowledge Workers and Contemporary Organizations,' *Journal of Management Studies*, Special Issue.
Bourdieu, P. and Coleman, J.S. (eds) (1991) *Social Theory for a Changing Society*, Boulder, Colorado: Westview Press
Bunce, V. (1983) 'The Political Economy of the Brezhnev Era: the Rise and Fall of Corporatism', *British Journal of Political Science*, 13: 129–58.
Burawoy, M. and Krotov, P. (1992) 'The Soviet Transition from Socialism to Capitalism: Worker Control and Economic Bargaining in the Wood Industry,' *American Sociological Review*, 57: 16–38.
Burchell, G., Gordon, C. and Miller, P. (1991) *The Foucault Effect: Studies in Governmentability*, London: Harvester Press.
Burnham, J. (1962) *The Managerial Revolution*, (first published 1942) Harmondsworth: Penguin.
Burrell, G. (1988) 'Modernism, Postmodernism and Organizational Analysis: The Contribution of Michel Foucault', *Organization Studies*, 9 (2): 221–35.
Castells, E. (1989) *The Informational City*, Oxford: Blackwell.

Child, J. (1972) 'Organizational Structure, Environment and Performance: The Role of Strategic Choice', *Sociology*, 6 1–22.

Child, J. (1973) 'Organization: A Choice for Man', in Child, J. (ed.) *Man and Organization*, London: Allen and Unwin, pp. 234–57.

Clarke, S. (1992) 'Privatization and the Development of Capitalism in Russia', *New Left Review*, 196: 3–27.

Clegg, S. (1990) *Modern Organizations: Organization Studies in the Postmodern World*, London: Sage.

Collins, R. (1985) *Weberian Sociology*, Cambridge: Cambridge University Press.

Comisso, E. (1990) 'Crisis in Socialism or Crisis of Socialism?' *World Politics*, 42: 563–96.

Cook, L. (1992) 'Brezhnev's Social Contract and Gorbachev's Reforms,' *Soviet Studies* 44, 1.

Cooper, B.C. (1992) 'Formal Organization as Representation: Remote Control, Displacement and Abbreviation', in Reed and Hughes, *Rethinking Organization*, pp. 254–72.

Crook, S., Pakulski, J. and Waters, M. (1992) *Postmodernization: Change in Advanced Societies*, London: Sage.

Dandeker, C. (1990) *Surveillance, Power and Modernity*, Cambridge: Polity Press.

DiMaggio, P. and Powell, W. (1983) 'The Iron Cage Revisited', *American Sociological Review*, 48(1): 147–60.

Elson, D. (1988) 'Market Socialism or Socialization of the Market?' *New Left Review*, 172: 3–44.

Ernste, H. and Meier, V. (eds) (1992) *Regional Development and Contemporary Industrial Response*, London: Belhaven Press.

Fehér, F. and Arato A. (eds) (1989) *Gorbachev: The Debate*, New York: Humanities Press.

Fehér, F., Heller, A. and Márkus, G. (1984) *Dictatorship over Needs*, Oxford: Blackwell.

Filatotchev, I., Buck, T. and Wright, M. (1992) 'Privatization and Buy-Outs in the USSR', *Soviet Studies*, 44(2) 265–82.

Fincham, R. (1992) 'Perspectives on Power: Processual, Institutional and "Internal" Forms of Organizational Power', *Journal of Management Studies*, 29(6): 741–59.

Fitzpatrick, S. (1979) 'Stalin and the Making of a New Elite', *Slavonic Review*, 38: 377–402.

Flaherty, P. (1992) 'Cycles and Crises in Statist Economies,' *Review of Radical Political Economics*, 24: 111–53.

Foucault, M. (1979) *Discipline and Punish: The Birth of the Prison*, Harmondsworth: Penguin.

Gadamer, H. (1976) *Truth and Method*, New York: Seabury Press.

Getty, A. (1985) *Origins of the Great Purges*, Cambridge: Cambridge University Press.

Giddens, A. (1971) *Capitalism and Modern Social Theory*, Cambridge: Cambridge University Press.

Giddens, A. (1985) *The Nation State and Violence*, Cambridge: Polity Press.

Giddens, A. (1990) *The Consequences of Modernity*, Cambridge: Polity Press.

Giddens, A. (1991) *Modernity and Self-Identity*, Cambridge: Polity Press.

Gouldner, A. (1959) 'Organizational Analysis,'in Merton, R.K., Broom, L. and Cottrell, C. (eds) *Sociology Today*, New York: Basic Books.

Gross, J. T. (1989) 'Social Consequences of War: Preliminaries to the Study of Imposition of Communist Regimes in East Central Europe', *East European Politics and Society*, 3(2) 198–214.

Habermas, J. (1984) *The Theory of Communicative Action*, vol. 1, London: Heinemann.

Habermas, J. (1989) *The Theory of Communicative Action*, vol. 2, Cambridge: Polity Press.

Habermas, J. (1990) 'What Does Socialism Mean Today? The Rectifying Revolution and the Need for New Thinking on the Left', *New Left Review*, 183: 3–22.

Habermas, J. (1991) 'A Reply', in Honneth A. and Joas, H. (eds) *Communicative Action*, Cambridge: Polity Press, pp. 214–64.

Hankiss, E. (1990) *East European Alternatives – Are There Any?* Oxford: Clarendon.

Hankiss, E. (1991) 'The 'Second Society': Is There an Alternative Social Model Emerging in Contemporary Hungary?' in Féher, F. and Arato, A., *The Crisis in Eastern Europe*, New Brunswick: Transaction Books.

Harvey, D. (1989) *The Condition of Postmodernity*, Oxford: Blackwell.

Hausner, J. (1991) *System of Interest Representation in Poland*, Cracow Academy of Economics.

Hausner, J. (1992) *Populist Threat in the Transformation of Socialist Society*, Warsaw: Friedrich Ebert Stiftung.

Havel, V. (1988) 'Anti-Political Politics', in Keane, J. (ed.) *Civil Society – New European Perspectives*, London: Verso, pp. 381–98.

Hickson, D. and Lammers, C. (1979) *Organizations Alike and Unlike*, London: Routledge.

Hill, R. J. (1988) 'The *Apparatchik*i in Soviet Political Development', in Potichnyj, P. *The Soviet Union – Party and Society*, Cambridge: Cambridge University Press, pp. 3–25.

Hinings, C.R., Brown, J.L. and Greenwood, R. (1991) 'Change in an Autonomous Professional Organization', *Journal of Management Studies*, 28(4): 375–93.

Honneth, A., Knödler-Bunte, E. and Windmann, A. (1981) 'The Dialectics of Rationalization: An Interview With Jürgen Habermas', *Telos*, 49: 3–31.

Hosking, G.A. (1992) *A History of the Soviet Union 1917–91*, London: Fontana.

Hosking, G.A., Aves, J. and Duncan P. (1992) *The Road to Post-Commmunism – Independent Social Movements in the Soviet Union 1985–1991*, London: Pinter.

Hough, J. (1969) *The Soviet Prefects – the Local Party Organs in Industrial Decision-Making*, Cambridge Mass.: Harvard University Press.

Hyman, R. (1991), 'Plus ça Change? The Theory of Production and the Production of Theory', in Pollert, A. (ed.), *Farewell to Flexibility*? Oxford: Blackwell.

Jacoby, H. (1973) *The Bureaucratization of the World*, Berkeley: University of California Press.

Jessop, B. (1991) 'Polar Bears and Class Struggle?: Much Less than a Self-Criticism?' in Bonefield and Holloway (eds) *Post-Fordism and Social Formations*, London: Macmillan with Capital and Class. 145–69.

Jowitt, K. (1983) 'Soviet Neotraditionalism: the Political Corruption of a Leninist Regime', *Soviet Studies*, 35,(3) 275–97.

Jowitt, K. (1992) 'The Leninist Legacy', in Banac, *Eastern Europe in Revolution*, pp. 207–24.

Kerr, C., Dunlop, F.H. and Myers, C. A.(1960) *Industrialism and Industrial Man*, Cambridge, Mass.: Harvard University Press.

Konstantinova, V. (1992) 'The Women's Movement in the USSR: a Myth or a Real Challenge', in Rai *et al.*, *Women in the Face of Change*, pp. 200–17.

Korosic, M. (1988) *Jugoslavenska kriza* [Yugoslavian Crisis], Zagreb: Naprijed.

Kowalik, T (1991) 'Marketization and Privatization: the Polish Case', *Socialist Register*, pp. 259–77.

Kumar, K. (1978), *Prophecy and Progress: The Sociology of Industrial and Post-Industrial Society*, Harmondsworth: Penguin.

Lash, S. and Urry, J. (1987) *The End of Organized Capitalism*, Cambridge: Polity Press.

Leggatt, T. (1985) *The Evolution of Industrial Systems*, London: Croom Helm.

Levitas, A. and Strzalkowski, P. (1990) 'What Does "Vwlaszczenie Nomenklatury" [Propertization of the Nomenklatura] Really Mean?' *Communist Studies*, 2: 413–16.

Lipietz, A. (1992) *Towards a New Economic Order*, Cambridge: Polity Press.

Luhmann, N. (1982) *The Differentiation of Society*, New York: Columbia University Press.

Lyon, D. (1988) *The Information Society: Issues and Illusions*, Cambridge: Polity Press.

Lyotard, J. (1984) *The Postmodern Condition*, Manchester: Manchester University Press.

Machlup, F. (1980), *Knowledge: Its Creation, Distribution and Economic Significance*, vols 1 and 2, Princeton: Princeton University Press.

Mandel, D. (1991) 'The Struggle for Power in the Soviet Economy', *Socialist Register*, pp. 95–127.

Mandel, E. (1992) *Power and Money – A Marxist Theory of Bureaucracy*, London: Verso.

Márkus, M. (1982) 'Overt and Covert Modes of Legitimation', in Rigby, T.H. and Fehér, F. (eds) *Political Legitimation in Communist Regimes*, London: Macmillan, pp. 82–93.

Mintzberg, F. (1989) *Mintzberg on Management: Inside our Strange World of Organizations*, New York: Free Press.

Mommsen, W.J. (1992), *The Political and Social Theory of Max Weber*, Cambridge: Polity Press.

Morgan, G. (1992) *Organizations in Society*, London: Macmillan.

Mozny, I. (1991) *Proc tak snadno?* [Why so Easy?], Prague: SLON.

Mulgan, G. (1991), *Communication and Control: Networks and the New Economies of Communication*, Cambridge: Polity Press.

Murray, R. (1989), 'Fordism and Post-Fordism', in Hall, S. and Jacques, M., *New Times*, London: Lawrence and Wishart.

Murray, R. (1992) 'Flexible Specialization and Development Strategy – the relevance for Eastern Europe', in Ernste and Meier, *Regional Development*, pp. 197–218.

Nelson, R. and Winter, S. (1982) *An Evolutionary Theory of Organizational Change*, Cambridge, Mass.: Harvard University Press.

Neumann, L. (1992) 'Decentralization and Privatization in Hungary – Opportunities for Flexible Specialization', in Ernste and Meier, *Regional Development*, pp. 233–46.

Offe, C. (1985) *Disorganized Capitalism*, Cambridge: Polity Press.

Pahl, R.E. and Winkler, J.T. (1974) 'The Economic Elite: Theory and Practice', in Stanworth, P. and Giddens, A. (eds) *Elites and Power in British Society*, Cambridge: Cambridge University Press.

Parsons, T. (1966) *Societies: Evolutionary and Comparative Perspectives*, Englewood Cliffs, NJ: Prentice-Hall.

Parsons, T. (1973) *The Social System*, New York: Free Press.

Pettigrew, A. (1973) *The Politics of Organizational Decision-Making* London: Tavistock.

Pettigrew, A. and Whipp, R. (1992) *Managing Change for Competitive Success*, Oxford: Blackwell.

Pilkington, H. (1992) 'Whose Space Is It Anyway? Youth, Gender and Civil Society in the Soviet Union', in Rai, *et al.*, *Women in the Face of Change* pp. 105–29.

Piore, M. and Sabel, C. (1984) *The Second Industrial Divide: Possibilities for Prosperity*, New York: Basic Books.

Raelin, J.A. (1991) *The Clash of Cultures: Managers Managing Professionals*, Boston, Mass.: Harvard Business School.

Rai, S., Pilkington, H. and Phizacklea, A. (1992) *Women in the Face of Change – the Soviet Union, Eastern Europe and China*, London: Routledge.

Rakovski [Kis] J. (1978) *Towards an East European Marxism*, London: Busby.

Ray, L.J. (1993) *Rethinking Critical Theory*, London: Sage.

Ray, L.J. (1994) 'The Collapse of Soviet Socialism: Legitimation, Regulation and the New Class', in Brown, P. and Crompton, R. (eds) *A New Europe? Economic Restructuring and Social Exclusion*, London: UCL Press, pp. 196–221.

Reed, M. (1985) *Redirections in Organizational Analysis*, London: Tavistock.

Reed, M. (1989) *The Sociology of Management*, London: Harvester Press.

Reed, M. (1991) 'The End of Organized Society: A Theme in Search of a Theory', in P. Blyton and J. Morris (eds) *A Flexible Future?: Prospects for Employment and Organization*, Berlin: De Gruyter, pp. 23–42.

Reed, M. (1992) 'Experts, Professions and Organizations in Late Modernity', in *The Challenge of Change* (Conference Proceedings), Cardiff Business School, (ISBN: 0–902810–11–1).

Reed, M. and Hughes, M. (1992) (eds) *Rethinking Organization: New Directions in Organization Theory and Analysis*, London: Sage.

Reich, R.B. (1991) *The Work of Nations*, London: Simon and Schuster.

Ritzer, G. (1992) *The McDonaldization of Society*, Beverly Hills, Calif.: Sage.

Rizzi, B. (1985) *Bureaucratization of the World* (first published 1939) trans. A. Westoby, New York: Free Press.

Rose, N. (1991), *Governing the Soul*, London: Routledge.

Rustin, M. (1989) 'The Politics of Post-Fordism or the Trouble with New Times', *New Left Review*, 175: 54–77.

Sabel, C. (1982) *Work and Politics: The Division of Labour in Industry*, Cambridge: Cambridge University Press.

Sabel, C. (1991) 'Moebius-Strip Organizations and Open Labour Markets: Some Consequences of the Re-integration of Conception and Execution in a Volatile Economy', in Bourdieu, P. and Coleman, J. *Social Theory for a Changing Society,* pp. 23–62.

Sampson, S. (1985–6) 'The Informal Sector in Eastern Europe', *Telos*, 66: 44–67.

Sayer, A. and Walker, R. (1992) *The New Social Economy: Reworking the Division of Labour*, Oxford: Blackwell.

Scaff, L. (1989) *Fleeing the Iron Cage: Culture, Politics and Modernity in the Thought of Max Weber*, Berkeley: University of California Press.

Scarbrough, H. and Corbett, M.J. (1992) *Technology and Organization*, London: Routledge.

Schutz, A. (1972) *The Phenomenology of The Social World*, London: Heinemann.

Sciulli, D. (1992) *The Theory of Societal Constitutionalism*, Cambridge, Mass.: Harvard University Press

Scott, J. (1985) *Corporations, Classes and Capitalism*, 2nd edn, London: Hutchinson.

Smart, B. (1992) *Modern Conditions: Postmodern Controversies*, London: Routledge.

Smith, C. and Thompson, P. (eds) (1992) *Labour in Transition – the Labour Process in Eastern Europe and China*, London: Routledge.

Sprinzak, E. (1972) 'Weber's Thesis as an Historical Explanation', *History and Theory*, 11: 294–320.

Staniszkis, J. (1992) *The Ontology of Socialism*, Oxford: Clarendon Press.

Starbuck, W. (1992) 'Learning by Knowledge-Intensive Firms', *Journal of Management Studies*, 29(6): 713–40.

Stark, D. (1991) 'Comment', in Bourdieu, P. and Coleman, J. *Social Theory for a Changing Society*, pp. 56–61.

Stark, D. (1992) 'Bending the Bars of the Iron Cage', in Smith, C. and Thompson, P. *Labour in Transition*, pp. 41–72.

Szalai, J. (1989) 'The Dominance of the Economic Approach in Reform Proposals in Hungary and Some of the Implications of the Crisis of the 80s', in V. Gathy (ed.) *State and Civil Society: Relationships in Flux*, Budapest.

Toffler, A. and Toffler, H. (1985) 'An Appointment with the Future', *The Sunday Times*, 17 February.

Voskamp, U. and Wittke, V. (1991) 'Industrial Restructuring in the Former GDR', *Politics and Society*, 19(3): 341–71.

Voslensky, M. (1984) *Nomenklatura – Anatomy of the Soviet Ruling Class*, London: Bodley Head.

Walker, M. (1987) *The Waking Giant – the Soviet Union under Gorbachev*, London: Sphere.

Weber, M. (1976) *The Theory of Social and Economic Organization*, trans. A. Henderson and T. Parsons, London: Free Press.

Weber, M. (1978) *Economy and Society*, 2 vols, (ed.) G. Roth and C. Wittich, London: University of California Press.

Whitaker, A. (1992) 'The Transformation in Work: Post-Fordism Revisited', in Reed, M. and Hughes, M. *Rethinking Organization*, pp. 184–206.

Williamson, P.J. (1989) *Corporatism in Perspective: An Introductory Guide to Corporatist Theory*, London: Sage.

Wood, S. (1989) 'New Wave Management?', *Work, Employment and Society*, 3(3): 379–402.

Zaslavskaya, T. (1984) 'The Novosibirsk Project', trans. T. Cherfas, *Survey*, 28(1): 88–108.

Zaslavsky, V. (1982) *The Neo-Stalinist State – Class, Ethnicity and Consensus in Soviet Society*, New York: Sharpe.

Zon, H. van (1992) *Alternative Scenarios for Central Europe*, Brussels: Commission of the European Communities, Science Research and Development.

Zuboff, S. (1988) *In The Age of the Smart Machine: The Future of Work and Power*, London: Heinemann.

Conclusion: autonomy, pluralism and modernity

Larry J. Ray and Michael Reed

Why read Weber any more? The answer to this question has not always been self-evident, for at least three reasons. First, recent systems approaches and empirical research on organizational structure (such as the Aston studies referred to by Stuart Clegg) suggested the obsolescence of Weber's apparently mechanistic, monocratic and closed model of institutional organization. Secondly, critical social theorists tended to see Weber as a nationalistic anti-socialist theorist who predicted the inevitability of bureaucratic domination, in contrast to the more liberating theories of Marxists, Foucauldians or postmodernists. Thirdly, for those who view Weber as theorist of the iron cage, the organizational developments of the past two decades or so – flexibilization, post-Fordism, disorganization – further point to the irrelevance of Weber's conceptual framework for the late twentieth and early twenty-first centuries. However, it has been argued here that these are poor reasons for rejecting Weber, since each is open to challenge.

This is so first because Weber's work itself has undergone re-evaluation and reappraisal such that, freed from the deterministic baggage of the iron cage thesis, a new or neglected Weber has been brought to light who does appear to have important things to say about late modernity and the disorganization of monocratic structures. Secondly, recent political and intellectual challenges to the Western left, combined with the crisis of state socialism, have altered the agenda for critical social theory. In particular a new sensitivity is apparent to questions of democracy, value pluralism and the relationship between state and society, in which context Weber's concern with the social conditions of authority, bureaucracy and the state acquire fresh relevance. Both of these themes are reflected in the essays in this volume and it would be appropriate now to review the central points that have emerged in each of them.

The question of (mis)readings of Weber is placed in sharp focus by David Chalcraft who documents the interplay of rationality and emotion in two editions of Weber's *Protestant Ethic* essays. He has argued that Weber used the iron cage metaphor (perhaps better understood as a 'steel shell') to capture the transition from pre-modern to modern concepts of calling. Whereas the Puritans chose to follow a vocation, for the individual in modern secular organizations the calling is a necessity dictated by exigencies of economic existence. Even so, Chalcraft argues that for Weber the modern social cosmos was not necessarily a casing or barracks since a variety of human experience and personality remained possible, and people can choose whether to escape into non-rationalized frames of meaning. Further, freed from the hermeneutic baggage of the iron cage thesis, Weber appears to be claiming that a fundamental feature of modern culture is the intertwining of various inheritances, some of which are encumbrances while others need to be absorbed if we are to survive in modern capitalism.

On a similar theme of the dialectic between past and present, Eldridge reminds us of Weber's comment, again in *The Protestant Ethic*, that his work has attempted to demonstrate the complexity of the superficially simple concept of the rational. The context for this remark was Weber's insistence that the goal-rational action of the capitalist, to maximize accumulation, would appear quite irrational from the standpoint of a pre-capitalist producer, whose substantive goal was to maximize leisure time. Working through the tension implicit here between formal and substantive rationality is one of the central motifs of these essays, as they attempt to fashion new ways of understanding the dilemmas of a late modernity.

This point is made in different ways by the contributors, but several illustrate how formal rationality co-exists with substantive values in ways that structure the institutional patterns of modernity. John Eldridge, for example, challenges what he calls 'vulgar Weberianism' with the view that apparently traditionalistic rebellion deploys substantive values in the defence of endangered ways of life. He argues that tradition should not be viewed as a residual category to be equated with the irrational, since substantive values and culture are resources for organizational renewal and resistance to capitalist rationalization and organizational values. The central focus of Clegg's chapter is the inescapability of substantive values, which are at the core of contemporary organizations.

Martin Albrow approaches the question of substantive values with reference to the interplay of rationality with emotion in modern organizations. Weber's interest in irrationality, and especially affectivity, he argues, has been submerged by twentieth-century rationalistic models of organizational efficiency and for too long the recognition of organizational emotions has suffered from the repression exerted by rationalistic models. Though rehabilitating the importance of affect, Albrow is none the less dependent upon Weberian insights. In particular he retains the action frame of reference as a central methodological principle which regards organizations as realities that exist through people's behaviour; that are constructed out of motives and systems of meaning; as systems of action that cohere only so long as people sustain them. However, Albrow proposes a new context for understanding the impact of affective relationships in organizational behaviour, in which emotion ceases to be viewed as peripheral or incidental but as an essential feature.

Challenging the assumption that the trajectory of modernity tends towards greater impersonality, Albrow highlights the paradox that the growing weighting of the advanced economies towards the service sector has led to increasing emphasis on innovation, greater demands on the whole personality, and the public presentation of emotion in dealing with customers. Dealing with the public involves managing both the emotional demands of clients and the emotions generated in the workplace itself, as his examples of the air steward and waiter indicate. However, this return to the 'whole personality' does not necessarily mean an end, but might on the contrary be an intensification of alienating work conditions. Organized work in late modernity does not always demand cold efficiency and affective neutrality, although it might require a more intensive organization and regulation of affective behaviour. In other words, as we argue in Chapter 7, modernity is a two-sided process with the potential for both disarticulation of rationalized structures and deeper colonization of everyday life.

Weber's comment about the only superficially simple concept of the rational to some extent ran counter to his belief in the organizational superiority of bureaucracy compared with earlier organizational forms. His expectation that the future belonged to bureaucratization was grounded in the view that bureaucracy represented the optimally efficient organizational form. In common with many others, such as Marxists like Karl Kautsky, Weber assumed that large-scale organizations would become dominant through a quasi-natural process of economic selection. Indeed, insofar as Weber was pessimistic about the future this was because of the way rationalization and the ethic of calculation would erode substantive values. Yet as Clegg argues, efficiency itself is a cultural concept which is viewed differently in different organizational settings. Further, Weber was well aware of the ways in which the substantive values of work organization (such as demand-led production; the exclusion of workers from control; the external constraints on enterprises) limited the development of pure rational forms. It is not self-evident, then, that a particular model of organizational efficiency will become dominant, and Weber was more aware of this in his analysis of organizational values and culture than in his ideal-typical model of bureaucratic domination.

Several contributors here agree that the attempt to impose monolithic organizational structures on variegated social and cultural settings is in the long run a failure, and questions of value and politics, substantive questions, as Eldridge says, cannot be repressed by even the most powerful machine. However, the celebration of substantive rationality and affective commitments does raise a problem which is brought out in Bryan Turner's chapter. Namely, how will the traditionalistic identities deployed in resistance to rationalization cohabit in a world of post-conventional and decentred identities which take a sceptical distance from all metanarratives of justification? For example, the importance of the Polish Catholic Church in providing ideological and organizational resources for Solidarity is well known, but how are we to respond now to the religiously-inspired erosion of rights, especially women's right to control their fertility, in post-communist Poland? Again, Islam has constituted a powerful reservoir of resistance to colonizing capitalist rationalization, but poses an evident challenge not simply to 'liberal values' but to the very concept of the modern, sceptical post-conventional self which keeps a critical distance from all sources of ultimate authority. This issue has been thrown into sharp relief in Britain by the Salman Rushdie controversy in which the intellectual left have not always been able unambiguously to defend the right to publish material that some find offensive to their beliefs. Part of the problem here, as Turner points out in his re-evaluation of the debate over orientalism, is that the defence of universalistic values and civil rights can be cast, by those who seek indigenous sources of validity, as camouflage for Eurocentric cultural imperialism. Implicit here is the crucial question of whether we resign ourselves to a value relativity in which ethical claims conceal a will-to-power, or whether we can defend the possibility of universal ethics.

Turner points out how recent events (especially the disintegration of Soviet communism and the rise of Islamic 'fundamentalism') highlight the need to rethink the conventional sociological paradigm and to reassess Weber's relevance, especially to political sociology. These questions provoke us to redefine the foundations of our ethics and the ground upon which we might defend universal rights whilst escaping the accusation of cultural colonization. Turner suggests that democratic radical politics involves a reassessment of the conditions for democratization on which Weber's political sociology has something to offer. This involves reassessing the Western intellectual heritage in a more balanced way than occurred in the immediate aftermath of the orientalism debate. For Weber, after all, the threat to individual autonomy arose not only from modern bureaucracy but also from authoritarian despotic powers. Weber's fragmentary analysis of communism suggested that it was a precapitalist ethos based on the comradeship of rebellious soldiers, the utopian mentality of intellectuals, and the revolutionary aspirations of the peasantry. As we further suggest in Chapter 7, communism was in some ways a pre-modern form of domination that began to be undermined as the system became increasingly formalized.

Acknowledging that threats to autonomy are two sided, that they arise from both pre-modern and modernist structures might go some way towards creating the conditions for a balanced understanding of the potential for democratization. More specifically, we might follow Weber in examining the social preconditions for the liberal democratic potential in Western societies. Turner suggests that Weber identified three historical conditions for liberalism: (1) autonomous urban areas (as opposed to the city as a military centre); (2) Christianity as a universalistic ideology that undermined tribalistic affiliations, which were superseded by the community of faith; (3) rational law-making as opposed to *ad hoc* justice. Whether or not we accept these as the most significant preconditions for liberal democracy, Weber's work opens a debate, within a comparative context, about the economic and ideological milieu within which autonomous structures are institutionalized. Further, rather than contrast the enlightened West with the barbarous East (as he is sometimes accused of doing) Weber points out how liberalism is *always* fragile and is continually threatened by the countervailing tendencies of political oligarchy and state bureaucracy.

This notion of modernity as a field of tensions has been developed here, again with reference to the continuing relevance of Weber's sociology. In his analysis of the educational system, Keith Tribe re-examines the interplay of science and scholarship and argues that we can gain insights into the development of our educational system by fashioning fresh perspectives. Weber is of value in this exercise in that he poses the right questions. Weber is not in any straightforward sense an uncritical defender either of traditional or of modern higher educational systems but on the contrary argues that the ethos of free academic inquiry, a product of the modern world, is equally threatened by modern commercial interests and traditional demands to produce loyal servants of the state. Thus Weber's problem of academic freedom reflects the dual nature of threats to autonomy in capitalism and is a call to resist the rationalizing tendencies of bureaucratic power. Value freedom does not imply (as is often suggested) a subjective attitude of 'objectivity' so much as an institutional condition of autonomy from external constraints. That this is a hard line to hold in late twentieth-century universities in Britain and many other developed democracies should be reason to pause before dismissing the iron cage tendency of bureaucratization.

Indeed, as we argue in Chapter 7, the development of late modernity does not preclude the appearance of new invidious forms of control, but rather opens up the terrain for divergent outcomes. We suggest that by using a Weberian understanding of formal rationality one can begin to formulate an answer to the problem of universalistic ethics referred to above. We argue that Weber was overly pessimistic in assuming that the differentiation of cultural value spheres, the condition for modernity, also entailed a privatization of belief, leaving the public sphere open only to the cold ethics of impersonal calculation. Drawing on Habermas, we argue that formal rationality need not restrict itself to matters of calculation but contains a procedural rationality which is indeed anticipated (counter-factually) in modern communication structures. The essential condition for value pluralism and autonomy then is procedural ethics that demands respect for the rights of the other as an equal dialogue partner. If this condition is abrogated on either traditionalistic or modernist grounds, we are entitled to object. Thus when technocratic rationality excludes democratic participation it introduces substantive values covertly in a way that is immune to public scrutiny. We are entitled to protest *through appeal to reason* on the grounds that open public debate is the only adequate way of arriving at decisions that have some chance of gaining consensus. If, as Turner says, liberty is denigrated as a Masonic ideology, secularization as a Jewish plot, and the doctrine of equality as a challenge to the authority of God, then we are entitled to protest too, on the grounds that only procedural rationality and public dialogue can create conditions for the negotiation of difference in a world where substantive values (as a number of contributors have argued) are inevitably present. Weber might not have expressed himself in these terms but the argument here is that he provided the intellectual apparatus with which to approach the modern problem of ethics.

So, Weber is still relevant after all. There is, as Clegg concludes, a continuing relevance in his thought for the sociology of organizations today, even if it is not what might be expected. Weber's iron cage prognosis, insofar as he believed it himself, no longer represents the necessary fate of modernity and is balanced by the potential for organizational forms that expand participation and democratic structures. The theme of bureaucratic rationalization and its implications for the organizational choices available to us is one to which we have had cause to return throughout this volume. Weber's analysis of this theme is central to any appreciation and assessment of his sociological work and its contemporary relevance. Yet his analysis is itself highly ambiguous in terms of the way in which he characterizes and explains the dynamics of bureaucratization and its impact on the way we are able to live. We have argued that alongside the analysis of bureaucratic rationalization there is an alternative reading of Weber that treats bureaucratization as a contested and contingent outcome of struggles between social groups whose long-term consequences cannot be predicted. While the former interpretation anticipates the inevitability of more pervasive and unobtrusive forms of organizational control in which individual autonomy and collective resistance are virtually extinguished, the latter reading suggests that the trend towards bureaucratic rationalization can be slowed, if not reversed, to allow more open and participatory decision-making structures to emerge.

This underlying ambiguity in Weber's work is reflected at a theoretical level in his oscillation between a logic of analysis which implies a form of historical determinism, and one in which the strategic choices of powerful institutional actors exert a dramatic influence on the course of events. Is history relatively open in the sense that it consists of a series of power struggles between contending interests, the outcomes of which can never be predicted, or is it a matter of the inexorable workings of a process that largely occurs behind people's backs and over which they have little influence, much less control?

The ambiguities and dilemmas which Weber confronts in his socio-political analysis of bureaucracy speak directly to those we encounter in our attempts to understand and explain the process of modernization and the condition of modernity. In particular, his analysis and those which have been developed in this volume focus on the contradictory dynamic of the modernizing process and its unpredictable impact on the constitution and organization of power within late modernity. His work suggests that modernization is simultaneously a process of incorporation *and* liberation; that is, it signals to us that there is an emancipatory potential *inherent* within the institutional dynamics and organizational forms characteristic of late modern societies which might be exploited if resistance is strong and skilful enough to take advantage of that potential. The possibility of 'rusting iron cages' and the potential for breaking vicious circles are made available by Weber's analysis of the contradictions and dilemmas of modernity in such a way that the misplaced idealism of Sabel's reading of post-Fordism and the restrictive determinism of Aglietta's neo-Fordism can both be avoided by contemporary approaches more sensitively attuned to the opportunities and threats which late modernity presents.

As a new international social and political order takes shape in the twenty-first century the development of democratic structures for negotiating divergent substantive interests and values, such as those of national, ethnic and religious identities, will be of fundamental importance. Perhaps, as Habermas claims, the revolutions in Eastern Europe involved overcoming distance with the West. The metaphor of a journey might be more instructive than he imagines, in that all journeys involve risks and one does not know quite what to expect on arrival. In particular, it is uncertain towards exactly what organizational forms the transition in Europe is leading, and whether transforming societies will find Western pluralism intact on their arrival. Political and economic restructuring, such as that occurring throughout post-Cold War Europe, involves heightened uncertainties, in response to which traditionalistic identities can serve as a focus for populist mobilization.

This situation arises because the values and practices of modernity are constituted through both contrast and combination with a traditionalism which modernity must presuppose in order to be 'modern' at all. We have seen in this book how the structures of both tradition and modernity contain alternatives – in the case of tradition, for autocracy *and* resistance; in that of modernity, for rationalization *and* autonomy. These four potentials exist in dynamic combination such that increases in organizational complexity are likely to be followed either by altered power relations manifest in pluralization and internal differentiation, or by systemic closure that blocks social development. The latter could be facilitated by political movements able to deploy primordial affiliations such as ethnicity, nationalism or religious revivalism. Perhaps these alternatives are not of equal weight though, in that the increased capacity for cognitive and moral learning embedded in formal-rational communication structures might prove a more durable form of social organization than either those based on nostalgia for pre-modern forms of life or monocratic bureaucracies. The struggle for participatory modernity involves the creation of open communicative structures in which alternatives are built into the system that facilitate command over the possibilities of change. In this quest Weber is a resource for concepts and frames of analysis that illuminate our present dilemmas.

Index

academic freedom 9–10, 152–3, 155, 202
action 72, 171, 188; communicative
    164–5, 189; *see also* economic action;
    social action; traditional action
Adorno, T. 3
affectivity 101, 111, 199
affinity 49–50
Albrow, M. 5, 11, 49, 55, 66, 199
Alexander, J. 159
alienation 102, 103, 107
Althoff, Friedrich 144–5, 152, 154
Althusser, L. 126
Andrzejewski, S.L. 108
anti-magical practices 8, 130, 131
Arato, A, 191
asceticism 26, 27, 41, 57, 58, 87, 88–9,
    130; Islam and 8, 131; rationality and 5
Ashley, Sir Maurice 36
Aston studies 63–6
atmosphere 115–18
Austrian Marginalist School 4
authoritarianism 10, 124, 126, 127,
    131–2, 201; citizenship and 136
authority 65, 111–15; and bureaucracy
    55–6, 58, 90–1, 93–4; and language
    188; in Soviet systems 169–70, 173
autonomy 11, 179, 201, 202

Baltic States 130
Barnard, C. 49, 61, 71
Bauman, Z. 3, 51, 167
barracks, capitalism as 28, 29, 30, 32
Baxter, R. 41
Beck, U. 4, 186, 190
Beetham, D. 184
beliefs 58, 112, 163
Bell, D. 3, 178
Bendix, R. 9, 90, 91, 159

Bentham, J. 133, 134
Blau, P. 48, 112, 117
Book of Orders 86
Boulding, K. 61
Braverman, H. 49
Brubaker, R. 88
Bunce, V. 171
Bunyan, J. 29
bureaucracy 82–3, 93–4, 177, 201, 203;
    authority and 55–6, 58, 90–1, 93–4,
    112, 113, 161; capitalism and 93–5;
    efficiency and 3, 4, 66–9, 71; iron cage
    of 2–4, 16, 51–4, 76, 160; in Islam 125,
    127; as method of control 171–2, 180,
    182, 184–5; over-developed 171–2,
    175; in socialist societies 83, 90–3,
    132, 158, 168–73; variable tendencies
    of 55–60, 63
bureaucratic particularism 171
bureaucratic rationalization *see*
    bureaucracy
bureaucratization 12–13, 160, 161, 165,
    169, 171, 186, 200, 203; resistance to
    4, 89, 92, 97, 166, 175
Burns, T. 94, 100
business colleges 147, 151, 152, 154
business ethos, in universities 150–1,
    155–6

calculability 56, 57, 58, 70, 104, 163; and
    formal rationality 82
calling 5, 20–1, 26, 27, 34, 35, 39, 198–9
Calvinism 5, 20, 27, 57, 131; dominance
    of 24, 25
capitalism 17–18, 22, 39, 56–7, 70–1, 83;
    bureaucracy and 93–5; Calvinism and
    5; Franklin and 34–5; iron cage of
    28–32; Islam and 126, 128; and

liberalism 133–4, 135; in *Protestant Ethic* 25–6, 27, 28, 31; and socialism 129–30; and traditional behaviour 84–5
career structure 59
Castells, E. 177, 178
centralization 59, 64, 65, 161, 177
Chalcraft, D. 3, 5, 198, 199
charisma 111, 112, 169, 170
checks and balances 12, 95
Child, J. 65
Christianity 102–3, 137, 201
citizenship 10, 135; and liberal democracy 135–7
city states 137
civil society 173; in Eastern Europe 123; in Islam 8, 125
Clarke, S. 174, 175
Clegg, S. 3, 4, 49, 60, 64, 66, 98, 161, 178, 200
climate, organizational 117–18
cognitive models, of organizations 117–18
collegiality 12, 174, 178, 190
Collins, R. 159
Comisso, E. 173
commonality of purpose 102–3
communication 165, 188, 204; of feeling 108–11
communicative action 164–5, 189
communicative rationality 166, 184, 186, 188
communism 130, 133, 138, 201; collapse of 166–7, 173, 188
competitiveness 179, 180
Comte, A. 48
configuration 59, 64
conflicts 86–7, 94, 95, 189; in capitalism 86–7, 89; in USSR 92, 93
consent 161, 187; rule by 160–1, 163, 172
contractualization 58
control 13, 71, 94–5, 180; dialectic of 185, 186; bureaucracy and 171–2, 182, 184–5; new technology and 14, 178; Weberian model of 166–7, 177–8, 184–5
convergence theory 3, 176, 184
Cook, L. 171
cooperation 106, 108
Corbett, M.J. 177
corporatism *see* Fordism
corruption 170, 171, 172
credentials 58, 59
Crook, S. 2, 182, 183

Crossman, R. 21, 109, 110
cultural imperialism 50–1, 201
cultural pessimism 3, 50, 52, 65
culture 67, 89, 163, 199; differentiation of 161, 162, 177, 182–3, 187–8; of organizations 4, 56–7; plebeian 86
custom, social integration and 161
cynicism 12, 175, 189

decentralization 67, 171, 173, 177, 178, 181
democracy 12, 92, 129, 135, 137, 169, 189
democratic participation 95, 135, 202, 203
depersonalization, of social relations 52
destandardization 183, 186
dictatorship of the official 90, 91, 92
differentiation 47, 48, 62; of culture 162, 177, 183, 187–8, 189; of spheres of existence 52, 161; in universities 150, 154
Dimaggio, P. 46, 73, 186
disarticulation of organizational structures 188
disciplinization 59
disenchantment 53, 57, 160
dominance 25, 26; of Calvinism 24, 25; of capitalism 27
dominant coalitions 180
domination 7, 161, 166, 168, 200; bureaucratic 56, 163, 168–9, 172, 184–5
Donaldson, L. 64
dramaturgical action 164, 190
Dunford, R. 49
Dunkerley, D. 49, 64, 66
Durkheim, E. 47, 133–4

Eastern Europe 123, 129, 130, 204
economic action 57, 70–1; and modes of rationality 73,.81, 82
economic restructuring 177, 180–2
Economy and Society (Weber) 82–3
efficiency 66–9, 71, 75, 91, 182, 200
egalitarianism 131, 171
Eisenstadt, 127, 159
Eldridge, J. 4, 5, 98, 199, 200
Elias, N. 104
elites 175, 187; recruitment to 169
emotions: authority and 113–15; communication of 108–11; in objective setting 104–6; in organizations 98, 99, 100–1, 112, 115–19, 200; and

rationality 98, 198, 199; and task
    performance 106–8
Enlightenment project 50
entrepreneurship 84, 85
entrinnen 32
entweichen 32
environment 61–2
ertragen, meaning of 24–5, 28
ethical-charismatic movements 173
ethics 27, 201, 202; Franklin and 34–5
ethnic nationalism 2, 92
Etzioni, A. 48
Eulenburg, F. 145, 146
Eurocentricity of modernity 3, 50, 201
evolutionism 1, 11, 177, 192
expert knowledge 177, 184; and power
    179–80, 186

Farrell, R.B. 32
Fayol, H. 49, 63
Fehér, F. 168, 191
feng-shui 74
Fiedler, F.E. 117
Filatotchev, I. 175
Fine, G.A. 101, 107
Fish, S. 21
Fitzgerald, Rev Charles 86
Flaherry, P. 170
Flam, H. 118
flexibility 174, 178, 181, 188, 189
flexible accumulation 180, 181
Fordism 176, 177, 181, 182, 185; crisis of
    180, 181
formal-rational legitimation 12, 160–1,
    163, 172
formal rationality 57, 95, 160, 163, 199,
    202; calculability of 58; and efficiency
    67; in money economy 70–2, 82
Foucault, M. 127
Fox, A. 73
Frankenstein 51–2
Frankfurt School 132
Franklin, Benjamin 34, 42
Franklin Bridge 33–5
freedom 68; academic 152–3, 155, 202;
    of modernity 54; uncertainty and 53
freedom of expression 153
Friedrich, C. 112
Fukuyama, F. 3
functionalism 116

Gambetta, D. 73

Gehäuse 3, 26, 27, 29–30, 31, 32
General Education Board 149, 150
Germany: democracy in 129, 135, 137;
    universities in 142, 143, 144–7, 152–4,
    155
Giddens, A. 4, 10, 13, 123, 178, 188
globalization 7–9, 122–3, 177, 181, 185
goals, organizational 68, 101–6
Goethe, J.W. 29, 40–1
Gorbachev, M. 175, 191
Gouldner, A. 48, 63, 76, 113, 117
Grimm, Wilhelm 41
Gross, J.T. 168
Grumley, J. 52, 54
Grundberg, C. 132

Habermas, J. 4, 163–5, 171, 188, 189,
    190, 204
Haferkamp, H. 52
Hankiss, E. 171, 174
Harré, R. 115
Harvey, D. 181
Hassard, J. 110
Havel, Vaclav 167
Hayek, F. von 67–8
Hearn, J. 118
Heller, A. 168
Hennis, W. 22, 142, 143
Herrschaft, meaning of 23–4, 26
Hickson, D. 3, 64, 66
hierarchy 47, 58, 59; in Soviet system
    169–70
Hindess, B. 68
Hobbes, T. 103, 134, 135
Hobsbawm, E. 88
Hochschild, A.R. 100, 101, 107, 118
Holgate, N. 116
Holton, R.J. 129
Horkheimer, M. 3
Hough, J. 170
Hull school 125
human rights 128
humanity 51, 52
Hungary, post-socialism in 173–4
hydraulic societies 127, 132

ideal speech situation 165
ideal types 60, 76, 81
idyllic state 86
impersonalization 59
incorporation 100
individualism 102, 103; and liberalism

133, 134; Weber and 129, 131, 135, 201
information technologies 177, 178–9
innovation 73, 86, 200
instrumentality 13, 177, 189; Weber and
    89, 163, 165
integration, horizontal 174, 189
interests 71, 73, 86, 171
intersubjectivity 129
'iron cage' 3, 16, 27, 28, 38, 158, 186,
    189, 203; of bureaucracy 2–4, 16,
    51–4, 76; and organizational analysis
    63–8, 160; resistance to 166, 175–6;
    translation of 29–32
irrationality 12–13, 70–1, 88, 199; in
    objective setting 102, 104; substantive
    83
Islam 8, 124–8, 130–1, 138;
    traditionalism of 200–1

Jessop, B. 7, 8

Kahn, R.L. 61, 118
Kalberg, S. 119
Karpik, L. 72
Kasler, D. 89
Katz, D. 61, 118
Kautsky, K. 200
Kent, S. 29, 41
Kerr, C. 3, 66
Kets de Vries, M.F.R. 99
knowledge 143, 150; of experts 179–80;
    in organization 75, 76, 179
Korosic, M. 170
Kosmos 29, 31

LaCapra, D. 21
Laclau, E. 133
language 165, 188; and meaning 23–32;
    of organizational practice 100–1, 118
Lash, S. 7, 119
Lauenstein, B. 142
leadership 105–6, 108, 111–12; political
    129
legitimacy 162–3; formal rational 160–1,
    172; new types of 188; of
    organizational action 55, 58, 59
legitimation 171, 172; crisis of 173
Leonard, E. 36
Levy, H. 36
liberalism 10, 133–5, 138, 201; and
    democracy 135–6
lifeworld 168, 170, 187, 190

line control of workflow 65
Lipietz, A. 177
Littler, C.R. 49
Litwin, G.H. 117
localization 7, 8
Locke, J. 134, 135
Luhmann, N. 104, 189
Lukács, G. 9
Lyon, D. 178
Lyotard, F. 178

McGann, J. 40
McGregor, D. 99, 115
McLuhan, M. 109
McMillan, C. 64
Macpherson, C.B. 133
Maier, C.S. 49
Mandel, E. 175
Mann, Thomas 42
Mannheim Business College 151, 152
Mansfield, R. 65
March, J.G. 62
Marcuse, H. 9
markets 47, 57, 88–9, 129; in Eastern
    Europe 174; and order 67–8; saturation
    of 181; and universities 143
Markus, G. 168
Marshall, D.H. 136
Marx, Karl 47, 126, 133
Marxism 133; and human rights 128; and
    liberalism 133–4
Mayo, E. 49
meaning 38; author's intentions and 21,
    37–8; local frameworks of 74; loss of
    159, 160; textual changes and 18–19;
    and use of language 23–32
Merton, R. 48, 116, 117, 159
metanarratives, Islam and 128
Methodism 36, 86, 87
Michels, R. 137, 152
middle class 8
Mill, J.S. 133, 134, 135
Miller, D. 99
modernity 161, 166, 170, 202, 204; and
    bureaucracy 51; dilemmas of 183–7;
    fate of 12–14; and iron cage metaphor
    16–17; and organizations 3, 46, 47–8,
    50, 56, 61; and rationalization 52–3,
    54; repressive and participatory 187–9
modernization 3, 47, 130–1, 203
Mommsen, W. 9, 81, 83, 89
money economy, rationality in 70

Morgan, G. 61, 99
Mozny, I. 174
MPR (military participation ratio) 108
Mulgan, G. 177, 178
Murray, R. 167, 190
myth of the vanguard 171–2

nation state 7, 96, 122, 123
nomenklatura 169, 170, 173, 174, 191
normatively regulated actions 164
Nove, A. 83, 91–2, 95

Offe, C. 7
officialization 59
order 67, 69, 161
organizational agencies 74
organizational behaviour 4, 109, 113
organizational communication 109–11
organizational structure 63–6;
    disarticulation of 188; emotions and
    115–19
organizations 4, 67, 75–6, 99–101; Aston
    studies in 63–6; bureaucracy and
    55–60; conflict in 94; emotions in 112,
    115–19, 200; goals of 68, 101–6; and
    modernity 3, 46, 47–8, 50, 56, 61; and
    rationality 98–9; rules of 55–6, 59,
    180; substantive values of 200; in
    systems theory 61–3; Weber's analysis
    of 46, 48–51, 69, 72–5
oriental despotism 131–3
orientalism 126–8

Parkin, W. 118
Parsons, T. 3, 113, 127, 159, 167; and
    'iron cage' translation 29, 31, 42
participatory organizational forms 185–6
participatory rationalization 174–5, 189
patriarchy, in post-socialist economies 175
patrimonial bureaucracy 125
Patterson, M. 117
Pauchant, T.C. 100
Payne, R.L. 64
perestroika 168, 172
personality 13, 41, 142, 143, 200; in
    capitalism 39; and charismatic leaders
    112; differentiation of 161, 162; and
    feelings 117; in Protestant Ethic 5, 31,
    33; Puritan 27
Peters, G. 98
Petty, Sir William 36
Piore, M. 177

planned economies 168–9
planning 67, 68, 92, 129
Plannwirtschaft 168–9
plebiscitary democracy 169
pluralization 168
Poggi, G. 20
political deregulation 177
politics 122, 123, 124
popularist-authoritarianism 175
✷ post-Fordism 176–83 HOLLYWOOD .
post-industrial analysis 176, 178
postmodernism 2, 11, 101, 202; culture
    and 182–3; and orientalism 18
post-socialism 167–76
post-Stalinism 170–1
Powell, W. 46, 73, 186
power 186; bureaucracy and 93–4, 131–2,
    182, 186; in expert knowledge 179–80,
    186; in organizations 59, 75–6
Preobrazhensky, E. 129, 130
privatization, post-socialist 174–5
professional practice 73
professional training, in universities 146,
    147, 148
professors 146, 149, 153
Protestant Ethic (Weber) 5, 20, 81, 83–4;
    author's intentions 21–3, 37;
    intertextual content of 35–8; linguistic
    and organizational principles of 23–35;
    omitted footnote in 28–9; text of 18;
    theme of 39
Protestant ethic 5, 104
Protestantism 25, 41; Franklin and 34, 35;
    see also Calvinism; Methodism;
    Puritanism
Prussia 154
psychoanalysis 99
Pugh, D. 3, 64
Puritanism 190
purposive rationality 160, 166, 184

rational action 85–6, 161
rational law 12, 56, 137, 201
rationality 53, 88, 160, 165; and
    bureaucratization 12, 13;
    communicative 4, 166, 184, 186, 188;
    and emotion 99, 198, 199; and
    goal-setting 103, 104; iron cage and 16,
    54; modes of 57, 69–72, 72–5, 85–6;
    purposive 160, 166, 184; and social
    action 4–5; substantive 57, 72, 81, 82,
    160, 191; see also formal rationality

rationalization 11, 12, 52–3, 158–9, 160,
    176; cultural conditions of 67; and
    globalization 7–9; of markets 57; and
    organizational objectives 103–4; of
    party democracy 137; repressive and
    progressive 173–4, 188–9; resistance to
    175; in socialist societies 168
Ratner, Gerald 114
Ray, L.J. 4, 7, 11, 12, 175
reality, in organizational theory 99, 100
realpolitik 7, 9, 11
reason 50, 52, 70
redistributive principle 170, 171
Reed, M. 4, 7, 11, 12, 98
reflexive modernization 186
reform, in Soviet systems 91, 92–3, 173
religious fundamentalism 2, 5, 124, 201
research 146, 147, 148, 155
resistance 11, 14; to bureaucracy 4, 89,
    92, 97, 175; tradition and 5, 87–8
Ritzer, G. 8
Robbins, L. 102
Rudé, G. 88
rules, of organizations 55–6, 59, 180; and
    authority 113, 161
Russia 130; Weber and 123, 124
Rybakov, A. 13

Sabel, C. 177
Said, E. 127
Saint-Simon, C.H. 48
Scarborough, H. 177
Schiller, J.C.F. 29
Schluchter, W. 119, 159
scholarship 9–10, 141, 142, 150, 156, 202
Schwartzman, H. 109
science 127, 142, 150, 156; philosophy of
    9; and scholarship 202
'Science as a Vocation' (Weber) 9, 142,
    144, 155
Sciulli, D. 12, 190
second society 4, 158, 168, 171–2, 174
sedimentation 73
self-discipline 104
Selznick, P. 48
seminars 146
service sector 100, 200
Shariati, Ali 131
shell, Gehäuse transalated as 30, 31, 32,
    33, 39
Simon, H.A. 62
Sinnverlust 159, 163, 164, 188

situational logic 114
Skinner, Q. 21
Smart, B. 178
Smith, Adam 47
social action 4–5, 163–4; Weber and 123,
    187
social change 122–3, 128, 130
social contract 171
social movements 96, 141, 166, 188
social organization 204
social relationships 55, 100;
    depersonalization of 51, 52
social stationariness 125, 126, 135
socialism 28, 95; bureaucracy and 83,
    90–3; Weber and 28, 83, 90–4, 123,
    129, 168
socialist societies 92–3, 129–30, 167–8;
    bureaucracy in 83, 91, 158, 160, 167,
    168, 170
society 7, 129, 161, 162
sociology 9, 47; classical tradition and
    10–12; of liberalism 122–3, 133–5; of
    religion 124, 125, 126, 130
Sombart, W. 152
Soviet Fordism 167, 185, 190
Soviet systems 167–71
specialization 52, 54, 58, 62, 64, 65; in
    universities 148, 149
spontaneous privatization 174
staatraison 7, 10, 11
Stalinism 132
Stalker, G.M. 100
Stammler, R. 113
standardization 59, 64, 65; in universities
    149
Staniszkis, J. 172
Starbuck, W.H. 64
state: control by 171; intervention by 95;
    power of, in German universities 153,
    155
State Property Committee 174
state socialism, crisis of 168–73, 175–6
Stinchcombe, A. 73
stratification 59
strikes 92
structures of dominance 69, 70, 72
structuring of activities 64–5
student fraternities 154
subordination 100, 113, 185
substantive rationality 57, 72, 81, 82, 160,
    191
substantive values 74, 188, 199, 200

surveillance 13, 96, 178
systems theory 61–3

Tagiuri, R. 117
task performance 106–8
Tavistock school 99
Tawney, R.H. 84
Taylor, F.W. 61, 63
technological innovation 65, 181
technological-organizational fatality 160
technological rationalization 177
teleological action 164
text 6, 17, 18–20; and author's intentions
    22; and intertextual context 35–8; and
    intratextual context 23–35
textile industry 85
Thiselton, A.C.T. 21
Thompson, E.P. 5, 86, 87
Thompson, J.D. 61
TINA (there is no alternative) 3, 4, 66
Tocqueville, A. de 135
Tönnies, F. 103
totalitarianism 126
Touraine, A. 48, 61, 96
traditional action 81, 88; and capitalism
    84–5; and rational action 85–6
traditionalism 4–5, 84, 175, 199, 204;
    Islam and 8, 125; and resistance to
    rationalization 200
transitions 159, 189
Tribe, K. 9, 10, 202
Trist, E.L. 99
trust 4, 73, 174
Turner, B.S. 5, 7, 8, 9, 10, 12, 166, 201, 202

uncertainty 11, 53, 54, 104, 180
Unger, R. 132
United States of America, university
    system in 143, 144, 147–51, 154, 155
universities 9–10, 60, 141, 142; American
    147–51; German 145–7; objectives of
    150; Weber on 143–5, 151–6
University of Cologne 154
Unwin, G. 36
urban associations 137, 201
Urry, J. 7
USSR 90–1, 92–3, 132, 167, 191;
    bureaucracy in 169; reform in 123;
    Stalinism in 132

value 9, 67, 69–70, 202

values 96, 161, 189, 201; substantive
    57–8, 74–5, 82, 188, 199, 200; ultimate
    96
Veblen, T. 150–1, 155

ways of life 39
wealth 36, 37, 38
Weber, Marianne 20, 21
Weber, Max 2, 4, 9, 10–12, 20–1, 98,
    203–4; alternative views of 11, 13, 98;
    on bureaucracy 51–60, 64, 66, 69,
    93–4, 184–5; on bureaucratic control
    177–8, 182, 187; and bureaucratization
    12–13, 93–4; and capitalism 5, 22,
    84–5, 89; and charisma 111–12; and
    citizenship 136–7; and communism
    130, 201; *Economy and Society* 82–3;
    and efficiency 66–7, 71; and Islam 8,
    124–5, 130–1; and liberalism 135, 138,
    201; and modernity 8, 11, 16, 52, 161,
    183, 187, 189; and organizational
    analysis 46, 48–51, 72–5, 76, 119; past
    and present in 17, 25, 39; philosophy of
    science of 9, 122; political sociology of
    7–8, 122–4, 128–9, 136–7, 201; and
    rationality 54, 69–72, 88; and
    rationalization 11, 57, 67, 160;
    rereadings of 159–66; on science 142;
    'Science as a Vocation' 9, 142, 144,
    155; and socialism 28, 83, 90–4, 123,
    129, 168; and society 7, 129; on
    universities 9–10, 143–5, 151–6;
    writings as texts 18–20; *see also*
    Protestant Ethic
Weick, K.E. 62
Wesley, John 36–7
Whimster, G. 119
Williamson, O.E. 69
Wilson, Harold 109
Wittfogel, K. 127, 131–3
women, in post-socialist economies 175
Woodward, J. 65
work, 39, 54, 89, 106–8
working class 87

Zaslavsky, V. 171
Zaslavskaya, T. 191
Zon, H. von 175
Zuboff, S. 14, 178, 179
Zwangsjacke 30–1
Zweckrationalität 163–4